The French Hit Back

Verdun 1917

The French Hit Back

Verdun 1917

Christina Holstein

Pen & Sword

MILITARY

AN IMPRINT OF PEN & SWORD BOOKS LTD.
YORKSHIRE - PHILADELPHIA

First published in Great Britain in 2020 by
Pen & Sword Military
an imprint of
Pen & Sword Books Ltd, 47 Church Street
Barnsley, South Yorkshire, S70 2AS

ISBN 978 1 52671 708 5

A CIP catalogue record for this book is
available from the British Library.

Typeset in Times New Roman by
SJmagic DESIGN SERVICES, India

Printed and bound in the UK by TJ Books Ltd,
Padstow, Cornwall.

Pen & Sword Books Ltd incorporates the imprints of
Pen & Sword Archaeology, Atlas, Aviation, Battleground, Discovery,
Family History, History, Maritime, Military, Naval, Politics,
Railways, Select, Social History, Transport, True Crime,
Claymore Press, Frontline Books, Leo Cooper, Praetorian Press,
Remember When, Seaforth Publishing and Wharncliffe.

For a complete list of Pen & Sword titles please contact
PEN & SWORD BOOKS LIMITED
47 Church Street, Barnsley, South Yorkshire, S70 2AS, England
E-mail: enquiries@pen-and-sword.co.uk
Website: www.pen-and-sword.co.uk

Contents

Acknowledgements

The preparation of this work on the little known fighting at Verdun in 1917 would have been more difficult without the help of many expert friends. I am particularly grateful to Tom Gudmestad, who once again allowed me the full use of his extensive archive, and to Wim Degrande, Jan Carel Broek-Roelofs and Harry van Baal who shared photos and information. My thanks go also to Mme Annick Eloy of Vadelaincourt, who generously shared her knowledge of Hospital 6 and provided an introduction to M Hubert Philippe, an expert on the medical services in the area and much else. The map tiles for the tours came from Openstreetmap.org. Once again, Laurent and Patricia Labrosse of the Hôtel du Commerce, Aubréville, provided food, good cheer and a place to relax after long days on the ground. As always, responsibility for any errors is mine alone.

Kent
2020

List of Maps

Author's Note

The fact that there was serious fighting at Verdun in 1917 is a surprise to many and investigating it takes the researcher into areas of the battlefield that are unvisited even by normal Verdun standards. Cote 344, the Butte de Caurières, the deep ravines of Bois des Fosses or the upper slopes of the Fond du Loup rarely see anyone other than hunters or forestry workers. That is a pity, because the 1917 fighting represents not only the French push back against the German assault of 1916 but also the triumph of planning, training and morale over the army mutinies of May and June 1917, a small number of which had occurred in the Second Army. There is a different feel to the fighting in 1917. The French war diaries and regimental histories of that period show a determination to be rid of the enemy once and for all and have no qualms in describing how it was done, whether by industrial levels of shelling, the bayonet, incendiary grenades or flamethrowers. 'No quarter was given' is a frequent refrain French war diaries in 1917.

A French heavy cavalryman at the start of the war. *Tom Gudmestad*

The massive change in warfare which had taken place since 1914 is nowhere more evident than in the villages south of Verdun which saw fighting in the first weeks of the war – an almost forgotten period of cavalry, red-trousered French infantry, officers with gloves and swords and Germans in spiked helmets. Into that sleepy countryside came French and German regiments during the First Battle of the Marne, soon to be followed by modern hospitals, new roads and railways, prison camps, massive dumps, huge guns, airfields, tanks and thousands upon thousands of men of varying nationalities, many of a type local people had never seen before. Visiting the area today it is hard to imagine that it ever saw such activity as almost all traces have gone. But the memorials remain, not only to men who fought the First World War but also to British bomber crews in the Second, shot down by German aviators whose fathers may well have flown there in 1917.

The aim of this book is to introduce visitors to parts of the battlefield and the wider Verdun area that they might otherwise not visit. The walking tours cover areas of the Right Bank which do not figure in the guide books but which explain the difficult ground over which the battle was fought, and why. It does not include walking tours of the Left Bank, which were covered in *Verdun – The Left Bank* some years ago. The driving tours provide an introduction to the air war, medical services and logistics of 1917, the contribution of Austro-Hungarian troops to the German effort, and touch on some aspects of fighting in the area at the very start of the war.

Series Editor's Introduction

Verdun is firmly associated with 1916; the fighting that raged around this city (with varying degrees of intensity) from February to December was fought in horrendous conditions and at a huge cost in men and materiel. It was one of the two massive offensives, one German and one Allied (the Somme), that dominated that year on the Western Front; and two that have lived on in national memories – and myth – ever since.

The literature on the French army in 1917 focuses on the failed Nivelle offensive along the Chemin des Dames in April-May and the subsequent mutinies. This is, at the least, unfortunate. The significant contribution of the French during the Third Battle of Ypres (Passchendaele) is often reduced to a few paragraphs. The successful French attack on the Verdun front in late August 1917 is almost unknown and hardly ever finds coverage in the histories of the Great War. In turn this means that there is no acknowledgement of the innovative approach by the French staff to the planning of this limited offensive, which took into account hard won lessons from 1916 and the spring of 1917.

Look at the figures; for the attack on 20 August – essentially a two-day affair, although related fighting did drag on into the winter – the French deployed more men and more guns than the British did for the first day of the Somme in 1916 and over about sixty percent of the length of front. The weight of artillery employed was extraordinary – over 2,200 pieces, of which just over 1,300 were heavy. Preparation was meticulous and the Germans were swept off Cote 304 and Mort Homme on the Left Bank and were pushed back on the Right Bank in line with the plan, all within forty-eight hours. Fought over the last ten days of August 1917, the attack cost the Germans 7,000 prisoners, significant numbers of dead and wounded, great quantities of materiel and the impact on morale of the loss of practically all the gains made in the area in 1916 at such expense and with so much effort; the French suffered the relatively modest loss of 21,000 casualties.

This was a supremely accomplished military operation, launched by an army that is popularly supposed to have been reduced to a discontented force, only capable of waging a defensive war. In this action it tied up no less than twenty-five German divisions. The fighting, occasionally very fierce but at a much reduced tempo, went on for the rest of the year, almost exclusively on the Right Bank. It was dominated by vicious, localised struggles for significant features (and you have to stand on the ground to appreciate how significant these features were, even if the post war forestation programme provides visual challenges).

Well over fifty percent of the book is devoted to the tours section. Verdun was an unusual scene of operations on the Western Front; it was the only major battlefield on that front that was so centred on a city on whose protection, in the late nineteenth century and even the early years of the twentieth, so much money was spent and great building efforts, largely in the form of modern fortifications, were undertaken. Verdun is one of the most difficult of the major Western Front battlefields to understand today. Mercifully free from intrusive development over the last century or so, much of it is, however, covered in rather haphazardly planted forestry. This makes the task of providing coherent walks very demanding. One of the most notable features of all of Christina's Verdun books is the way that she makes sense of the course of the fighting by putting it firmly in the context of the ground that was at issue; no small feat, given the fact that so much of the Verdun battlefield is a mass of woodland.

One of the tours, the second, is of the French rear areas, looking at aspects of the war that are all too often ignored or taken for granted. It gives an opportunity to consider the issue of communication and supply lines in the rear to support, reinforce and replace the almost unimaginable numbers of men and guns who were deployed on the Verdun front. Considerable space is given to the care of casualties, their evacuation and to the field hospitals, supported by first hand accounts of the men and women who were engaged in this dangerous and emotionally exhausting work. Several airfields are included in the tour, which provides an opportunity to look at the role of air power in the battle and the heroics of these pioneer military aviators.

The other three tours are of the battlefield, for the most part on the Right Bank, although Tour 1 – a driving tour – includes points of interest on the Left Bank. It is an irony that successful offensives in the Great War (and is often the case in all wars) have generally left little trace on the ground. However, the ground relevant to 1917 on the Left Bank is well covered in the walks in Christina's *Verdun: The Left Bank* and *Walking Verdun* in this series. The two walking tours provide a pathway to an understanding of the ground and the significance of particular points and features in the battles for Verdun throughout the war. To illustrate the intensity of the combat she directs the readers to relics of earthworks and the occasional reinforced concrete remnants, which more often than not would have been difficult to locate without her clear instructions and excellent maps.

This book has brought an important, neglected offensive to the attention of an Anglophone readership and has thereby done a service to the achievements of the French army of the Great War. Christina Holstein's six books on the Verdun battlefield provide a comprehensive guide on the ground to what took place in this area during 1916 and 1917, backed up by a coherent narrative that makes full use of both French and German sources and a wealth of personal accounts. They have achieved the best of what was hoped for in the Battleground Europe series when Roni Wilkinson and I started it some thirty years ago.

Nigel Cave
Montauban de Picardie, November 2020.

Introduction

While the 1916 Battle of Verdun has received a reasonable amount of attention over the years the same cannot be said of the major French counter offensive of August 1917. Known to the French as the Second Offensive Battle of Verdun, it recaptured much of the ground lost in 1916, and although it did not achieve all its objectives, there was no substantial change in the lines between the end of the offensive in November 1917 and the start of the Franco-American Meuse-Argonne battle in September 1918.

The operation of August 1917 was the third successful French counter offensive at Verdun. The first two, launched on the Right (east) Bank of the Meuse in October and December 1916, had pushed the German lines back, returned Forts Douaumont and Vaux to French hands and re-established the main line of resistance around the city. Shocking though that was to the Germans, there was little reaction on the ground. Instead, it was decided that in future serious French threats would be met by tactical withdrawals and only 'minor offensives' would be carried out. There were indeed minor offensives in the first six months of 1917 but no serious German attempt to re-establish the lines of October or December 1916.

In fact, the German failure at Verdun had brought significant change to their command structure. At the end of August 1916, General Erich von Falkenhayn, the Chief of the General Staff and the man behind the Verdun plan of attack, had been replaced by the duumvirate of Field Marshal von Hindenburg and General Ludendorff. Command of the Fifth Army, which had fought the battle since February 1916, passed from Crown Prince Wilhelm of Germany to General von Lochow, and the Army Chief of Staff was also replaced. The deep disappointment represented by these changes

General Erich von Falkenhayn, Chief of the German General Staff.

Field Marshal von Hindenburg.

was a far cry from the optimism with which the offensive had been launched in February 1916. Verdun was to have been the battle which brought the war to an end, and although for some of the parties involved the means chosen may have been difficult to understand, the reason for it was clear enough.

In January 1916 the German strategic situation on the Western Front was stable but weak and General von Falkenhayn was no closer to achieving his goals than at the end of 1914. All the efforts made on the Western Front in 1915 had failed to divide the Allies and force France, the major enemy, to the negotiating table, while on the Eastern Front Russia, despite devastating losses, had refused to consider a separate peace. As a result, Germany had to maintain considerable forces on both fronts and could not gather enough resources to inflict a decisive defeat on either of them. With British Army numbers increasing month by month and no new fresh supply of men available to either Germany or Austria-Hungary, bringing the war to a successful conclusion was becoming more urgent by the day. The question was how to do it, as no tactic tried so far had been successful.

As, in the late autumn of 1915, General von Falkenhayn believed Russia to be incapable of launching offensive action for the foreseeable future, he turned his attention back to the Western Front and devised a plan to force France to the negotiating table without draining the remaining fronts of German troops. With France out of the war, there would be no reason for Britain to go on fighting, and if Russia chose to continue the war without its French ally Germany would have the manpower available to deal with it. With intelligence reports indicating France to be on the point of military and economic collapse, it would not be necessary to seek defeat in a great decisive battle if the same could be achieved by striking with limited resources at a place that the French would defend to the last man. Such a place did not have to be of overwhelming military importance; importance to morale would be sufficient. In Falkenhayn's view, Verdun, a *place forte* (fortress), was such a place. In 1914 the most important bulwark in the new chain of defences along France's eastern frontier built after the Franco-Prussian War of 1870, surrounded by a massive interlocking defensive system and too strong for the Fifth Army to attack frontally, by 1915 it was ten kilometres behind the front, drained of resources, weakly held, surrounded by a salient divided by a river, and dependent for supply on a narrow road, a light railway and one standard gauge railway line, part of which was under German guns. The Germans, on the other hand, had the massive coal, iron and steel resources of the Briey basin under fifty kilometres away and an extensive railway system, originally developed for pre-war industrial purposes but now massively developed. Considered logically, the German ability to supply an overwhelming artillery assault at Verdun – for such was the plan – was many times greater than the French ability to defend against one; and if the Germans were to knock out the remaining standard gauge line in the first hours of the offensive, thus making it next to impossible for the French to supply the needs of the battle, the speed and shock of their advance would allow them to break through and reach their objectives before the French could get themselves together. Falkenhayn's aim was not to take Verdun but to reach certain strategic heights while inflicting such a shocking level of casualties on the French *in so short a time* that on top of the enormous losses already suffered – of which the 191,797 casualties of the Champagne and Artois battles in September-October

1915 were a recent terrible memory – it would be military and politically impossible for France to continue; either the Government would collapse or it would be forced to the negotiating table by pressure from the army and the home front. This was not to be a long drawn out struggle but a short sharp blow and speed was of the essence; the operation was to be launched on 12 February 1916 and the Kaiser was to attend a victory parade in Verdun sixteen days later. The Fifth Army was commanded by the Crown Prince of Germany and there could be no failure.

Crown Prince Wilhelm of Germany.

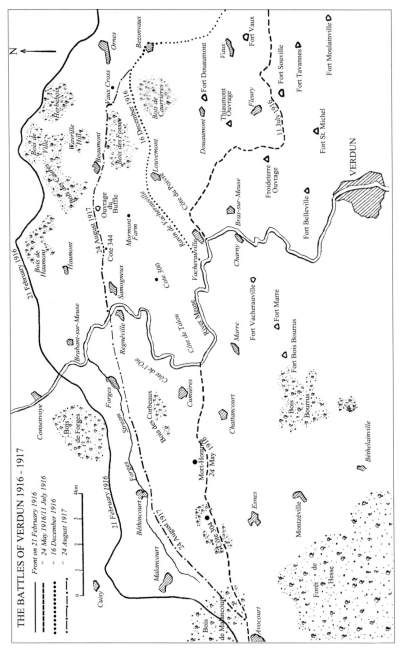

The Battles of Verdun 1916 and 1917.

As always, things did not go according to plan. Limiting the attack to the northern front of the salient on the Right Bank meant that French guns on the Left Bank could be turned on them; and French supply lines did not fail. Although the standard gauge line was swiftly put out of commission and not repaired for several days, the extraordinary and rapid organisation of the road later known as the Voie Sacrée into an endless rotating convoy of trucks and other vehicles meant that the supply lines did not break down. The Germans attacked the Right Bank with three Army Corps backed by over a thousand artillery pieces, but

General von Lochow.

against all the odds the two infantry divisions and 270 guns defending the French lines fought to the last man and reinforcements were thrown in so fast that one week into the battle there were as many French troops on the Right Bank as there were German. After early success, the battle became a slogging match which reached its high point in July 1916, still short of the strategic heights; and with Germany by then heavily involved on other fronts, the Fifth Army was ordered on the defensive. Then the French pushed back. By the end of the year they had recaptured their lost forts, re-established the main line of resistance and retaken some important high ground in a prelude to another ambitious operation the following year. Their success in August 1917 in an operation far more violent and industrial than the 1916 fighting, and with troops equipped and trained to the highest degree, recaptured most of the ground lost in 1916 and removed the threat to Verdun for good.

Chapter One

Worthy descendants of the Revolution

The 1916 Battle of Verdun divides into two parts: the period from 21 February to 1 August, which was offensive for the Germans and defensive for the French, and the period from 1 August to 18 December, during which the roles were reversed. The action was violent for the first six months of the battle but from August 1916 fewer local operations were launched and a relative calm descended. On the French side this masked feverish activity as they prepared for another major offensive to relieve pressure on Verdun by pushing the German lines further away from the city and recapturing certain important positions on the Right (east) Bank of the River Meuse. These included Fort Douaumont and Fort Vaux, two works in the main line of resistance around Verdun which the Germans had captured months earlier.

After weeks of preparation and training, the offensive was launched on 24 October 1916; and while it failed to recapture Fort Vaux, which

Part of the damaged facade of Fort Douaumont after its recapture in October 1916.

was evacuated a week later, the other objectives were achieved. In a triumphant Order of the Day, issued on 25 October, General Nivelle, the commander of the Second Army and the man in charge of operations at Verdun, declared that the ground which the Germans had taken eight months to capture at the cost of devastating losses and unimaginable quantities of shells had been reconquered in a single dash in four hours.

On the French side some senior commanders considered that Verdun was now safe and that operations could be reduced. However, General Nivelle saw things differently. Whilst Fort Douaumont, the most important of the permanent works around Verdun and a position of the greatest tactical importance, had been recaptured, it was still very close to the front line and open to a surprise attack. In addition, artillery observers on high ground to the north of the fort could still direct fire on the new French positions. If the Germans were to be persuaded that there was no point in trying another offensive at Verdun, a further operation was needed.

The defeat of 24 October 1916 was a bitter blow to German commanders at Verdun and an investigation was ordered into what went wrong. Some voices raised the possibility of attempting to recapture Fort Douaumont on the grounds that too much German blood had been spilt in holding it and that to fight back would show that the battle was not yet over. However, this idea was quickly quashed (not least because considerable resources were tied up in the continuing severe fighting on the Somme)

and instead, the German High Command turned its attention to the immediate needs of the front, which included shelters, fieldworks, machine gun posts, and communication lines. Terrible weather and French artillery fire hampered the work and the front line troops, who were also labourers, suffered severely, but no one was very worried. German aerial reconnaissance during November showed what looked like offensive preparations but French prisoners were reporting that a new operation was unlikely, so with any luck there was still time to get everything in order before spring.

General Nivelle.

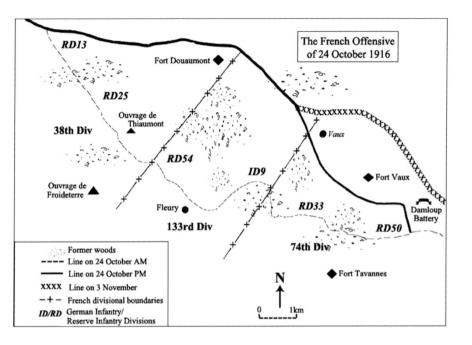

The French Offensive
of 24 October 1916

Former woods
- - - - Line on 24 October AM
———— Line on 24 October PM
XXXX Line on 3 November
- + - French divisional boundaries
ID/RD German Infantry/
       Reserve Infantry Divisions

N
0   1km

Preparing the new offensive
However, the French were not going to wait until spring and preparations
for the new offensive had already begun. The difficulties involved were
even greater than in October and the ground itself constituted a major
obstacle. Violently shelled for months and reduced to a landscape of
waterlogged craters, it was almost impassable to men and completely
impassable to guns. Despite torrential rain, snow and deep mud, and at
the cost of immense effort, some twenty five kilometres of road were
repaired, new roads created and 60cm and 40cm gauge railway lines laid
or extended. That allowed tools and materials to be brought forward to
create the other positions needed - observation posts, communication
and assault trenches, camps, assembly areas, ammunition and supply
dumps, telephone cables, machine gun posts, batteries, first aid posts,
evacuation routes, water supplies and optical communications. The two
forts also had to be repaired enough to defend themselves and support
the attack. All hands were needed and regular army units, technical and
specialized detachments, territorials, engineers, colonial labourers and
prisoners were all put to work.

The aim of the new offensive was to regain control of a number
of key positions on the Right Bank between the River Meuse on the

3

General Mangin.

left and the Woëvre Plain on the right. They included a high ridge called the Côte du Poivre, the villages of Vacherauville, Louvemont and Bezonvaux, and a series of important fieldworks, all of which would be strongly defended. The plan drawn up by General Mangin, the attacking general who had also devised the plan for the successful operation of 24 October, required eight infantry divisions supported by hundreds of guns and howitzers of calibres from 65mm to 370mm, with further firepower coming from the 155mm and 75mm turret guns of various forts, including Fort Douaumont.

During November, French aerial reconnaissance had spotted almost two hundred and fifty German gun emplacements, most of them situated in a cordon two to three kilometres deep running parallel with the front. Counter battery fire began at the end of November and continued every time the weather and visibility were good enough, with systematic destruction starting on 9 December. Two types of batteries received particular attention from French gunners: those that were active and those armed with heavy calibre guns that were difficult or slow to repair or replace. Between 9–14 December guns were blown up, shelters collapsed on gun crews, ammunition dumps exploded and gunners were killed, wounded or gassed. At the same time bombers, assisted by "Champagne", a dirigible based at Toul, ranged over the German rear areas, targeting stations, marshalling yards and junctions, bivouacs, ammunition depots, air fields and factories. Fighter squadrons prevented German pilots from attacking French planes or balloons and flew low enough to machine gun troops on the ground. The effect was stunning. 'I've served on many parts of the front' wrote Joseph Coulet of the tough and highly decorated Régiment d'infanterie coloniale du Maroc, which had recently added the recapture of Fort Douaumont to its battle honours:

'but I've never seen such a deluge shells of all calibres swamping the enemy trenches. It was like a continuous roll of thunder, broken only by the huge guns, which boomed like the big base drums of an orchestra. Shells were hitting the ground like enormous raindrops and the dirt was just blowing up like dust.'

In order to trick the Germans into betraying the position of any field guns which had so far escaped punishment, General Nivelle ordered a simulated attack on 14 December – a tactic already tried successfully the previous October. German gunners were tricked again and the batteries were swamped by counter battery fire. By the time French troops moved off on 15 December over one hundred German batteries had ceased firing, some had been completely annihilated, and at least thirty guns had been destroyed.

In December 1916 the German lines on the Right Bank of the River Meuse stretched for ten kilometres and were held by elements of four army corps and one Bavarian formation: from the German right by the River Meuse to their left on the Woëvre Plain these were the 14th Reserve, 39th, 10th, 14th, and 39th Bavarian Reserve divisions (respectively VII Reserve Corps, XV Corps, V Corps and VII Corps). Of the five, the 14th Reserve had held a quiet sector for months and only taken part in local actions. The 10th and 14th were good solid troops but had suffered physically from too long a period of service in the arduous Douaumont sector, which had resulted in high levels of sickness. The 39th was deeply disillusioned by being transferred from Verdun to the Somme without the promised rest, and furious at later being returned to Verdun with the same unfulfilled promise. As for the 39th Bavarian

French colonial troops on parade.

General Passaga, commander of the 133rd Division, with his staff.

Reserve Division, they had spent almost two years on the quiet Vosges front and lacked experience of a major battle.

By contrast, the French divisions moving up for the attack all had major battle experience; their morale was high and they were well trained. The gaps in the ranks had been filled and every man had spent time on the firing range, practised throwing grenades, and learned how to fire, dismantle and re-assemble an automatic rifle. The distribution of relief maps of the Verdun region had allowed similar terrain to be identified near to the training camps so that troops could practise their part in the operation and work out how to solve any problems that might arise. There were eight assault divisions in all: 126th, 38th, 37th and 133rd in the first line and the 123rd, 128th, 21st and 6th in the second line. Two of the first line divisions, the 38th, commanded by General Guyot de Salins, and the 133rd, commanded by General Passaga, had played major roles in the victorious operation of 24 October. The 37th and 38th Divisions comprised colonial and African troops with a reputation for hard fighting, including the Régiment d'infanterie colonial du Maroc. Major Nicolay, commander of the battalion that, on 24 October, had cleared Fort Douaumont of its last German defenders and was the first commander after its recapture, was again leading his men into battle.

The final decision on the start of the offensive depended on the weather, so during the night of 13–14 December the assault troops moved into position and waited for orders. Throughout the day heavy guns continued pouring shells into German camps, observation posts and

6

communication lines, while field guns hit trenches and secondary defences. Any battery that responded was swamped with gas and gas filled the ravines, hampering resupply.

Under the pounding German morale, already affected by the peace proposals put forward by Kaiser Wilhelm on 12 December, fell even lower. After the war, a veteran of the 1st Battalion, Infantry Regiment 126 – formerly the 39th Division's strongest and most homogenous regiment but now as disillusioned as everyone else – remembered bitterly that:

Kaiser Wilhelm II of Germany.

'When Mangin's artillery went over to destructive fire on 12 December [we had] fifteen battalions in the front line, another fifteen in the ravines behind them and the same number in the shelters at the foot of the ridge. Fighting and labouring had exhausted every man; all of them had shed blood here and on the Somme. The artillery preparation lasted for three days. Clouds of dust and gas spread [*right across the Right Bank*], blocking out what pale daylight managed to penetrate the snow clouds…It was when wire, obstacles, trenches and shelters had been destroyed, front line companies as good as wiped out, and the battalions in the ravines overcome with gas, that the French infantry attacked; and it was rested and fresh troops that Mangin sent into the fight.'

The night before the assault his commander, Hauptmann Tobias, reported that the chances of defending the position were slim:

'After seven days in the front line under continuous artillery fire and without any hot food the fighting strength of the battalion has been almost exhausted by labour and fatigues in the mud filled trenches. The position has been flattened along half its length; in many places the line of the trenches can no longer be seen, and pools of mud, anything up to one metre deep, make movement impossible.

With the trenches in this state, without wire or obstacles, and with the enemy so close, there is little prospect of successfully resisting an energetic assault launched after a preliminary heavy barrage.'

Poor visibility hampered aerial reconnaissance on 14 December but the photos that came back showed sufficient destruction for the assault to go ahead the following day, and at 10am on 15 December a round fired from the 155mm turret gun in Fort Douaumont gave the signal to move off. The terrible battering the German guns had received had not knocked all of them out and for several hours the waiting troops had been subjected to a violent bombardment. It gradually diminished as French counter battery fire grew but some formations suffered heavily. The weather was terrible. The combination of prolonged shelling and persistent rain had destroyed the ground and turned the trenches into rivers of mud, which quickly put rifles out of action, so it was with a grenade in one hand and a bayonet in the other that many of the assault troops moved forward. The Germans had put the increasing levels of fire down to retaliation for a recent local operation on the Left Bank, rather than as preparation for an offensive, and they were taken by surprise when the attackers, following closely behind a rolling barrage, reached the German line. Grenades and flamethrowers dealt with any resistance, while planes flew low overhead, machine gunning anyone who escaped.

With the exception of one part of the Côte du Poivre, where undamaged machine guns held up the 126th Division's advance for several hours, the first objective was reached quickly along the whole line, and at noon the three other divisions moved off again without waiting for the 126th to catch up. However, reaching the second objective did not go so well. The second and third German lines were less damaged than the front line and German resistance was strong. In the centre of the front a handful of men from the Fusilier Battalion of Grenadier Regiment 6 (10th Division), swearing

The 155mm revolving gun turret on Fort Douaumont that signalled the start of the French offensive of 15 December 1916. *Author's collection*

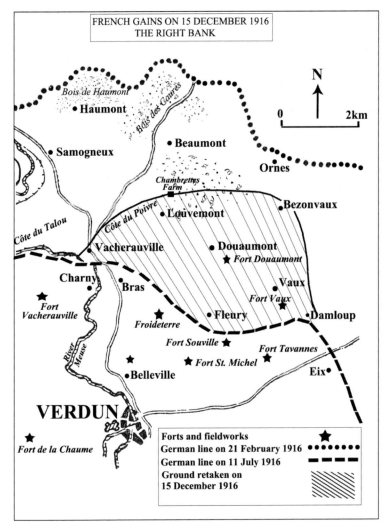

The French offensive of 15 December 1916.

'those dogs won't take us alive', managed to recapture a couple of bits of trench but they were soon surrounded. As Hauptmann Koeppel reported:

'The others handed me rifles and I just fired at any Frenchman who stood up. One man on either side of me and one by my feet kept on loading and I kept on shooting, helped by my best hand grenade thrower and my faithful orderly…The two of them

9

threw grenade after grenade as calmly if they were on the training ground …Then Lieutenant Balan came up. "Oberstleutenant von Kaisenberg [the regimental commander] is down. The MGs are all smashed and the reserve company's had it!"…We carried on firing all round and even upwards, where planes flying really low were machine gunning us. More and more men were falling. In the end Balan and I only had four unwounded men left but we did what we could. Then a French hand grenade exploded in our grenade dump and two more men were wounded. That was it. We fired our last rounds and tried to get back to the dugout, where we knew we still had a rifle and ammunition and our revolvers, but the French were on us.'

Resistance was particularly strong in the 133rd Division's sector on the French right. The Ouvrage de Bezonvaux, a small fieldwork comprising three concrete shelters and an earth rampart surrounded by wire, which had been perched on top of the Meuse Heights in 1889 to block an infantry attack in the direction of Fort Douaumont and Fort Vaux, had to be cleared by incendiary grenades, despite having been comprehensively worked over by French guns before the attackers reached it; while the batteries, stores dumps and camps in the steep ravines running down from the Meuse Heights to the Woëvre Plain were defended tooth and nail. The 321st Infantry, whose task was to recapture the village of Bezonvaux lost the previous 25 February, was

German soldiers of Verdun in 1916. *Tom Gudmestad*

10

held up for hours by the resistance of the Tranchée de Deux-Ponts, a position on the edge of the Meuse Heights which, together with the Ouvrage de Bezonvaux, commanded access to the village below; and night fell with the village still in German hands. With most of the other French objectives already captured a fresh plan was needed and at midnight General Passaga issued a new order. There was to be no waiting for daylight; Bezonvaux was to be taken in a surprise attack to be launched at 2am by a group formed of the 102nd Chasseurs and the 6th Battalion, 321st Infantry. The 102nd would advance on Bezonvaux and occupy it, while the 6th Battalion would turn sharp left on arriving level with the Ouvrage de Bezonvaux and attack the Tranchée de Deux-Ponts from the rear, distracting the defenders and allowing the 4th Battalion to attack from the other side. Three companies of the 5th Infantry were to have relieved the 102nd but when the moment came they had not arrived. 'It did not matter', wrote the clerk responsible for the 102nd's war diary,

> 'the order was imperative; there could be no delay. The machine guns were left behind. There was very little ammunition because it had been given to the 116th Chasseurs but it made no difference. It was a night attack. We would use the bayonet.'

There was no doubt about the difficulties involved. The plan involved advancing by the compass in darkness and deep snow over chaotic ground strewn with fallen trees and deep shell craters, with the added difficulty of the Fond du Loup, a deep ravine housing an extensive German camp

Part of the original entrance gate to the Ouvrage de Bezonvaux, with a heavily shelled shelter behind. *Author's collection*

that would have to be cleared before they could continue. The 321st's commander, Lieutenant Colonel Picard, made no bones about what was involved:

'The difficulties were enormous: black night and thick snow, troops scattered [*by the previous day's fighting*], knowledge of enemy resistance pretty well nil. I was asked to send two companies: we would never have seen them again. I telephoned to say that I would need at least two battalions.'

The operation was to be led by Major Gatinet, commander of the 6th Battalion. Colonel Picard again:

'When he received the order, Gatinet expressed the view that it was absolutely impossible and I believe he was right. But there was no time to discuss it; if we let the enemy reorganize we would fail and might have to withdraw, with incalculable consequences. So I wrote to Gatinet: "Military honour is at stake; you are responsible for carrying out the order. Whatever it costs, you must attack tonight. It is 2am; I will give you until 5am but no more. I will hold you personally accountable." ... Gatinet, who is a warrior, said to his officers: "It's absurd, but in war the absurd sometimes succeeds. Let's do it!"'

Part of the Tranchée de Deux-Ponts. *Author's collection*

A night which Colonel Picard swore he would never forget if he lived to be a hundred ended with complete success:

'… that night operation, which was the epitome of recklessness and audacious to the point of madness, was carried out under unimaginable difficulties, but succeeded. Orders got through the darkness, the snow and the bombardment. If even one runner had been hit, everything would have collapsed. In the ravines, in pitch darkness, everyone moved off together but it more or less fell apart later. Major Gatinet was alone for three hours with fourteen men against 200 Germans who fired from their dugouts without daring to come out… Finally, the other companies came up and relieved them. At dawn, the 4th Battalion seized the Tranchée de Deux-Ponts. It had held out all night.'

In the meantime, the Chasseurs had got to the bottom of the Fond du Loup where:

'…there was not a German in sight apart from four scared men in a shallow dugout … who surrendered without a word. From there to the bottom of the valley there was just glutinous mud and we slipped and stuck. There had been a camp there; some of the dugouts had been burned and were still smoking. On the left, rockets were going up everywhere along Deux-Ponts ridge. We maintained a really impressive silence and advanced as quietly as possible. We arrived at the bottom of the Fond du Loup, 250 metres south of the village, feeling that we had not been seen…to the left there were four small calibre guns that had been destroyed. The ground was boggy and shelling had turned it into a real quagmire'.

They were quite close to Bezonvaux before things changed:

'Twenty five metres from the hollow way [a deeply worn track into Bezonvaux], there was a prolonged fusillade. It was about 6am. The front lines [two companies] stopped and lay down. In an instant, the Chasseurs opened violent fire. Rifle grenades were flying in all directions and making a hellish noise. It was scarcely ten minutes before two buglers suddenly sounded the charge… It made everyone leap up. Like a whirlwind the two companies rushed to the village and raced through it. Two columns of prisoners, about eighty men each, were sent back to the Ouvrage de Bezonvaux. Germans were fleeing in all directions [and] seeing his men completely outnumbered the battalion commander sent the two front line companies to hold the northern and eastern edges of the village while he remained behind a hedge with the reserve company 150 metres to the south. Numbers were so low that it was only by including the pioneers, runners and signallers that he could form two sections and that was insufficient to allow the village to be searched'.

It was 7am when the battalion commander, by now feeling rather anxious, caught sight of movement near the Tranchée de Deux-Ponts and saw the 321st heading towards him. The 6th Battalion's surprise attack had been a complete success; two hundred prisoners had been taken, and machine guns, trench mortars and masses of other equipment captured. There were now more men available to mop up shelters and round up the Germans still holding on, but even so the situation was precarious, and

German soldiers in a well built trench prepared for a gas attack. Note the box of *kugel* **hand grenades.** *Tom Gudmestad*

14

once it was properly light and the German batteries opened up, it got much worse. Within an hour:

> 'the runners could no longer get through…We could only use the [last] pigeon. All the equipment had been lost when the Pigeon Sergeant was killed [so] we just wrote the message on a scrap of paper and tied it on with thread. We watched anxiously as it flew off… The command post had been set up in the last house on the western side of the village. It still had walls and a bit of roof but there was not much left by evening. At 10.40am the machine gunners by the Ouvrage de Bezonvaux were ordered down to the village. That was the last order…that arrived at its destination. All the runners…were killed or wounded, even when they went out in pairs'

By 3pm the trenches dug that morning had disappeared, ammunition was running out and some sections were down to four men; but despite general exhaustion they managed to establish a continuous defensive line around the village and link up with the Ouvrage de Bezonvaux.

By 9am on 16 December all objectives had been achieved and at last the filthy, exhausted and frostbitten troops could be relieved. The weather had been awful throughout, with rain and snow and temperatures dropping to several degrees below zero. On both sides of the line men suffered severely from frostbite. Captain Félix Pourailly, 283rd Régiment d'artillerie longue, watched a group of frostbitten Zouaves slowly making their way out of the line:

> 'The Zouaves had beaten everything in their path but even they could not beat the cold.

Major Nicolay, commander of the 8th Battalion, Régiment d'infanterie coloniale du Maroc, and first commander of Fort Douaumont after its recapture. He lies in Plot 164 of Bevaux Military Cemetery, southeastern outskirts of Verdun.

They came past me in an unending line, in little groups, or two by two. They had pulled their shoes apart and were just wearing the soles tied on with rags; most of them were walking barefoot, their feet wrapped in scarves, bonnets or handkerchiefs…Shuffling, staggering, using their rifles as crutches, leaning on one another, or crawling on all fours, they came towards me…their uniforms stiff with mud, their faces filthy and drawn with pain…'

It was a victory but it had come at a substantial cost in officers and men and they included Major Nicolay, who had been killed clearing shelters in a ravine to the south of Louvemont within minutes of the start of the offensive. Nevertheless, the front was now solidly established along a series of ridges and hills which provided the French with invaluable observatories. The German lines had been pushed a considerable distance from Verdun and Fort Douaumont was protected from a surprise attack. German losses for the period of 15–18 December were estimated at roughly 25,000; over 11,000 prisoners had been captured, some of whom had had no food for days, and more than 280 guns, mortars and machine guns had been taken or destroyed. It had been a great success and General Mangin, addressing his troops as *Mes Amis*, praised their magnificent efforts as worthy descendants of the Revolution and ambassadors of the Republic.

On 17 December 1916, General Nivelle took over from General Joffre as Commander-in-Chief of the armies in France. Believing that Verdun could now be regarded as a purely defensive sector he ordered that the resources available there should be reduced. However, the

General Guillaumat.

new Second Army commander, General Guillaumat, protested that the difficulties of organizing a sector convulsed by months of violent shelling, together with the terrible effects of the weather on the front line regiments and the continuing aggressive attitude of the Germans, required a strong force to be maintained. In his view the Battle of Verdun was not over. While the fighting was no longer continuous, any of the local operations currently being undertaken by the Germans could be the prelude to a large scale operation.

Chapter Two

Decisions

The December offensive had been a disaster and for the German High Command the two successive defeats demonstrated 'serious tactical failures of the sort our Army had rarely suffered since the start of the war'. Moreover, they raised serious concerns for the future of the war, especially in the light of the number of prisoners taken and guns and material captured or destroyed. Field Marshal von Hindenburg, who had taken over as Chief of the German General Staff at the end of August 1916, wasted no time in taking action. On 17 December, he requested the dismissal of the commanders of the Fifth Army, VII Reserve Corps and the 39th Bavarian Reserve Division and threatened other commanders with court martial. There were to be no proposals for decorations other than the Iron Cross, and in a blistering letter officers and men were reminded of their duty. The following day, General von Gallwitz took command of the Fifth Army and General Ludendorff, First Quartermaster General, travelled from Silesia to join other senior commanders in Stenay, north of Verdun, for a discussion about what had happened. Ludendorff's conclusion was that there had been no failure of defence; the troops' ability to resist had simply been exhausted by the sheer enormity of the demands made on them in 1916.

It was all very well to draw that conclusion but what was to be done about it? At the end of December senior German commanders at Verdun were expecting another major assault. None came and activity gradually died down. On the Right Bank senior commanders considered plans to recapture some of the most important positions lost on 15-16 December but these were not supported by Crown Prince Wilhelm, now commander of Army Group Deutsche Kronprinz, which covered the front from Champagne to the Swiss border.

General Ludendorff.

17

He believed that it would be impossible to supply the replacements needed for offensive action at Verdun and that the ultimate solution lay in withdrawal to the positions of February 1916. The problem was that the weather and the state of the February 1916 lines made it impossible to withdraw before the spring, quite apart from the effect on morale withdrawal would have. The only alternative was to remain where they were, improve the lines, particularly the supply lines which, as things stood, could barely provide the troops with their daily needs. In the end the combination of winter weather, supply problems, the state of the ground and the continuous labouring needed to bring the defences up to scratch wore out the troops so much that by mid-January four of the five Right Bank divisions brought in as replacements after the December defeat had to be relieved, leaving the High Command with no alternative but to face the fact that Verdun had to become a secondary front.

General Ludendorff took the final decision: there would be no attempt to recapture the ground lost in December, serious threats from the French would be met, if necessary, by tactical withdrawals, and only 'minor offensives' would be carried out.

That did not stop the Germans from launching limited operations in tactically important sectors such as on the Left Bank, where they attempted to break the stalemate on Cote 304 and gain control of a position they called the Backenzahn (*Back Tooth*), which offered clear observation over French lines. It had already been attacked unsuccessfully several times. To ensure success this time the assault troops trained over ground as similar as possible to the area of operation; whilst absolute secrecy was maintained at all times. During the preparation, thirty trench mortars concentrated on the French front lines, cutting the wire and smashing the machine guns, while a field gun barrage prevented the arrival of reserves and long range guns dealt with the French artillery and when the leading waves moved forward on 6 December there was little resistance.

This success was followed by a second 'minor' operation, this time along a 1500 metre front with flanking operations to keep the French busy. Preparation for it followed the same formula, with specialized training for the assault troops and hand grenades, planks, rolls of wire, sandbags, entrenching tools and other material dumped in the front line to avoid shortage at the vital moment. In the run up to the operation each unit received detailed plans of their sector and the relevant timetable, signallers were forbidden to use telephones to transmit orders or messages, and every night assault troop leaders reconnoitred No Man's Land and got to know the terrain. With so much activity behind the lines it was fortunate that weather prevented aerial observation of the German preparations, whilst fog could have hampered the guns too;

18

but 25 January dawned sunny and clear. After three hours of pounding with gas, high explosive and mortar bombs, the Germans moved forward to find the French lines completely destroyed. Once again it was a complete success; the German front line had been pushed forward to a point where they could observe the French positions behind Cote 304 and bring them under rifle fire.

As winter went on the troops on both sides had to find ways of surviving in the ocean of icy mud that formed their new lines. Having conquered the high ground on the Right Bank, the French now found that many of their positions were in clear sight of the Germans and they were constantly shelled. Gas forced men to wear their masks for hours at a time. Snow and frostbite added to the general misery and the temperature fell to -20C. Trees exploded as if hit by lightning, bread could only be cut with an axe, the wine came up frozen in sandbags and the ground was too hard to dig. Sergeant Bonfils, 217th Infantry, was on the Mort-Homme:

> 'We all do what we can to keep warm. It's so cold that you can't even think. All our food is frozen; bread, wine, coffee; the sardines we have for every meal are just a solid block in the oil and have to be thawed out. Since solid fuel [paraffin blocks] was distributed every man keeps some in an old chocolate tin and makes a little stove out of an empty stew tin with holes in.'

A German position on Cote 304 after the offensive of 25 January 1917. *Tom Gudmestad*

A snowy German camp on the Right Bank. *Tom Gudmestad*

Fortunately, some men retained an appetite whatever happened: Maurice Bouquet, 5th Infantry, was:

> 'Going up to the line … I fell in a shell hole half filled with mud and water. The shelling was terrific but the runners and … the acting battalion commander rushed to pull me out. I was covered in mud … To make myself feel better when I got to the command post I pulled a pickled herring out of my haversack, wiped the mud off and cooked it over a candle.'

Scores of men were evacuated every day. Following their success on 15-16 December, the 133rd Division returned to the Bezonvaux sector on 10 January. Jean Norton Cru, a sergeant with the 321st Infantry and later the author of an acclaimed critical review of works on the Battle of Verdun, recalled that:

> '…during the six days in line I lost my entire section, a quarter of the men being killed or wounded and three quarters evacuated for frostbite… [our division] was effectively half destroyed by the first relief'.

When it thawed water filled the trenches and dugouts, men and guns sank in the mud, rations failed to get through, and the wounded could not be evacuated. Moving in or out of the line was slow and exhausting. In some sectors the opposing lines were very close together. Sergeant Bonfils again:

'Our front lines on the Mort-Homme were more like jump off lines than real trenches. There were sentry posts at regular intervals and one of them, which was more important than the others, was commanded by a sergeant, who was posted by a sand bag barricade topped by stakes and wire. On one side our grenadiers and on the other side Fritz. On both sides you could hear boots stamping up and down on the hard ground. From time to time one of our men hummed a popular song and then a German soldier repeated it on his harmonica. Musical harmony or not, we were always on the alert.'

In May 1916 General Pétain had moved from being in charge of Second Army operations at Verdun to overall command of the Group of Armies of the Centre. It was in that capacity that he now ordered every division to devote all possible energy to strengthening their lines, which were inadequate in every way. The Germans were doing the same thing. Determined not to be pushed back any further, they fortified their new positions heavily with wire, machine guns, trench mortars and deep underground shelters – veritable barracks, according to the French Official History. On the Right Bank their main centres of resistance were Cote 344 and the Butte de Caurières (two hilltops which offered the possibility of observation over wide areas) and the extensive forests and deep sheltered ravines of Bois des Fosses.

The effort of reorganization needed after the December defeat meant that for several weeks there was little German activity on the Right Bank; but once they were established in their new lines they began to attack again, starting with a major push by three divisions on 4 March. The aim was to recapture certain important positions lost in December, take prisoners and seize as much material as possible. One such position was Chambrettes

Géneral Pétain.

21

Chambrettes Farm before its complete destruction.

Farm, a cluster of ruined buildings commanding Bois des Fosses, which was attacked repeatedly throughout the spring and only held at the cost of substantial casualties. Soaked with gas, constantly shelled, with lines fragile and imprecise, the sector became, in the words of one French commentator, 'an empire of death'. In the Bois des Fosses, in which every narrow brush filled ravine became a little Thermopylae, conditions were unimaginable. Captain Paul Flamant, 332nd Infantry:

> 'We lived in foul mud. The rain fell in torrents and when the sun shone horrible flies swarmed over the mass grave in which we had dug our shelters and trenches. The mud was full of mummified corpses, both French and German, who had taken on the colour of the soil. [They] had been there since the terrible fighting of 1916. Here a hand stuck out of the ground; there a leg appeared after a mud slide. Our men, indifferent or perhaps philosophical about it, hung their canteens on it…At night, the scene in the ravine was hallucinatory. It was only because of [our previous experience] that we could cope with the strain of holding such a position under the threat of storm troop raids almost every night.'

Forcing the Germans to fight
The German withdrawal to the Hindenburg Line in March 1917 made the French High Command fear that the Germans would go entirely over to the defensive. As a result, General Nivelle began to consider forcing them to fight by launching offensive operations on those parts of the front which were too important for them to give up – a reflection

of General von Falkenhayn's thinking in 1916. On the Verdun front the possibilities were, first, an attack northwards towards Stenay and Montmédy, which would threaten the main German railway supply line and the vital Sedan rail hub; and, second, an action towards the northeast to recapture the important iron and coal mining areas around Briey.

After consideration, the Stenay project was rejected but the Briey project was accepted and extended to include the prior reduction of the St Mihiel Salient. This was a wedge-shaped bulge in the lines to the southeast of Verdun which, **General Max von Gallwitz, who took command of the Fifth Army on 18 December 1916.**

when it was formed in September 1914, had cut one of the two railway lines then supplying the city. Clearing the St Mihiel Salient would not only remove a threat to Verdun and allow supply trains to run again but would also shorten the French line and free up an extensive German rail network for French use. General Nivelle approved the proposal and a plan was drawn up for a two phase operation culminating in the recapture of the Briey area. However, the failure of his offensive on the Aisne in April 1917, which General Nivelle hoped would lead to a breakthrough and the decisive defeat of the Germans, resulted in a crisis of morale in the French army and there was open mutiny in many divisions.

On 17 May 1917, Nivelle was replaced as Commander-in-Chief by General Pétain, who acknowledged that for the time being the French army was unfit for major offensives. Two days later he issued Directive No 1, which stipulated that any future offensive would not only be strictly limited but would also use the maximum of artillery and the minimum of infantry to achieve its objectives. General Pétain had three main aims: to restore discipline and morale to the army, to keep the Germans fighting, and to husband French resources until the United States of America, which had entered the war on 6 April 1917, was able to take its full place among the Allies. In the circumstances, the planned two phase operation to reduce the St Mihiel Salient and recapture the Briey sector, which would have involved two armies operating together, had to be shelved until the

French army was once again in good health. But even if the two phase operation could not be undertaken for the moment, there was preliminary action which could. For any operation towards Briey to be successful, the roads and rail hubs serving Verdun would have to be protected from long range German artillery fire. The guns stood north of the Verdun salient and were guided by observers stationed on hilltops on both sides of the River Meuse which provided the Germans with clear views over French supply lines and allowed them to direct fire on to the main hubs. Capturing these observatories would force the German artillery to withdraw, thus putting French lines of communication out of range. By a letter of 23 May 1917 General Pétain approved this limited operation and ordered it to be launched around 15 July 1917. The date was later postponed by a month.

An operation on both sides of the river
The hilltop observatories in question were Cote 304, the Mort-Homme and the Côte de l'Oie on the Left Bank and the Côte du Talou and Cote 344 on the Right Bank. All had been the scene of violent fighting in 1916 and before any offensive could be launched everything – communication trenches, assembly points, supply and ammunition dumps, first aid posts, evacuation routes, batteries, signalling centres, reserve positions, shelters, dugouts, command posts and observatories, to say nothing of kilometres of roads and railways – had to be created from scratch or improved. The plan was pushed on as fast as possible, with goods and supplies moving at night or, if daytime movement was absolutely indispensable, along forested routes. Where possible, the

work was also done at night, although darkness made it difficult to protect the workers from German incursions. The ever present danger of men deserting or being captured meant that the true reason for the work was not given and troops were only told that they were reinforcing the defence of the sector. Thousands were involved.

A French medical detachment at a well prepared aid post on the Côte du Poivre. *Tom Gudmestad*

A light railway under construction.

Then there were the guns. The heavies needed platforms, several hundred ammunition depots, scores of command and control centres and hundreds of dugouts. Night after night, thousands of tons of equipment and supplies arrived at stations in the rear and were transferred to narrow gauge railways for transport to the front. While wagons on the 60cm lines were pulled by locomotives, the smaller 40cm lines, which ran much closer to the front, were pulled by teams of men who hauled the loaded wagons over planks laid across yawning craters, jumping from sleeper to sleeper and doing everything to avoid falling under the wheels of the wagons rocking behind.

A pre-emptive attack
It was impossible for such massive preparations to remain completely unknown to the Germans and in June French aerial observers reported increased traffic behind the lines and more batteries on the Left Bank. On 28 June, any doubt that the Germans were preparing to take action was swept away in an absolute hurricane of fire on Cote 304. Firing as fast as they could, German guns swept back and forth along the French first and second lines destroying everything; the batteries were swamped with gas and heavy howitzers smashed the observatories. Within an hour the enormous weight of steel had destroyed the French lines completely. With flame throwers and grenadiers leading the way the attackers moved forward but there was almost no resistance and it only took forty five minutes for them to reach their objectives. The scene was complete

The memorial to Lieutenant Gontran de Witte, 24th Dragoons, who was killed with eight companions in the German offensive of 28 June 1917. This handsome memorial is in the French military cemetery at Dombasle. *Author's collection*

devastation; all reference points had been destroyed and the maps issued before the assault were unusable. Pioneers and labourers were already scrambling forward with the tools and equipment needed to organise the new position; but it took time to clear it all and several days later French troops were still being dug out of collapsed bunkers.

The next day another whirlwind assault pushed the German lines even further forward and it was only the determined resistance of small isolated groups of men that prevented the French from losing Cote 304 altogether. These German assaults were a shock to the French and, although on 17 July they threw the Germans back and recaptured most of the lost ground, they had had an unpleasant lesson. In future, artillery and infantry had to be ready to take action at any time, day or night, without losing a minute. For General Guillaumat, the best way for troops to defend themselves was by attacking and that was precisely what the Second Army was intending to do.

The final plan
The final plan involved simultaneous assaults along an eighteen kilometre front using four army corps: XIII (General Linder) and XVI Corps (General Corvisart) on the Left Bank and XV (General Fonclare)

26

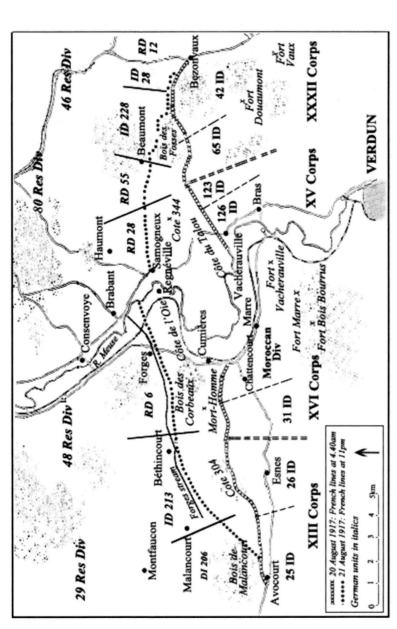

The French offensive of 20 August 1917.

and XXXII Corps (General Passaga) on the Right Bank. On each side of the river, four divisions would attack in the first line, with a further four behind to provide relief and to hold and defend the captured ground. On the Left Bank the main objectives were, from left to right, a section of the Bois de Malancourt, Cote 304, the Mort-Homme and the Bois des Corbeaux, with a second operation the following day to recapture the German positions on the Côte de l'Oie and liberate the village of Regnéville. On the Right Bank the objectives were the Côte du Talou, Cote 344 and flanking positions in Bois des Fosses, with a follow up operation to clear the village of Samogneux. As Samogneux and Regnéville faced each other across the Meuse valley at a point where it was less than one kilometre wide, recapturing the two villages would allow the French to control the river valley once again.

In keeping with General Pétain's assurance of the maximum possible artillery support for the infantry, the line-up of guns was prodigious:

XIII Corps: for objectives spread over six kilometres, fifty seven field gun batteries, eighty nine heavy batteries.

XVI Corps: for objectives spread over seven kilometres: sixty field gun batteries and seventy nine heavy batteries

XV Corps: as for XVI Corps.

XXXII Corps: for objectives spread over four kilometres, sixty field gun batteries and sixty three heavy batteries.

In all it made an average of ten field gun batteries and thirteen heavy batteries per kilometre. Further firepower came from almost 300 trench mortars and over one hundred of the heaviest guns and howitzers

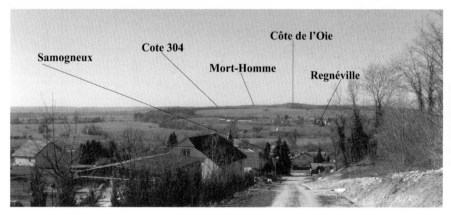

The view from Samogneux to Regnéville. *Author's collection*

28

available. These pieces, known as *artillerie lourde à grande puissance* (ALGP), were capable of firing over greater distance and with more destructive power than the field artillery and they would be needed to deal with the deep mined dugouts and tunnels on the Left Bank.

A subdivision of the artillery created during the war, the ALGP formed the general heavy artillery reserve and included various types of heavy gun, including those on railway mountings and on barges. While most of the heavies were of calibres between 140mm and 320mm, there were a small number of 370mm howitzers and two 400mm giants which had already demonstrated their terrifying power against Fort Douaumont and Fort Vaux in October 1916. The work of getting the guns into position, which involved men and horses by the thousand, began at the end of June and lasted until shortly before artillery preparation began. It was an arduous task and spared no one, as the Second Group of the 57th Field Artillery Regiment found on 3 August after slogging through deep mud to reach their intended position:

'There was nothing there except four small stakes with bits of white paper attached to show where the guns should stand. The next day we started digging trenches and shelters. We had to bring up enormous quantities of ammunition and the effort was prodigious but by 12 August we had stacked 25,000 shells, all brought up from the artillery parks, some as far as twenty kilometres away. The horses got hardly any rest, there was little shelter and with the terrible weather, mud, fatigue and misery many of them died.'

A French 400mm howitzer on railway mountings. *Tom Gudmestad*

Despite all the difficulties, when artillery preparation began 60,000 gunners, several hundred trench mortars and over two thousand guns of all calibres stood ready to support the assault. One hundred guns, corresponding to five for each kilometre of front, were heavies. As for the ammunition supply, a week of preparatory fire, plus three days' supply once the offensive had started, required almost 160,000 tonnes of shells, each of which needed handling and transporting, mostly in the dark and often in poor weather. Inspired by methods in use in the British Army, batteries of machine guns used indirect fire to harass and interdict along the whole front. Their fire was concentrated on sectors immediately behind the German lines, as well as on relief or reinforcement routes, important junctions and assembly points, communication trenches, groups of dugouts and supply lines. Any breach made in the German wire was immediately subject to continual blasts of fire to prevent it from being repaired. The consumption of ammunition was spectacular. During the eight nights preceding the attack on the Left Bank, the Moroccan Division (XVI Corps) alone fired over a million and a half rounds and wore out a substantial number of machine gun barrels, but the violent reaction of German artillery and the statements made by German prisoners made it worth it.

French machine gunners with a Hotchkiss. A note in the French Official History records that in the eight nights preceding the offensive of 20 August, harassing and interdiction fire by French machine gunners wore out one hundred St. Etienne barrels and fifteen Hotchkiss barrels. *Tom Gudmestad*

The plan also involved balloons, reconnaissance and spotter planes by the score, fighters, and night and day bombing groups, whose task was to harass the railway stations and industrial centres north of Verdun. Beginning in the middle of July, daily photographic missions provided scores of images of the front that were rapidly printed and put together in a series of panoramic views. These were distributed throughout the corps and provided daily updated information on the state of the enemy defences. The number of photos taken was phenomenal, XVI Corps alone taking almost 400 on a single day. Fixed and movable anti aircraft defence was provided to protect balloons and batteries and to prevent any enemy incursion over depots, rail hubs and airfields.

With so many men labouring night and day, tiny villages became immense hives of activity. A typical example was Lemmes, formerly a dot on the landscape by the Voie Sacrée, the main supply road into Verdun, but now surrounded by dumps, depots, airfields and an immensely busy narrow gauge railway capable of supplying daily rations for 50,000 men and 15,000 horses. Far more than that would be needed for the coming offensive, which was based on 200,000 men on the Right Bank and 160,000 on the Left Bank, plus horses, requiring altogether an overall daily supply of 4,500 tonnes of food. In Dugny, a logistical and supply centre on the River Meuse some five kilometres south of Verdun, 144 ovens baked enough bread each day to supply the whole of the Second Army. As General Guillaumat remarked, merely preparing for the assault was a full military operation but there could be no failure this time. Army morale demanded a complete success.

An ammunition dump at Lemmes

German positions on each side of the River Meuse

By mid-1917, the German positions at Verdun comprised, roughly speaking, five defensive lines on the Right Bank, with some positions still under construction, and three lines on the Left Bank, which included three tunnels on the Mort-Homme. The lines were served by an extensive railway network and supported by roughly 130 batteries, many of them heavy, and twenty air escadrilles, comprising bombers, fighters and spotter, reconnaissance and communication units. As regards infantry, French intelligence reports at the time named four German infantry divisions on the Right Bank, plus three with elements of a fourth on the Left Bank. As for reserves, there were two divisions available on the Left Bank and four or five which could be brought rapidly forward to support the Right Bank.

The existence of the tunnels was well known to the French from aerial observation and the interrogation of prisoners. Work on them had begun during the summer of 1916, when the really desperate fighting had died down, leaving the German lines visible to French observers. This made supplying them both difficult and costly and to solve the problem General von François, commander of VII Corps, ordered the excavation of three tunnels to provide safe, underground passage between the front and the rear. The work, which took almost nine months to complete,

A German railway yard on the Left Bank after a French bombing raid.

32

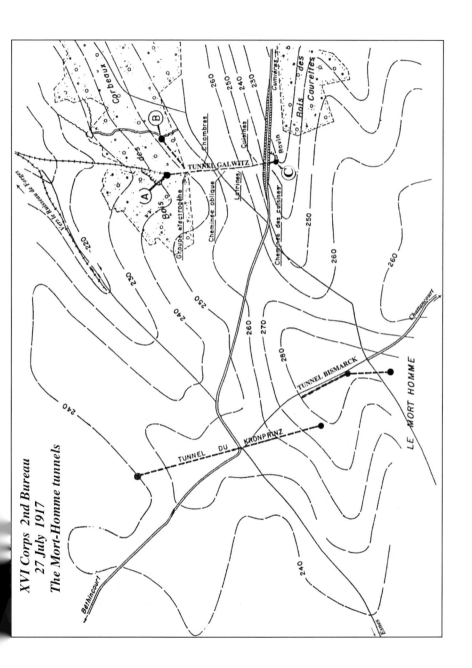

XVI Corps 2nd Bureau
27 July 1917
The Mort-Homme tunnels

33

General von François.

was carried out by pioneers and infantry, many of whom were miners, who also provided the nightly labour needed to bring the tools and building materials from the regimental pioneer park several kilometres back. Even ration parties were pressed into service once they had delivered the rations. All three were inaugurated by General von François in May 1917, an occasion on which decorations were handed out.

The Kronprinz Tunnel

Starting in a ravine on the lower slopes of the north side of the Mort-Homme, the Kronprinz Tunnel ran through the hillside to the Schlesier Graben, a deep trench forming part of the intermediate line. From prisoners' reports the French knew it to be just under a thousand metres long, varying from two to four metres wide and approximately two metres high. Tunnelling through limestone was hard work and even with jack hammers and pneumatic drills progress was only about seven metres per day. At first the spoil was dumped close to the main entrance and covered over; but as the tunnel progressed rails were laid and the spoil was loaded into wagons and hauled away by horses. In addition to the main entrances at the northern and southern ends of the tunnel, twelve side exits offered access by steep flights of steps to a series of rooms housing a regimental command post, a first aid post and beds for two companies. There was a machine room with a four horse power motor, a compressor, a power unit, and a generator providing power for the drills and lighting for the workface. The power unit, which comprised a petrol engine and a lighting dynamo, provided tunnel lighting. There were kitchens in a short branch tunnel at the northern end, while a captured spring at the southern end provided water for the machine room and a mineral water plant. All the exits had gas doors and internal barricades allowed the tunnel to be defended against attackers. General von François called it 'a masterpiece of civil engineering' but others had reservations. In May 1917, the commander of Reserve Infantry Regiment 35, one of the

34

A squad from Pioneer Company 108 outside their 'Rest Home' on Cote 304 in 1916. *Tom Gudmestad*

regiments using the tunnel on a daily basis, complained that 'inexcusable design flaws' made it weaker than it should have been. He had numerous complaints: the timbering was inadequate, particularly in the widest part where the kitchen tunnel branched off; the roof in the central section was weak; the entrances needed reinforcement; the kitchen tunnel had no independent escape route; and generally speaking the construction was amateurish. He was rebuked, told that other regiments would be pleased to have such accommodation, and his report was dismissed.

The Bismarck Tunnel
This short tunnel was first named after Generalleutenant von Runckel, commander of the 43rd Reserve Division, but the name was later changed. Starting in the Schlesier Graben, a short distance from the exit from the Kronprinz Tunnel, it ran for a little over 400 metres under the summit of the Mort-Homme to the German front line. Most of it was excavated by pioneers and progress was slow, with only about one metre being added each day. The Bismarck Tunnel was the same height as the Kronprinz Tunnel but it was only half as wide and differed in being entirely timbered. It had no electric lighting and, whilst there were multiple exits, there were few side rooms, as it was purely designed for the passage of troops, ie a subway.

35

The Gallwitz Tunnel

This ran from the north side of the Mort-Homme, passed under a hilltop and ended in the Ravin des Caurettes, a sheltered ravine behind the German front line to the east of the summit of the Mort-Homme. Although shorter than the Kronprinz Tunnel it was similar in many respects, being the same width and height and having the same sort of timbering, gas protection and barricades. It was also electrically lit, and had several side exits accessible by long flights of steps, including one of 165 steps known as the 'stairway to heaven', which led to an artillery observation post. The machine room was similarly equipped and there was a command post, a first aid post, kitchens, and side rooms with enough beds for one company. Rails ran the whole length of the tunnel, allowing spoil to be evacuated and equipment to be brought in.

During the summer of 1917 all three tunnels offered shelter, food, and accommodation for the regiments in the sector; but the weaknesses noted by the commander of Reserve Infantry Regiment 35 remained and in time they would prove disastrous.

Chapter Three

Artillery preparation begins

French guns began counter battery fire on 11 August, with preparatory and destructive fire starting two days later and involving the massive use of gas. The Germans responded with more gas and, fearing mass casualties among the gun crews, General Guillaumat ordered the constitution of a reserve. The 57th Field Artillery Regiment was typically affected:

> 'Serving the guns became more and more arduous. The enemy shelled us with a mixture of gases and men had to wear their masks all the time. The air was unbreathable. Handling the ammunition, aiming and manoeuvring the guns, became really difficult because we were half blind and half suffocated.
> Between 19–20 August our sector was hit by a real deluge of shells of all calibres, both high explosive and gas. Some men were knocked over by the blast, others collapsed half intoxicated. We had to keep our masks on all the time.'

Once the serious work of destruction was under way the Germans responded with violent, harassing fire on the French front lines and with zone fire where they believed the French artillery to be. German bombers ranged far and wide. In the ravines behind the front, and as far as fifteen kilometres back, German shells smashed into batteries, dumps and communication lines, and from the size of the explosions it was clear that heavies were in action. Deep in

German aerial bombs.
Tom Gudmestad

37

a ravine 700 metres from the German front line on 13 August, Alexis Callies, commander of the 1st Group, 58th Field Artillery, noted that:

> 'The German guns hardly stop firing now. The noise drives you mad and my dugout is a sounding box, which makes it worse. It's like living in a drum. French machine guns are firing on the other side of the ravine just a few hundred metres away and the noise they make is even more disagreeable than the shells.
>
> At 6pm, Boche concentration fire on [the] ravine. For half an hour the shells (105mm and 150mm) fall all round my command post at a rate of one every three or four seconds. This morning, a shell fell five metres from my command post at the entrance to a heavy artillery dugout…seriously wounding three men…Fifteen minutes later, when my three captains were at the command post, a heavy artillery ammunition dump blew up one hundred metres away. The blast knocked us all down. [One of the captains] was blown inside. The blast lifted the roof of the dugout in one piece….'

A particular objective of French guns on the Right Bank was the Bois des Fosses, an extensive area of woodland cut by several deep ravines and heavily protected by banks of wire, machine guns, trench mortar

A German 42cm howitzer. *Tom Gudmestad*

positions, fieldworks and observation posts. During the 1916 Battle of Verdun the Bois des Fosses had been a German staging post on the way forward where troops could rest and pick up what they needed at the front. As Infantry Regiment 67 recalled:

'There were ammunition and hand grenade depots and dumps of entrenching tools, rifles, steel helmets and every possible type of equipment. They were supplied by narrow gauge railways that ran right into the ravines [in the wood] and were controlled by long established stores clerks who would only release goods against a receipt...Several kitchens and some huge boilers provided men with hot food and coffee.'

A crowded place in which every square metre was taken up, it had always been under fire but the intensity increased when French heavies started targetting it in preparation for the offensive. Soon the forest was a wasteland of craters and smashed tree stumps. By 15 August the trenches were flattened, the kitchens were destroyed, the wire was blown to bits and the ravines and dugouts were full of gas. A trench mortar blew up with all its ammunition, others were knocked over, machine guns were buried, underground barracks collapsed on the men inside, contact with neighbouring units was lost and telephone cables were cut. 'Anyone who

A damaged light railway station in Bois des Fosses, known as the *Hundekehle*.
Tom Gudmestad

has been in the front line', wrote the historians of Fusilier Regiment 35, 228th Division, in 1929, when the events in question were long past but not forgotten, 'knows the real meaning of such a matter of fact description of the events of a single day':

'Just maintaining the telephone cables was in itself an immense achievement. The breakage men were permanently at work and had to patch the lines ten to twenty times. Once mended the connection worked for ten minutes or half an hour but then it was broken again...The signallers often worked all night only to have the line broken again as soon as they had mended it. With the lines down we had to use runners. That sounds a simple thing but what was it actually like to run 300–400 metres through a bombardment? How often did a runner have to throw himself down flat or crouch in a shell hole, how often did death miss him by a hair's breadth...?'

The German gunners were badly affected by gas but they managed to keep firing, although with mixed success. Fusilier Regiment 35 again:

German troops expecting a gas attack. *Tom Gudmestad*

'Shell after shell roared, whistled, screamed, growled, snarled, groaned and crashed around the command post and often we could not tell where they were coming from or whether they were theirs or ours...Mortar bombs and shells from our own guns hit us from time to time. That is really terrible, as men feel completely betrayed and abandoned... Soon you could not see the trench any more, just craters, all sizes...The sector was unrecognisable...The wire, which we had rolled out at night at such cost, was completely destroyed; there were tree stumps and branches everywhere and bits of bodies that the shells had thrown around, a trunk still in uniform, a leg, a hand.'

French shell consumption from 13 to 19 August 1917

D[ay]-7	D-6	D-5	D-4	D-3	D-2	D-1
110400	320000	346000	330000	300000	325000	425000

German shell consumption during the same period (almost all gas)

D-7	D-6	D-5	D-4	D-3	D-2	D-1
65000	44000	36000	37000	26000	27000	25000

Dr Raoul Mercier

It was the same on the Left Bank; between 12 and 20 August the whole sector was massively shelled with gas every night and casualty levels grew. Gas spread as far back as Forges Stream, a swift flowing tributary of the River Meuse on the north side of Cote 304 and the Mort-Homme, which shelling had turned into a swamp. The bridges and causeways over it were now a prime target of French guns, which swept back and forth across the area every night, blowing guns into the air and preventing their replacement. Men had to wear their masks all the time and while this was bearable for men who did not have to exert themselves, for ration or supply parties struggling up from the rear, ducking and diving into cover as they moved towards the line, it was simply unendurable. Unable to see once the eye pieces misted up and unable to breathe in the gas filled air, some men tried removing the eye pieces, holding the nose and breathing through the mouth as they hurried forward, but it was not very successful. The ration parties lost many men en route and even when they got through the gas soaked rations were often uneatable. That meant that once the

41

German pioneers building a bridge. *Tom Gudmestad*

iron rations had run out there was nothing to eat and, with the springs on the hillside destroyed, nothing to drink either.

In Reserve Infantry Regiment 35 on the western side of the Mort-Homme, gas casualties ran at roughly forty per cent; injuries, death, accidents, etc., brought the numbers down even more. By 15 August the regiment had 'no defensive position worthy of the name'. Their whole sector was a wasteland; companies were down to a handful of officers and men scattered here and there in shell craters, while the heavy guns, which were guided by spotter planes flying low overhead, methodically destroyed what was left of the trenches and shelters. Second Lieutenant Glitscher, Reserve Infantry Regiment 24, described the effect of aerial observation:

'On 15 August the sky was a clear blue, perfect for controlling artillery fire from the air. As expected, at around 9am the superheavies (350mm–400mm calibre) began to target our dugouts. Regularly every three minutes the battalion command post received a direct hit. The aeroplane guiding the fire was flying about 30 metres above ground [sic], high enough to be out of reach but low enough to see the tunnel entrances clearly…I was asked to report to the battalion commander… and after a direct hit on the command post I raced for the tunnel and got there before the next shell fell. I had scarcely got inside before the next shell destroyed the entrance. The entrances were being shelled systematically but were dug out by the men inside. In between we were hit by some

'No defensive position worthy of the name' in this trench. *Tom Gudmestad*

real 'tunnel smashers' which seriously weakened the roof. At midday the other men from my dugout rushed into the tunnel and reported that the company commander's dugout had been shelled and that there was nothing to be seen but a huge crater.'

Taking shelter in a dugout ran the risk of being buried alive or suffocated by gas; but for some men it was preferable to cowering unprotected in a shell crater under a rain of steel. Musketier Havemann, 6 Company, Reserve Infantry Regiment 35, saw a big group of men rush inside one of the last remaining dugouts and decided to follow them. Hardly had he got inside than there was:

'...a deafening roar. My mouth, nose and eyes filled with dust... the wooden cladding on the walls bent inwards like cardboard and then it all went dark...After a few minutes I managed to pull myself

43

A German working party takes a break from constructing a concrete dugout. *Tom Gudmestad*

out from under the debris that had fallen on me. I did the same for my comrade Neumann and then we managed to get another four comrades out. We were really lucky because we had been sitting closest to the entrance… [and] a direct hit over the unsupported passage between the two entrances had brought the roof down… Now we had to try to get the others out. The bombardment was raging but we carried on working all night to try to clear the roof fall and free our comrades. We knew that some of them were still alive because we could hear muffled knocking and cries for help but rescuing them was almost impossible. Debris was falling in as fast as we cleared it, the guns were roaring and iron shards were flying through the air. Towards morning we managed by a miracle to free [two more] and then we found some bodies. After thirteen hours we had to stop trying to free anyone else and by then their suffering was over. We had lost thirty one men, including our company commander.'

During the last days of the French preparation many of the men surviving in the trenches tried to take shelter in the tunnels but the sector was so ravaged that just finding the entrance became an almost impossible task. Second Lieutenant Hauschildt, Reserve Infantry Regiment 24, had to

A scene of destruction in the Bois des Corbeaux (Rabenwald). *Tom Gudmestad*

lead a battalion into the front line from a camp in the rear. He had been
in the sector a few days earlier and thought he knew it well:

'Everything went all right up to Bois des Corbeaux but then
we wandered all over the place for two hours trying to find our
destination, the entrance to the Gallwitz Tunnel. We couldn't
see anything of the position although we knew it very well;
communication trenches, fire trenches, shelters, everything had
gone. Even the tree trunks in Bois des Corbeaux, which even
without any branches showed where the wood used to be, had
gone. It had all been ploughed up and turned over in just a few
days. We decided to wait in a shell crater until dawn. At first light
we saw, just a few metres away, a soldier crawling out from under
a tarpaulin. It was the entrance to the tunnel we were looking for,
the only one still accessible, well hidden from spotter planes. At
4.30am, after almost five hours of searching all over the shell
blasted sector, I reported with the battalion to our regimental
commander, Major von Ahlefeld, who had moved into the tunnel
with his staff.'

By the time Major von Ahlefeld moved in on 13 August, the Gallwitz
Tunnel was already accommodating eight other staffs, a trench mortar
battalion, pioneers, several infantry companies and three field kitchens,
in addition to the normal garrison. Dr. Burmeister, senior medical officer
to the Third Battalion, Reserve Infantry Regiment 24, who had taken

45

refuge there earlier the same day along with the battalion commander and other medical personnel, found it dangerously overcrowded. Giant 400mm shells were targetting the tunnel, which rocked and crumbled with every explosion. As he later reported:

'The gas alarm sounded at any moment and gas in thick heavy clouds ...rolled down the steps and spread quickly throughout the tunnel like a black sack. It did not just affect the membranes of the eyes and the respiratory tract but the stomach too; the tongue soon acquired a slimy coating and there was nausea and vomiting. Despite the two electric fans the air was thick. As it was rarely possible to go outside the tunnel, emergency latrines had to be created. There must have been 400 men inside. The first aid post was constantly overcrowded with wounded, gassed and concussed men. It was not so much the poison gas that affected our men but rather the carbon monoxide from the explosions. The Ninth Company had twenty one men poisoned by carbon monoxide from a single shell and some of them could only be brought round with a lot of oxygen.

Inside the tunnel time became a blur; we did not know whether it was day or night. The wounded continued to arrive and

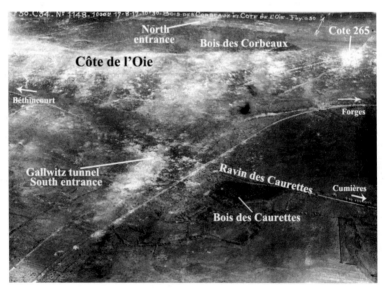

Aerial evidence of heavy shelling on the Côte de l'Oie in preparation for the assault on 20 August 1917. Image taken at 1,000m at 10.30am on 17 August. *Tom Gudmestad*

Dr. Schmidt and I were constantly at work. In the early days of the bombardment we could send the walking wounded back at night with their gasmasks, while the seriously wounded went back with the kitchen wagons; but that soon became impossible. The narrow gauge railway [along Forges Stream] had been completely wrecked. The springs in Bois des Corbeaux had been destroyed and the well in the tunnel provided nothing like enough water. Once the kitchens had taken what they needed, there was half a cup of water left per man. Most of the exits had been closed to stop gas coming in and despite the fans the air inside got thicker. Food ran out'.

Major Pachaly, commander of the Second Battalion, Reserve Infantry Regiment 35, decided to move his command post into the Kronprinz Tunnel after his command bunker was destroyed:

'It was difficult to get into the tunnel because all the entrances were under heavy fire. Once we were inside … we had to pass a section where a shell had recently come through the roof. The pioneers had already carried out makeshift repairs but we had to be careful because it could collapse again…

It was most unpleasant in the tunnel. The superheavy shells were crashing overhead all the time and everything groaned and

The spoil tip for the Gallwitz Tunnel stretches for over one hundred metres and is heavily shelled. This is a partial view from the north end. *Author's collection*

47

shook. We expected the roof to fall in at any moment and we lost all track of time…The air got thicker and thicker until we thought we would suffocate. In the hope of improving the air the pioneers placed fans at some of the entrances but it just made matters worse. The French were shelling with gas every night and the fans just sucked the air in so that we had to wear our gasmasks. Fires were lit at the entrances in the hope of driving the gas out but the draught of air from outside simply drove the smoke back in… It was impossible to make even the slightest improvement to the living conditions in the tunnel, which were very primitive, and the sufferings of the wounded and sick, who mostly could not move, were terrible. To make matters worse, men were forced to answer the call of nature where they were, so there were pools of urine on the floor and a terrible stench everywhere. The destruction in the tunnel made it impossible to use the wagons [which ran on rails] to evacuate either the refuse from the first aid post or the latrines. Thank heavens there was still some rum left to wet our lips and get the foul taste out of our mouths'.

Major Pachaly was shocked by the appearance of the men who managed to get into the Kronprinz tunnel from the front lines:

'In tatters, emaciated, filthy, deathly pale, with all the horrors they had gone through etched in their faces, they came into the tunnel hoping for rest and refreshment, only to find that even here it was not available and that it was scarcely less dangerous inside than outside. Worn out by the stress of recent days and overcome with exhaustion, some squatted silently with their rifles against the walls of the tunnel, while others, completely apathetic and unaware of what was happening, simply lay on the wet slippery floor between boxes and planks and wagon rails and tried to sleep. They slept like the dead and were not disturbed either when they were bumped or stepped on, or when the tunnel rocked under massive explosions.'

Two such explosions occurred in the evening of 19 August when two 380mm shells hit the Kronprinz Tunnel at the point where the kitchen tunnel branched off and the roof was thinner than elsewhere. An enormous mass of debris poured inside, blocking the entrance completely, preventing the explosive gasses from dissipating and suffocating a large number of men who were sitting or lying close by. That was bad enough but there was worse: the collapse had also blocked the entrance to the kitchen tunnel and the men inside – the staff of five kitchens – could not get out.

'...if the debris was not cleared away quickly another hundred men would die of suffocation. The tunnel commander immediately ordered the debris to be cleared but it was impossible. Earth and rocks kept falling in and we could not get through to the kitchen tunnel. A number of our comrades managed to escape via an air duct but most of them just died where they were.'

If conditions were grim inside the tunnels, outside they were unimaginable. Dr. Burmeister again:

'We had two companies outside, one in the front line and one in the intermediate line, with the machine gunners spread out in various nests; of all those men there was scarcely one who had not been buried at least three times...They were constantly being brought into the first aid post. They were soothed, given a little glass of rum and allowed to rest for a while but then they had to go out again. It was rare to see anyone despair of going back. Many were pale and ill and I would have liked to offer them more treatment but I had to be hard...11 Company (on the right) was hit by a concentrated bombardment of terrible fury...a runner sent out from the tunnel with orders found no trace of the dugouts, no trenches, no wire and no trace of life'.

A 370mm howitzer outside the Le Creusot factory in January 1917. *BDIC_VALGF11_73 https://argonnaute.parisnanterre.fr/*

49

The southern entrance to the Gallwitz Tunnel was blocked up during the August offensive and reconstructed for visitors after the war. This is what remains in the Ravin des Caurettes. *Author's collection*

On 19 August an attempt by the surviving German guns in the forward batteries to fire their own gas bombardment only resulted in increased shelling. During the night this rose to drum fire, which swallowed up any surviving machine guns or trench mortars and their crews. The south entrance to the Gallwitz Tunnel was blocked by a direct hit and the last fighting strength of the men drained away. Reserve Infantry Regiment 35 had expected to be relieved but it was not to be. Their regimental history did not mince its words:

> 'It was obvious that troops who had been gassed for eight days and suffered an almost unbroken bombardment of the most appalling type, day and night for eight days, with unbelievably high losses as a result, would not be able to withstand a major assault, especially as during that time hardly anyone had had warm food, fresh water or bread, or been able to rest and sleep. But the [6th Reserve] Division's urgent calls for relief went unheard…*Maasgruppe West* persisted, despite all our statements to the contrary – and it must be said despite clear evidence – in believing that the French objective was not the Mort-Homme but Cote 304…With

a complete lack of understanding *Maasgruppe West* refused not only the division's request for relief but also a request for reserves to be on standby, and even went so far as to withdraw several of the division's batteries to support [a neighbouring division]. By the time the *Maasgruppe* accepted that the Mort-Homme was to be attacked …it was too late for counter measures and too late to be relieved. In any case, new troops, however fresh and fit they might be, thrown into this terrible battle in a completely unknown position, would be less effective than the men of the 6th Reserve Division who, worn out though they were, had been tried and tested by all the fire and gas horrors of this terrifying war.'

Stunned by the hurricane of fire, the number of deserters increased day by day. For Reserve Infantry Regiment 24 'the heart and soul of the defence had been wiped out before the French attacked'. The fighting strength of the First and Third Battalions, Reserve Infantry Regiment 35, was down to 250 and 200 respectively, while the Second Battalion, which was in camp, had barely 120. Being in camp did not keep them out of the fight. Back in the rear, anyone who could hold a rifle and was more or less fit was gathered up and pushed forward in expectation of a French assault. It still did not amount to very many and they knew that

'Anyone who could hold a rifle.' German cooks in a field kitchen behind the lines. *Tom Gudmestad*

when the French attacked it would be with troops who were rested, well fed and well equipped.

German forces in position
Between 18–20 August Army Group reserves were pushed nearer the front and some of the *Eingreif* divisions (formations responsible for immediate counter attacks against an enemy that broke through a defensive position) moved forward to support the weakened front line units. The last reinforcement batteries took up position – too late for them to be really effective – and more fighters, bombers and reconnaissance planes made ready. The final line up was:

Left Bank, VII Corps (General von François);
Divisions in line from west to east: 2nd Landwehr, 206th, 213th
and 6th Reserve;
Divisions in support: 29th and 48th Reserve;
Right Bank, V Reserve Corps (Generalleutenant von Garnier);
Divisions in line from west to east: 28th Reserve, 25th Reserve,
228th and 28th;
Divisions in support: 80th Reserve and 46th Reserve.

There was no doubt that an offensive was imminent and a powerful German raid carried out on 16 August by units of the 28th Division brought definite information about French plans.

At 7pm, a violent bombardment by heavy guns cleared the way for an attack by roughly 1,000 men at a point on the French right where the opposing lines were very close together. They burst through the French lines and flooded along the communication trenches to reach and surround the battalion command post; some men even continued as far as heavy artillery batteries several hundred metres from where they broke through. Reinforcements were thrown in and after some hours the position was restored but not before over 600 men had been killed or captured, machine guns, trench mortars and automatic rifles seized and over forty dugouts destroyed. As if that was not bad enough, documents had also been found which detailed the plan for the entire offensive and indicated that the launch date had already been postponed because of bad weather. As a result of the raid it was postponed again. Late in the evening of 19 August, after another day of earth shaking bombardment, the commander of Fusilier Regiment 35 in the Bois des Fosses was informed by Brigade headquarters that the assault was to be expected the following day; a later message gave 5.15am French time as zero hour.

A German raiding party with trophies. *Tom Gudmestad*

The date was right but not the time; General Guillaumat had fixed it at 4.40am. Everything was ready. The assault divisions had been rested for a month. Every officer and man knew exactly what he was required to do. The liaison officer from General Headquarters had reported that weather and visibility were good, the programme of destruction and counter battery fire had been carried out as planned and two thirds of the active German batteries had been destroyed. Neutralisation of the remaining batteries and shelters began that evening and the Germans responded by shelling the French lines of communication with gas. This caused problems for heavily laden men making their way forward over broken ground and the machine gunners found it particularly exhausting, but as the war diary of the 81st Infantry (XVI Corps) remarked, 'no one wanted to miss the party and little by little the men who had dropped out rejoined their battalions'

The liaison officer reported a general air of confidence and in fact morale was at its highest. Each corps had been carefully chosen; they all knew the Verdun front, had previously distinguished themselves and were ready to do it again. For weeks infantry and specialist troops had studied the action in minute detail and trained together on ground laid out to resemble their sector of operations as closely as possible. They had learned new tactics, practised offensive reconnaissance, tunnel clearance, and combined operation with neighbouring divisions. Particular attention had been paid to crossing the German lines and reducing machine gun nests, while maps and plans had been prepared and circulated. The calamitous result of the April offensive on the Chemin des Dames and the army mutinies that followed it meant that it was absolutely imperative for this offensive to succeed.

53

Above and below: The Germans gassed the French approach routes to the front and some regiments suffered heavily, among them the 81st and 96th Infantry. Sergeant Jean Laguille, 81st Infantry, and Private Léon Malgloire, 96th Infantry, who died the day before the assault, may have been gas casualties. They are buried in the French military cemeteries of Dombasle and Chattancourt respectively. *Author's collection*

German wounded being loaded into a train for evacuation. *Tom Gudmestad*

54

Offensive of August 1917 Overall figures (French)	
Front of attack	18 kilometres
Total effectives	420,000
Percentage of total resources (2,500,000 men)	16.5%
Effectives per kilometre	23,333 men
Number of guns	1,308 heavies 918 field guns
Percentage of total resources (heavies and field guns)	30.2% (heavies) 18.5% (field guns)

Source : Les Armées Françaises dans la Grande Guerre, Tome V, 2nd Volume, Annex II

Chapter Four

20–21 August 1917

The Right Bank:
XXXII Corps
The Bois des Fosses position comprised a long central ravine and a number of branching ravines which provided the Germans with shelter and access between the rear and the front.

Chaotic after a week of artillery preparation, there was little German response in the gas filled ravines when the French assault units moved off behind the rolling barrage.

With the front line effectively destroyed, three companies from the sorely tried Second Battalion, Fusilier Regiment 35, had been forced to create some sort of position in shell craters but they were in a hopeless position; the neighbouring regiment had been moved a kilometre sideways, leaving a huge gap on their right. At 4.40am the 16th Chasseurs (light infantry) swept forward behind the rolling barrage and flooded through the gap. They overwhelmed the Second Battalion, reached the intermediate objective a mere seventeen minutes after zero hour and ploughed on to the next objectives, a fieldwork and a ravine

A comfortable German camp in a ravine. *Tom Gudmestad*

full of shelters. The shelters, which were energetically defended, were to be cleared by the mopping up squads but a sizeable group of Germans managed to evade capture and attacked the 16th in the rear. Turning back and destroying the shelters did not hold them up for long and the final objective was reached at 5.50am. On their right two battalions of the 94th Infantry reached their intermediate objective on time at 4.52am and continued to the final objective, arriving 5.55am, having covered roughly 600 metres. Prisoners were rounded up and the captured equipment, which included machine guns, trench mortars, grenades, a sizable dump of 150mm shells and a fully equipped first aid post, sorted through.

Losses among the assault units ran to almost 400 and they included a considerable number of officers, but it had been a great success and without any delay names were put forward for the Légion d'Honneur, the Médaille Militaire and other awards. However, it had been devastating for the Fusiliers, only sixteen of whom managed to avoid capture. German reinforcements came up during the night but they were fed in here and there and the result was total confusion. However, it was enough to prevent the French from advancing further that day. The northern half of Bois des Fosses, with its defended camps and strongpoints, remained in German hands.

Albert Foucaud, one of the 211 casualties suffered by the 16th Chasseurs in their assault on Bois des Fosses. He is buried in the French military cemetery in front of the Osssuary. *Author's collection*

XV Corps

On the right of XV Corps, the 123rd Division was heading towards the formidable challenges posed by Cote 344 and Cote 326. The former was protected by an advanced line of fieldworks, while the latter was secured by a strong position that the French called the Ouvrage du Buffle. The gap between the two was covered by another fieldwork (the Ouvrage de l'Oursin) and backing all three was a strongly organized trench system, which included the main line of resistance, the Tranchée de Trèves. This protected three ravines of vital importance to the Germans because they offered sheltered access to the front lines and steep hillsides for deep underground barracks.

So formidable was this German position that the French Official History described it as 'two bastions linked by a curtain wall of trenches'; and its strength meant that on 20 August it was the objective of four French regiments. These were the 6th and 12th on the right to capture the Ouvrage du Buffle, the 411th on the left to seize Cote 344 and, in the centre, the 412th to break through the trench lines and dig in at the head of the main German supply ravine in order to sweep it with cross fire. With the rolling barrage crashing ahead of them, they reached the advanced fieldworks, found them to be evacuated, and hurried on. At 7.30am the Ouvrage du Buffle was in French hands and fifteen minutes later the 411th reached the summit of Cote 344. However, the 412th, which had first suffered from friendly fire and then found that their artillery preparation had not been as destructive as they expected, was stopped by heavy machine gun fire and could get no further. The Tranchée de Trèves remained in German hands but the Ouvrage de l'Oursin was captured the next day.

The divisions on the left of XV Corps faced the Côte du Talou and the flanks of Cote 344, positions which provided observation over both sides of the river and allowed German guns to enfilade the Left Bank. The assault troops were so anxious to get going that they moved off before 4.40am, following so closely behind the rolling barrage that one war diary described them as 'almost imprudent'. However, the preparatory bombardment had done its work; and aided by fog and smoke so thick that the leading ranks could not see the hill in front of them, the attackers reached the German front line, found it to have been evacuated, and carried on to the final objective, which they reached soon after 7am.

Less than three hours later, two of the assault regiments, the 55th and 173rd, were ordered to continue the advance to the objectives originally planned for the following day. These included Samogneux, a village situated one kilometre ahead on the River Meuse, and a section of the strong trench system linking Samogneux to Cote 344. The assault troops got ready but before they could move off the operation was postponed

The fieldworks defending Cote 344 were anchored at the northern end by Mormont Farm, a cluster of buildings forming a strong redoubt. Completely destroyed during the fighting, it has never been rebuilt and only the faintest outline remains. *Author's collection*

until 5am the following morning. Samogneux was known to be a strong centre of resistance but fortunately for the 55th Infantry:

> 'Dense fog meant that at first [the troops] advanced without the enemy seeing them but it was not long before machine guns began to fire from the banks of the river or the canal, causing us serious

The main street in Samogneux in 1916. *Tom Gudmestad*

losses. It did not diminish the ardour of the troops, who were fired by the finest patriotic zeal and continued their advance with a remarkable scorn for danger, electrified by the extraordinary dynamism of Captain Juanahandy, the battalion adjutant. Roughly 300 metres from the edge of the village [the battalion] came under machine gun fire and stopped. Our machine gunners brought their guns into position and replied energetically…in the direction of Samogneux. The German defences were intact. The situation was becoming critical. The sun was beginning to pierce the clouds and it would not be long before the enemy knew exactly where we were and concentrated its fire on our new positions. It was then that Lieutenant Mayné took advantage of a lull in the firing to throw two sections forward. They cut through the wire blocking the road and jumped into [the nearby trench], taking a number of prisoners.'

Led by specially trained assault detachments, the battalion moved off again and, seeing that the French showed no signs of stopping, the Germans withdrew. While some of the attackers continued to the other end of the ruined village, others went through the cellars and shelters and secured the ferry, the lock on the canal and the footbridge. The result was well over three hundred prisoners and several machine guns that were immediately turned on the retreating Germans. At 7.30am on 21 August, Samogneux was in French hands. (*See Tour No 3 for more on the fighting in this sector.*)

Dummy machine guns lined up on top of a German trench. *Tom Gudmestad*

60

A relaxed group of Germans in a deep trench not far from the summit of the Mort-Homme before the August offensive. *Tom Gudmestad*

Left Bank:
XVI Corps

On the left, facing the Mort-Homme, the 31st Division found that their only difficulty was making their way through the chaos caused by the week-long bombardment. The ground was so destroyed that compasses had to be used and even so it was almost impossible for men to be sure of where they were. It was only when the rolling barrage stopped that they realised they had reached the first objective. At 7am, with the summit of the Mort-Homme once more in their possession, three mountain guns were hauled to the top and the troops moved off again.

The Bismarck and Kronprinz Tunnels

Reaching the Bismarck Tunnel, a platoon from the 81st Infantry, supported by a sapper section and flame throwers, went inside to carry out a reconnaissance. The tunnel had been smashed in two places by direct hits from huge 400mm shells, so that it was difficult to get through. Inside, they rounded up a group of about thirty Germans and sent them back through the lines as the mopping up troops began their work. While that was happening, a specially trained detachment of the Second Battalion, 96th Infantry, was securing the entrances and exits to the Kronprinz Tunnel. Despite heavy German gas shelling before jump off, which meant that some companies had to wear their masks throughout the advance into the line, morale was very high. The regimental commander himself stood in the jump off trench to watch the

61

The former German front line on the Mort-Homme after its capture on 20 August 1917.

96th, officers in the lead, move off 'to destiny and glory with heads high, eyes open and confident hearts'. A few minutes later they reached the German front line, where the war diary reports:

> 'The harvest of Boche has begun and promises to be abundant. The few sentries remaining in the advanced line were immediately captured. Any that tried to resist were pitilessly killed.'

Shelling had blocked the main entrances, while the side entrances were guarded by machine gunners. They were quickly overcome but resistance from inside kept the 96th out. Hearing from German prisoners that there were about 800 men in the tunnel, the battalion commander sent one of them forward with an order to surrender. The tunnel commandant, Major von Orloff, who was desperately hoping that help would arrive in time to save the situation, delayed replying for as long as possible but in the end the threat of flame throwers proved too much. Almost 1,000 men were captured and sent back through French lines.

The 96th may not have known it but there were already French troops inside. The 122nd Infantry had been clearing a deep trench lined with dugouts when they noticed a sign reading 'Kronprinz' and thought they would take a look. Lieutenant Monestier, commander of the 2nd Machine Gun Company, described what happened next:

81. MORT-HOMME — Entrée du Tunnel du Kronprinz pris par la 31ᵉ Division d'Infanterie le 20 août 1917. La Legion nettoya le tunnel y trouva plusieurs fractions de régiments et tout un bataillon d'un 20ᵉ de reserve. Parmi les officiers se trouvait le comte Bernstorff neveu de l'Ambassadeur allemand aux Etats-Unis Entrance of the Kronprinz tunnel.

The entrance to one of the Mort-Homme tunnels, probably Gallwitz, despite the caption. The inscription states that inside the French captured elements of several regiments, a reserve infantry battalion and Count Bernstorff, nephew of the German ambassador to the United States.

'Going inside, we saw that the electric light was still on. Taking every precaution, we went down the first thirty steps of the entrance and came to a landing where there were two other entrances. These had been destroyed by the bombardment but an observation post with a telephone, binoculars and artillery plan was intact. Continuing our inspection, we saw two parallel staircases which were also electrically lit. We started to go down ... and found ourselves in a rest area through which light rails ran. Moving on carefully, we arrived at a reinforced door which we thought might be closing off the entrance to the tunnel.

At that moment we heard German voices and quite a lot of noise. Later, we learned that the noise came from building a barricade. My first thought was to barricade the reinforced door on our side, so that the Germans could not attack us from the other side. Going back to the exit to make sure that the machine gunners were on guard, I found one of my men…bringing five prisoners captured at another entrance. They brought useful information. They warned us, first, that all the tunnel entrances were mined, and that the men wanted to surrender but were prevented by their officers, who did not want to be taken prisoner. We also learned that the strength of the garrison was about two companies.

I immediately reported this information and asked for specialist sappers to be sent up to deal with the mines.

While we were waiting, we went back into the tunnel and began to examine the walls of the rest area. I discovered… two electric wires which disappeared behind planking and I realised I held the key to the mines. A few blows with a pickaxe broke down the planking and behind it we saw a small tunnel packed with explosives and charged. It was the work of a minute to detach the fuses from the wires …. Now we had to capture the garrison. I had asked for someone who spoke German and

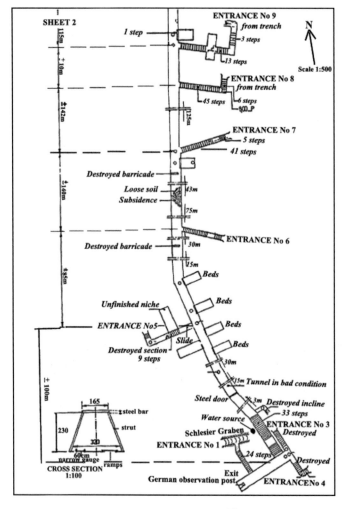

A section of the Kronprinz Tunnel from a plan prepared by XVI Corps, 2nd Bureau.

Captain Py, 2nd Génie, brought along a prisoner. The Captain ordered a machine gun to be brought in and set up in front of the reinforced door. He then ordered the prisoner to tell the men inside to surrender and to make it clear that at the slightest sign of resistance, we would open fire. After waiting for ten minutes, Captain Py ordered him to tell the officers that if they did not surrender immediately, he would blow them up. The threat worked. A German officer …came through the barricades and with an impeccable salute informed us that his men were demolishing the barricades and would surrender. The prisoners soon came out, three officers, two officer aspirants and 170 dirty and tired men whose faces showed just how pleased they were to have finished with the war. By 3pm… the tunnel was clear.'

Operating on the right of the 31st Division was the Moroccan Division, an elite formation comprising light infantry raised in the French African colonies and the Régiment de marche de la Légion Etrangère (the

Avove and below: **Two casualties of the Moroccan Division, Corporal Jean Badetz, 4th Tirailleurs, and Private Robert Guillemoto, 8th Zouaves, died on 20 August 1917 and are buried in the French military cemetery at Chattancourt.** *Author's collection*

Foreign Legion). While on the left Tirailleurs and Zouaves followed the rolling barrage through the German front line towards their final objective, in the centre the Third Battalion, 7th Tirailleurs, looked for the Gallwitz Tunnel.

The Gallwitz Tunnel

At jump off, the only problem reported by the 7th Tirailleurs was thick smoke from shelling and incendiary grenades that darkened the sky and made the air unbreathable. Aerial reconnaissance had shown the south entrance to the tunnel to be damaged, so having reached it the Tirailleurs left guards outside and moved on to find the ventilation shafts and side entrances. According to the war diary:

'At 4.54am…reconnaissance patrols found a brick chimney with an iron ladder extending above the top. The sappers and Tirailleurs threw grenades into the opening. Flame throwers were directed down the chimney but the flames and smoke were blown back by the air current from inside.'

According to Dr. Burmeister, some Tirailleurs managed to get into the tunnel through a ventilation shaft and the northern entrance, but were driven back. The side entrances were also defended, so the Tirailleurs threw grenades inside and blocked them up. It was clear to Dr. Burmeister that:

'We were buried alive. Our last hope was a German counter attack. It had to come soon. The last rations, the last piece of bread, had been shared out, the well was nearly dry. The [tunnel] commandant, Major von Ahlefeld, called me. He was outraged because men in the south part of the tunnel had been talking about surrender … he told them in no uncertain terms that the tunnel would be defended to the last man…

The defence of the entrances had cost us many killed and wounded…We two doctors had our hands full. Part of the tunnel had to be cleared to make room for the wounded. The air was horrible. The dead, who could not be taken outside, soon began to decompose. The emergency latrines could not be emptied. Everywhere I saw men vomiting. When it began to get light on 21 August a slim young officer climbed up a ventilation shaft, which was still open, and looked around. It was hopeless. The wood was full of French soldiers; sentry posts had been pushed far forward, the whole valley [of Forges Stream] was full of gas and German guns were not firing.

The enemy soon discovered this ventilation shaft, threw hand grenades inside and closed it off. Then there was no more fresh air. The effects were soon seen. The wounded, particularly those with lung wounds, suffered terribly but we healthy men also became faint and nauseous, with blue lips. It would not be long before we were done for. Everyone craved water and there was none.'

If, for the men inside the tunnel, the situation seemed hopeless, outside it still looked dangerous, and having waited all night the Third Battalion commander, Major de Saint-Léger, lost patience. What happened next is described in the battalion History:

'Major de Saint-Léger…told the machine gunners not to fire without his order and going up to the entrance to the tunnel he shouted "Oi, Fritz! Come here, we won't hurt you!"

Heavy calibre shell splinters and other debris close to the northern entrance to the Gallwitz Tunnel. *Author's collection*

We soon heard steps and a German officer appeared. Major de Saint-Léger gave him his conditions:

1. The garrison must capitulate within fifteen minutes or the tunnel would be blown up;
2. The tunnel commandant and his officers must surrender immediately;
3. The officer carrying the message had to give his word to return and surrender if these conditions were not met.

Hiding his emotion, the German officer returned to the tunnel. Ten minutes later he returned followed by Major von Ahberfeld [sic. Ahlefeld], commander of Reserve Infantry Regiment 24, and thirteen other officers. The commandant's only request was to evacuate the tunnel by the south entrance to avoid the shelling. His request was accepted and Captain Poulet, Captain Chavanas and Chaplain Borde d'Arrère entered the tunnel accompanied by a group of armed Tirailleurs.

A steep and slippery staircase defended by machine guns led to the main gallery…It ran through the Côte de l'Oie and ended in an entrance in the Ravin des Corbeaux [sic. Caurettes]. Electrically lit, served by a light railway, with pumped water, a power unit and generators, the Gallwitz Tunnel was a prodigious piece or work.

At each end there was a horrible cesspool of stinking mud mixed with blood and excreta and in dark corners piles of corpses. Rifles, helmets and equipment were thrown about everywhere pell-mell, showing how demoralized the [Germans] had become.'

The Germans were indeed demoralized but before leaving the tunnel they had time to destroy maps and papers, and put machine guns, rifles and revolvers out of action. Then things got worse. Dr Burmeister again:

'Everyone, officers and men, were robbed of everything, watches, money, even puttees and caps, supposedly for 'souvenirs' but it was mostly at gunpoint. Even the officers took part. It was an officer who ripped off Major Büttner's Iron Cross First Class and his epaulettes…'

The Tirailleurs captured 800 officers and men in the Gallwitz tunnel, together with field guns of various calibres, trench mortars, machine guns, masses of rifles and much other material. Dr Burmeister,

German dead, hurriedly buried in Bois des Corbeaux. *Tom Gudmestad*

who wanted to stay with the wounded, refused to leave the tunnel and in the end he was allowed to remain there with his staff:

> 'Soon the regimental medical officer arrived, a polite and distinguished man. The Tirailleurs respected the first aid post and nothing was touched. Only one of my medical NCOs, who despite my express order to the contrary stepped outside, was robbed at gunpoint of his watch, money, etc. From a captain who came through the tunnel with his company I requested and immediately received a guard of three men, who worked hard, both for the wounded and for me and my staff. They made coffee and provided bread, meat, chocolate and cigarettes, which a French doctor had promised. Later ... stretcher bearers arrived ... a really disreputable, garrulous, thieving bunch. Immediately everything moveable disappeared, including the small parcels, some of them named and already fastened up, containing the belongings of our dead. I beat one of them with my stick. In the meantime the light had gone out and it was pitch dark in the tunnel. I had an acetylene lamp and a few candles. I had been

German prisoners in an organized camp. *Tom Gudmestad*

ordered to bring out all the dead and bury them outside but when I began to do so I was not allowed outside. A colonel arrived, a man of very distinguished appearance, and said we should be allowed to bury our dead….He told me to leave the tunnel when the wounded had been evacuated.'

Dr. Burmeister was one of almost 7,000 German prisoners captured on 20 August; he was first sent to the prisoner of war camp at Souilly, south of Verdun, and then transferred to another camp in southwest France. French casualties on the Left Bank that day, which included many victims of gas, ran to over 8,000; but all that was forgotten when not only the rations but also the post came up to the trenches as soon as the troops were established on their objectives.

The Régiment de marche de la Légion Etrangère (Foreign Legion)
Serving for the first time at Verdun, the task of the Foreign Legion on 20 August was to recapture the village of Cumières, clear the Bois des Corbeaux and take several fieldworks, including a redoubtable position on the top of the Côte de l'Oie. They had broken camp on the evening of 18 August and begun the march to their jump off positions, with each man carrying two days' rations of chocolate, biscuits, tinned beef and sardines but no overcoat or blanket. The continuous German gas bombardment meant that they spent the next day wearing their gas masks

and at about 3am on 20 August the attacking battalions moved forward to shallow positions between the lines. This was an uncomfortable place to be, as the guns on both sides were firing short, and it was with some relief that they could move off at 4.40am. In the fog and smoke, some units drifted off course but they soon caught up again. An American machine gunner with the Legion, Christopher Charles, described the action:

'At twenty to five the order came to go forward and you can be sure we were all glad to get out of the living hell we had been under for nearly two hours. We got through the curtain fire pretty easily… with a few quick steps we were beyond the most dangerous point. We got to the first German lines without any trouble and found a few lost Germans who did not seem to know whether they were in France or Russia, and I do not think they cared very much, for they had been under the bombardment for six days and were glad to get out of it.'

The officers had difficulty holding the men back and progress was swift. Despite strong resistance, the final objective, three kilometres from the jump off line, was reached well ahead of schedule. Christopher Charles again:

'We kept on going with a little grenade fighting here and there, and by seven o'clock we had gained three kilometres in depth

Bois des Corbeaux   Côte de l'Oie

A view of total destruction: Cumières after it was retaken by the Foreign Legion.

and two in width. We took Cumières or what was left of it, which was just a few stone walls, also a wood and a hill. There we rested until the afternoon, for we had done some hill-climbing and were pretty tired out.'

The planners had assumed the Foreign Legion would reach its objectives towards the end of the day and would then be relieved. However, the regimental commander, the redoubtable Colonel Rollet, had no intention of stopping when more could be done and after another bombardment aimed at demolishing any remaining German resistance on the Côte de l'Oie, the Foreign Legion moved off again at 4pm. By 6pm the redoubts at the top were in French hands and everyone began to organize the new lines. Sentries were posted and reconnaissance patrols went out, while convoys of donkeys brought up the rations and the post. As it was vital to establish liaison with XV Corps on the other side of the River Meuse,

Colonel Rollet in his favoured desert uniform with the colours guarded by an Adjudant-chef [senior warrant officer] and three corporals, all holders of the Légion d'Honneur.

72

it was decided that the following day all three battalions of the Legion would continue to advance along the Côte de l'Oie to the river. This involved retaking Regnéville, a village which had been in German hands since 7 March 1916. Christopher Charles described the action in laconic terms:

'We were pretty lazy on the 21st and did not start forward until the afternoon, when we were told to take a village. Our seventy-fives kept a barrage just ahead of us as we advanced…In a dugout we found a badly wounded German who had been there for three days. He lay cursing his comrades for stealing his watch and money and leaving him to die. We sent him back to a stretcher-bearers post. We pushed on about five hundred metres farther and there the fight ended. We installed ourselves in the orchards overlooking the Meuse beyond the village and worked all night long putting the position in shape to be defended should the Germans counter-attack. We had a nice party in a shell-hole with German wine and jam, and under our tent covers we smoked a few cigars which the Boches forgot in their hurry to get away.'

Telephone liaison with XV Corps was established at 7pm on 21 August. With the Legion's new line established far beyond their objectives, a messenger soon arrived asking where they were and what they were doing, to which Colonel Rollet merely replied that the assigned objectives had been too easily achieved and he had been obliged to give

Guido Agostini was killed near Regnéville on 21 August 1917 and is now buried in Chattancourt military cemetery. *Author's collection*

The French 240mm naval gun at the foot of the Côte de l'Oie as seen in July 1917. The barrel has been sawn in two and part has been removed. *Tom Gudmestad*

his men new tasks. In two days the Legion had pushed the line forward by over three kilometres and captured 680 prisoners, fourteen guns of various calibres, machine guns, automatic rifles, masses of ammunition and piles of equipment. They had also recaptured a French 240mm naval gun, which had been abandoned in the German assault of March 1916 and their losses – fewer than four hundred in all – had been smaller than in any of their earlier battles.

XIII Corps

The one area in which matters had not gone so well was in XIII Corps sector on the French left, where Cote 304 remained in German hands. Part of the problem was the state of the ground. There were no trenches or communication trenches to speak of, just a chaotic mass of overlapping shell craters half filled with water from the recent rain. Dominating the horizon was the hill of Montfaucon, from where enemy observers could see every detail of the French lines. Moving up the assault regiments found a lunar landscape without a single reference point; not a tree, not a road, not a path. The only way to reach their assigned objectives was to follow the compass.

With a direct frontal attack on Cote 304 out of the question, the final plan involved a two stage operation aimed at securing the flanks before any attempt was made on the summit. A covering operation in the Bois de Malancourt kept the Germans occupied while successful flanking operations were carried out, but the attack on the summit

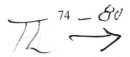

Cote 304 on 24 August 1917. The Tranchée des Zouaves after recapture. *BDIC_VAL_185_005 https://argonnaute. parisnanterre.fr/*

The 1917 side of the Cote 304 memorial. The divisions which fought there in 1916 are commemorated on the other side. *Author's collection*

failed. The Germans withdrew, leaving only rearguards in place, and when the French attacked again after three days of furious bombardment they reached their objectives without serious difficulty. By nightfall on 24 August the Germans line had been pushed back over two kilometres to the far side of Forges stream and with that final success – and at the cost to XIII Corps of almost 4000 casualties – the French line on the Left Bank of the River Meuse was once again firmly established.

American observers on the Left Bank on 20 August

On 26 September 1918 the final French line of August 1917 became the jump-off line for another offensive, this time one launched by III and V Corps, American First Army, on the first day of the Franco-American Meuse-Argonne offensive. That was not the first day that Americans had been on the Left Bank. On 20 August 1917, General Pershing, commander of the American Expeditionary Force, accompanied Generals Pétain and de Castelnau to the Left Bank, where he followed the actions of the Moroccan Division with the corps commander, General Corvisart, who was an old friend. George Marshall, later a famous General and author of the Marshall Plan but then a young captain, was one of several officers also invited to observe the operation. Pleased to find himself with elite troops, and especially pleased that no French officer was available to accompany him or prevent him from exploring, Marshall seized the opportunity of heading towards the front, where an astonished German prisoner told him their officers had assured them that the United States was not sending troops to France. They all agreed that their officers had lied.

On the Mort-Homme after the Battle

The following letter from a gunner in the 3rd Battery, 9th Artillery, was published in the *Messager de Millau* on 8 September 1917.

26 August 1917

This afternoon, I visited the Mort-Homme. There was nothing left of the Boche lines. The first line had been 'toadied' [shelled by the French trench mortars known as 'crapouillots' or little toads]. The others, hit by every calibre of shell, were even more destroyed, with overlapping craters everywhere. An extraordinary sight, a fantastic chaos like a stormy sea with picket posts, barbed wire, wooden beams, stick grenades, broken planks, unexploded shells and thousands of those sad wrecks that you find on every battlefield emerging from it. Some of the shell holes had equipment in them left behind by men who had been evacuated; we saw that every hundred metres. Here and there we saw a body, a crushed limb, a shoe with a foot inside, etc.

A heavy French trench mortar shell. *Tom Gudmestad*

The second Boche line was particularly smashed. I say 'second line' but I should really say 'what had been the second line', because we searched in vain for the slightest trace of a trench. The few trench mortars and 'toads' be to seen are a mess, the saps have fallen in completely. It makes you wonder how anyone managed to hold on in ground that was changing all the time. Not a single metre of it was intact. Our shells had ploughed craters everywhere, some of them six metres deep and eight or more wide. Stones and great blocks of earth had been blown up and come down like an avalanche, crushing anything underneath. It was a scene of complete devastation…It was like that all the way to the command post…and from there we continued to the Kronprinz Tunnel. Going and coming was two kilometres and the smell was so repugnant throughout that we had to hold our nose. The battlefield smelt bad in places but inside the tunnel the stink was just everywhere. We went in through an ordinary opening in the side of the trench, no wider than that. There were two staircases each one metre wide, one for going down and the other for coming up. The corridor was flooded because the pipes which carried water as far as the front lines had been smashed by our shells. We splashed along …Down below, twenty metres below ground level (the depth of earth above the tunnel varies between fifteen and twenty metres) it was surprisingly cool and damp. We passed a steel door fifty centimetres in diameter. Our troops were lying on beds or stretchers along the walls. The tunnel ran straight as far as the third

German dead in the Kronprinz Tunnel.

German line. It is fairly roughly made and offers nothing but the security of being underground. The roof had not needed much support. One wooden prop per metre supports a double-T bar on which the ceiling planks are laid. Electric light, lamps every twenty metres along the wall; along the bottom, water pipes. In the middle, a well made duckboard so we don't walk in the mud. On each side, a line of beds made of planks. After five hundred metres the beds stop and 60cm wagon rails begin. Officers' rooms with wood panelled walls and wallpaper are dug into the sides of the tunnel. Then a model infirmary with a central reception area, operating theatre, kitchen and various annexes. There we met a battalion doctor who had remained behind with three Boche prisoners taken the day before. They had spent five days in a collapsed sap with a lot of corpses and they had completely lost their wits; the doctor had taken pity on them and kept them in the infirmary for forty eight hours. We got to talk to them; they had had to be pulled out of the sap with ropes, one of them had been wounded and a fourth man who was pulled out at the same time had died…

Opposite the infirmary, the pharmacy: indescribable disorder. They must have had to take care of a lot of wounded in the last hours in the tunnel. All sorts of stuff on the table: a chest full of wooden and cardboard boxes, paper wrapping from pharmaceutical bottles and products. It smelt so strongly of ether and phenol that I went out

78

Water tanks and a stairway in the Kronprinz Tunnel.

quickly. Next to it, a really formidable machine room with model factory machines: two 180hp petrol-driven engines, two compressors for pumping water to the various parts of the tunnel, a petrol tank, a pump, a control panel with voltmeter and ampere meter on a marble plate almost one metre square. There was a comforting smell of hot oil and petrol. This extraordinary installation was not finished; only one of the machines was in working order.

Finally, making our way through the jumble of weapons, blankets, clothing, equipment, ammunition and particularly helmets lying in the mud (there must have been about 2,000 of them), we arrived at the place where our 400mm broke through the thirteen metres of earth above the tunnel. Crushed bodies were still lying there. The explosion had killed 178 men who had been fifty metres away. Rations everywhere: biscuits, tinned meat, empty bottles, cooking pots, mess kits, packs, etc. The same disorder as everywhere else but made much worse by the roof collapse, which had completely blocked the tunnel. We left by the same route, happy to be getting out of the putrid atmosphere and into fresher air... We went to look at the front lines. I took some interesting photos of the poilus, who are in shell holes because as yet there aren't any trenches. That's actually an advantage because it means that the Germans, who have been completely disorganized for days, have no organized line [of ours] to target.

Everybody was really enthusiastic about our artillery preparation. Twice I heard somebody say: "If we did that every time, we'd soon be in Berlin". The officers said...that they couldn't hold the men back once they saw the Germans weakening. In some places they even went too fast and had to be held back behind the rolling barrage. At the moment, morale is higher than it has been for the last three years. We should take

A view of destruction inside the tunnel.

advantage of it to push on: the Germans would soon flee…Our counter battery fire was exceedingly good. The Boche barrage started ten minutes after the first wave had moved off, when there was nobody left in the trenches, and it was very weak. All our telephone communications worked and our old trenches are completely intact. Let us hope that this success is only the prelude to greater ones and that instead of advancing two kilometres, we advance…to the Rhine.

A poilu from Millau

Chapter Five

August–December 1917: Unfinished business

On the Left Bank fighting died down after the recapture of Cote 304. The important hilltop observatories were back in French hands and the lines had been pushed far enough forward as to make it impossible for the Germans to retake them without the use of massive resources in attacks against an entrenched enemy over unfavourable terrain. However, a 'zone of friction' remained on the Right Bank, where the Germans still held a number of commanding positions in close proximity to the new French lines. As originally conceived, the plan for 1917 had been to capture all the high ground on the Right Bank running east from the Ouvrage du Buffle to the Woëvre Plain and push the French line back sufficiently far north as to render it safe from recapture; but following the mutinies and the decision to limit the operation, some of the objectives were dropped. These included Wavrille Hill, the ruined village of Beaumont, Bois le Fays and a long hilltop on the French right named the Butte de Caurières, which overlooked the Woëvre Plain. The Butte commanded a major section of the French front line between the Bois des Fosses and the village of Bezonvaux and provided the Germans with observation

A French observation post. *BDIC_VAL_231_02/ Lt Barbier 2 https:// argonnaute.parisnanterre.fr*

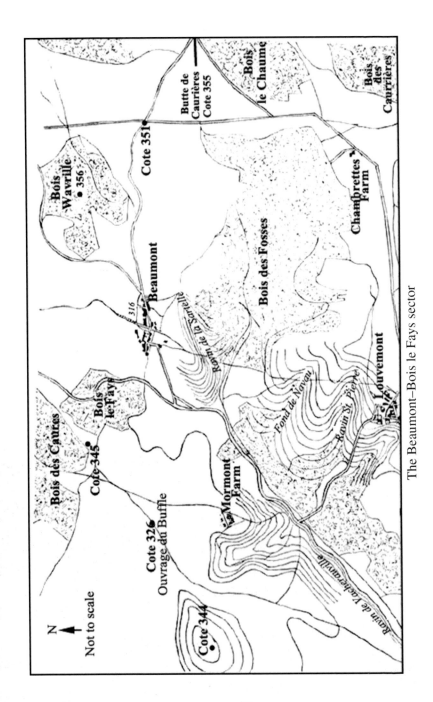

The Beaumont–Bois le Fays sector

over their new lines and supply routes; while from Beaumont and Bois le Fays machine guns sweeping the Ravin de Vacherauville made it difficult to supply the French front line in the Cote 344 sector. Another problem was the continuing resistance in front of Cote 344 where the objectives of 20 August had not been fully achieved.

There was no ignoring the dangers of leaving the situation as it was and on 22 August the commander of XXXII Corps, General Passaga, issued orders for a series of local operations to wipe out the 'zone of friction', two of which – far from being short – led to months of fighting.

26 August: Bois le Fays and Beaumont
For five days corps and divisional artillery pounded the entire area, targeting Beaumont and the surrounding ravines with heavy calibre guns and howitzers and harassing German batteries on the Woëvre Plain. The strong German response hampered French preparations for their next step, which began at 4.45am on 26 August and, once again, did not go according to plan. While the 154th Infantry reached their objectives in Bois le Fays, machine gun fire from Beaumont tore such holes in their ranks that they got no further. On their right, two battalions of the 155th Infantry reached Beaumont in only a few minutes – so fast, in fact that the left hand battalion continued past the objective for several hundred metres and had to be pulled back to avoid friendly fire. Casualties were very high and the right hand battalion had to bring up two of its

A former dugout and rubble on the site of Beaumont. The site is cleared and safe to visit. *Author's collection*

Twenty one year old Private Henri Michelet, 154th Infantry, who disappeared without trace during the assault on Bois le Fays on 26 August 1917.

reserve companies to fill the ranks and hold off counter attacks. Over three hundred prisoners were taken and a considerable amount of materiel captured. While that could be counted a success, the 155th was in a weak position, with a gap on the right and a left hand battalion so weakened by its bold assault that it was unable to resist the inevitable counter attacks.

During the night the remains of all the assault battalions – mere debris, according to the 155th's War Diary – were ordered to withdraw. It had been a bloody affair. The 155th's casualty list for 26-27 August ran to twenty six officers and 429 men, with another eight officers and 342 men out of action in Bois des Fosses. The 154th's War Diary gives no figure. There were no further attempts on Bois le Fays or Beaumont and the plan to recapture Wavrille Hill, the highest point on the Right Bank and with controlling views over French positions, was also abandoned.

7 September – 25 November: Cote 344 and Cote 326
(the Ouvrage du Buffle)

Although the offensive of 20 August had carried the 123rd Division over the top of Cote 344 and Cote 326, they had failed in their primary objective, to capture the main German line of resistance, the Tranchée de Trèves. Having come to a stop, all four attacking regiments dug in and resisted a number of counter attacks but their hold on the sector was precarious and, to make matters worse, organizing the new position required large numbers of men who worked without shelter in full view of German machine gunners. As a result, daily casualty levels were very high. The Germans, on the other hand, had the advantage of a series of sheltered ravines offering access from the rear to the front line, with secure bases in scores of dugouts and deep underground barracks on the steep north side of Cote 344. These were in dead ground to French artillery fire and it was clear that the only way to deal with them was to push the French line so far forward that the Germans would be forced to evacuate them. The 20 August operation had left six hundred metres of the Tranchée de Trèves in German hands, and new defensive positions were being developed all the time, so action had to be taken without delay. The exhausted 123rd Division was relieved, the 14th Division took over, another operation was planned, and in a lightening assault on 7 September heavily armed assault troops attacked the Tranchée de Trèves and managed to clear the barracks.

They did not enjoy their success for long. Two days later specially trained German units burst out of thick fog and pushed the French back. The preliminary bombardment had cut the telephone lines and it took some time for news to reach the command post but, when it did, it was dramatic. The battalion holding the Ouvrage de l'Oursin had given way with heavy casualties, the Germans were heading into the French support positions behind it, and Cote 344 had been captured. The only good news was that the Ouvrage du Buffle was still holding out. Reserves were thrown in, ammunition and grenades rushed forward, and with heavy artillery support the position was re-established and even a section of the Tranchée de Trèves recaptured but it had again been at great cost. Between 7–9 September, the two French regiments involved lost over 800 officers and men and if the number of German corpses was anything to go by, their losses had been substantial too.

Re-entering the Ouvrage de l'Oursin the French were astonished at the number of German dead and the heaps of equipment thrown everywhere. However, for both sides the sector was too important to give up and fighting went on.

If the French lines were precarious, the German positions were no better. Situated on steep slopes below the French, they were open to rifle grenade and machine gun fire, while gas filled

„Herr, dein Wille geschehe!"

Zum frommen Andenken
an meinen lieben Gatten und guten Vater
Joseph Maier
Hauptlehrer in Schiftung
geboren am 17. Nov. 1884 in Fischbach, A. Lillg.
gefallen am 8. Sept. 1917 bei Verdun.

Gebet.
O Gott! Herr der Gnaden, verleihe der Seele deines Dieners **Joseph** den Wohnsitz der Erquickung, die Seligkeit des Friedens und die Herrlichkeit des ewigen Lichtes durch Jesum Christum, unsern Herrn. Amen. Vater unser ꝛc. Jesus, Maria, Joseph! (7 Jahre, 7 Quadr.) Barmherzigster Jesus, gib ihm die ewige Ruhe!

A memorial card for thirty three year old Joseph Maier, who was killed in the fighting of 7 September 1917. Unfortunately, his regiment is not mentioned. *Tom Gudmestad*

85

French battlefield burials close to a first aid post on a rubble strewn hillside.
Tom Gudmestad

the dugouts and barracks and German guns fired short. One of the units in position was Infantry Regiment 91.

'In the continuing cold wet weather the approach tracks became mud pits. The supply parties and fighting troops often went for eight to ten days without dry clothes. The shell craters were full to the brim with water, which meant that no one could use them as emergency cover during sudden shelling and in pitch darkness many men ended up taking an unexpected cold bath. Despite every effort and the best will in the world, it was impossible to get as much ammunition and equipment forward as ordered and even the superhuman efforts of the front line companies could scarcely prevent the trench sides from collapsing into the water. There were hardly any dugouts and rising water levels forced the evacuation of the few that were available. Over half the troops were outside day and night. The relief planned for 8 October had not taken place. As before, relief orders were issued and withdrawn, which complicated day to day administration and tactical planning.'

Ramshackle accommodation in a German trench. *Tom Gudmestad*

The situation became so bad that the regimental commander felt obliged to inform the division that his three battalions were so exhausted that they would be unable to defend their 1400 metre front from serious assault unless they were regularly relieved. Nobody listened to him. The higher command was so dissatisfied with the lack of success in the Cote 344 sector that when on 10 October an attempt to recapture a section of the main line of resistance failed again the Army Group commander, Generalleutnant Kühne, ordered that the assault troops should not be withdrawn until the operation had succeeded and then only with his express permission. Another attempt was hastily planned and great quantities of material rushed forward but once again it was a failure. Rather than keep trying the same thing, the Germans decided to outflank Cote 344 by first capturing the Ouvrage du Buffle, as this would provide them with observation over Cote 344 and make life difficult for the defenders. In a surprise assault launched under cover of fog at 4.30am on 23 October, elements of Infantry Regiment 78 not only captured the Ouvrage but also pushed the French several hundred metres back to a position dominated by German machine guns. However, it was a short lived success. While the first hastily launched counter attacks failed, a later assault using fresh troops broke German resistance and the French were back. (*For more on Cote 344 and the Ouvrage du Buffle, see Tour No 3.*)

87

A trench and field memorials at the Ouvrage du Buffle. *Author's collection*

25 November

And so it went on. In the opinion of General Guillaumat the Cote 344 lines would not be secure until the Germans evacuated the ravines. In early November, VII Corps (128th and 37th Divisions) took over and a major operation was planned for 25 November with the aim of clearing the German trenches once and for all, destroying the barracks and establishing an outpost line sufficiently far forward as to prevent the Germans from launching surprise attacks. The new operation involved four infantry regiments in the first line, three more in reserve, 216 field guns, 288 heavies and nine trench artillery batteries. For several days before the offensive, officers and NCOs from the assault battalions reconnoitred their positions, ammunition and supply dumps, approach routes and command posts. In mocked up trenches near Verdun they carried out combined training exercises involving aviation and specialist flamethrower sections, while sappers practised blowing up the underground barracks and at the front troops armed with automatic rifles and rifle grenades prevented the Germans from repairing the damage done by shelling.

On 23 November the attacking regiments – from left to right the 168th Infantry, 2nd Tirailleurs, 2nd Zouaves de Marche and 3rd Zouaves de Marche – drew their rations and began to move up. The next day was

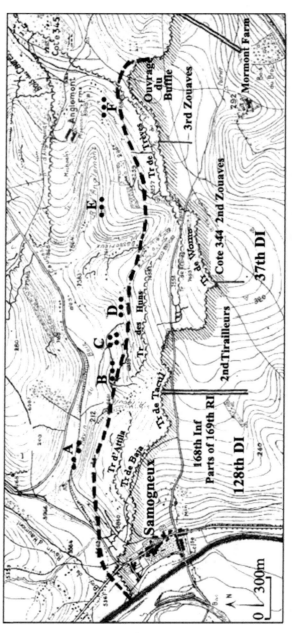

Les Armées Françaises dans la Grande Guerre
Tome VII, Vol. 1

French front on 25 November before the assault
French front on 26 November after the assault
Underground barracks
Barracks: **A:** Landwehr **B:** Meiningen **C:** Cologne
D: Hamburg **E:** Lüder **F:** Schubert

Cote 344: 25–26 November 1917.

89

A French 280mm howitzer.

spent in detailed reconnaissance but during the night a powerful, storm troop led, raiding party burst out of the ravine between Cote 344 and the Ouvrage du Buffle and fought a short pitched battle with the 2nd Zouaves, who had just arrived. The German aim was to capture prisoners, equipment and useful information and ten minutes after the first grenades were thrown, they withdrew. From the prisoners they learned of the imminent operation and all available reserves rushed forward. In the French lines preparations resumed; last minute reconnaissance parties went out, breaches and ramps were made in the jump off lines and groups of machine gunners concentrated harassing and interdiction

German troops moving up. *Tom Gudmestad*

fire on ravines, camps, tracks, assembly points and counter attack routes. Then, after four hours of destructive fire all four regiments moved off behind the rolling barrage. Conditions were appalling. According to the French Official History:

'The weather was frightful. Torrential rain turned the clayey soil…into a swamp. From the moment our guns opened fire, the Germans replied by violently shelling our jump off lines.'

The French positions had been bombarded for days; they offered little shelter and casualties were high among the waiting men, among them the 2nd Tirailleurs:

'Accurate shelling with every calibre of gun smashed our two battalions in their jump off trenches. From 6am until noon on 25 November, without a break, officers and men endured the fire, crouched in the bottom of shell craters, pressing themselves down as far as possible into the mud. The dirt thrown up by the shells came down all over our weapons. It jammed the rifles and machine guns, buried our stores of ammunition and knocked out many of the flamethrowers. At 11am, 5 Company had forty seven men left, 1 Company had just a handful more and only four machine guns were still working'.

A confident group of 2nd Tirailleurs takes time for a photograph on the way forward. They are commanded by Sergeant Royer. *BDIC_VAL_220_186* *https://argonnaute.parisnanterre.fr/*

When zero hour came there were plenty of unarmed men among the leading waves but, despite the horrors of the morning, morale was high and the 168th, 2nd Tirailleurs and 3rd Zouaves soon reached their objectives. While a covering force went forward to establish an outpost line, clearance parties and sappers went to work on the shelters and barracks with incendiary grenades and explosives. The 2nd Tirailleurs had three barracks to clear and it was not long before 2 Company reached the first one (Cologne). Surrounding it, they began by hurling grenades into the openings:

'… the underground galleries shook with the shock of the explosions. Flamethrowers were directed into the openings and thick black smoke poured out. The last men rushed out with their hands up. A few minutes later the Meiningen barracks were attacked by the remnants of 2nd Battalion. The flamethrowers were covered in mud and out of action…so grenades were thrown in. Amid the explosions we could hear shrieks and cries and more men poured out.'

The men inside the Hamburg barracks did not wait for the flamethrowers. Seeing what had happened to the others they fled down the ravine but found the Tirailleurs already there and digging in. No quarter was given:

'Some of the grenadiers tried to fight but our flamethrowers soon put a stop to that and the survivors joined the other men whom the flames had driven out. They were soon heading towards our lines, while behind them the shelters were blowing up with the last occupants inside.'

Altogether about 600 prisoners were taken and the Tirailleurs were soon firing tricolour flares to show they had achieved their objectives. However, while the operation had gone well on the right, on the left the 168th had been pushed back to the main line of resistance, leaving the Landwehr barracks in German hands; and in the centre the 2nd Zouaves were held up by deep mud, machine guns in the Tranchée de Trèves and fire from the Lüder barracks, which was still holding out. On 26 November, the Germans evacuated the Landwehr barracks but the 2nd Zouaves only cleared the Lüder barracks the following day, so it was 27 November before the new lines were established. With French machine guns finally sweeping the bottom of the ravines, the French hold on Cote 344 was secure at last. It had taken them ninety eight days.

Collapsed entrances on the site of the Lüder barracks. *Author's collection*

Pioneers spent the next few days blowing up the barracks, just to make sure the Germans could not use them again. The Germans withdrew to the Brabanter-Stellung, a defensive line two kilometres to the north, and were now too far back to launch a surprise attack. The former barracks remained between the lines.

An aerial view of the Brabanter-Stellung and the Haumont defence line showing heavy French shelling. *Tom Gudmestad*

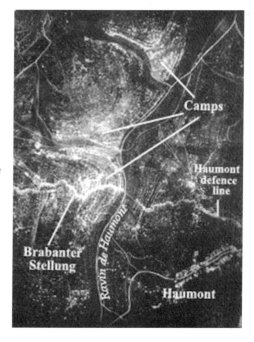

The Butte de Caurières: September – December

The third local operation concerned a sector which had not been attacked on 20 August. This was the Butte de Caurières, a bare hill on the French right between the Bois des Fosses and Bezonvaux, which had been captured by the Germans in February 1916. There were several reasons for its importance to the Germans: the summit – originally marked by a wayside cross (the Vaux Cross) – commanded several ravines offering access to their front line, provided an outstanding platform for artillery observers and signallers, and dominated Bois des Fosses. It was precisely for these reasons that the French wished to capture it. For months the Butte had been shelled, raided and gassed by both sides and by August 1917 it was an expanse of shallow trenches, water logged craters and collapsing shelters. The aim of the new offensive, which was to push the line north of the Butte de Caurrières and link up with French positions in Bois des Fosses, was entrusted to the 128th Division and supported by huge masses of artillery of calibres up to 280 mm. General Passaga also requested more fighter planes, the single escadrille available being seriously hampered by German fighters which, as the French Official History ruefully remarks, 'control fire on our batteries and communication routes with incontestable superiority'.

The date fixed was 8 September and destructive fire began as soon as the order was issued, concentrating particularly on the German supply ravines. The Germans responded violently, causing massive casualties

German soldiers investigate a crashed French aircraft near Romagne-sous-Montfaucon, roughly fifteen kilometres northeast of Cote 304. *Tom Gudmestad*

during the preparation, and counter attacked repeatedly when the assault came, but some progress was made and the all important summit position was captured. However, losses were extremely high, particularly among officers, and as on Cote 344, fighting went on.

In the autumn of 1917, French intelligence assessed German strength on the Right Bank at six divisions, of which two were regarded as good, plus ten in the rear, of which three were worn out. If that encouraged them to believe that the Germans would be unable to resist, they were mistaken. Following the fall of Riga, the German high command transferred a number of formations to the Western Front. These included the Guard Ersatz Division (Guard Infantry Regiments 6 and 7, Infantry Regiment 399), which had already served at Verdun twice: the first time between May and August 1916 losing 50% of its infantry, and the second time in December of the same year. They arrived in the area in mid-September and rested for a few days before beginning retraining:

'Every infantry company received three light 08/15 machine guns. That involved a considerable increase in fighting strength and made the companies independent of the regimental machine gun companies. Special training was arranged ... so that every officer and NCO and many of the men could become familiar with this important weapon. Everybody trained hard with hand grenades because the training offered in summer had been superficial... Hand in hand with this individual training went – helped by wonderful autumn weather – battalion and regimental training, so that commanders and troops could learn to cooperate in the use of the heavy infantry attack weapons, become familiar with artillery, trench mortars and aviation, as well as the important communications and intelligence services.'

It was not all work. The distant thunder from the front did not disturb sports days and theatre visits and it was only on 10 October that the Guard Ersatz Division entered the Vaux Cross sector. From a tactical point of view the position they took over was unfavourable. In addition to the fact that their positions were clearly visible from the French front line less than a hundred metres away, their right wing was more or less in the air. In the view of Guard Infantry Regiment 7:

'A precondition of a successful assault is a good jump off position with plenty of secure communication trenches leading to the rear. In this respect the position [the regiment had taken over] left much to be desired. The front lines of the two divisions were

95

not always contiguous and the communication trenches were too shallow. There was such a severe lack of dugouts that many of the men had to sleep sitting or squatting. The whole position needed extensive work. As a result, the First Battalion…and in particular 1 and 4 Companies, which were in the front line, had to work intensively right up to the day of the assault.'

It was all made more difficult by continuous rain and the need to do most of the work at night but the awful conditions meant that the French did not notice the increased activity and failed to realise that an assault was imminent. On 28 October, the Second Battalion, reinforced by flamethrower troops, pioneers and detachments from Sturm-Bataillon Rohr, climbed into trucks and set off for the front. The communication trench was merely:

'A shallow trough, almost without sides …constantly under fire, full of shell holes and craters, [which] led to the front past smashed and smoking dugouts and literally over corpses.'

A direct hit on the column meant thirteen men had to be evacuated but the rest plodded on and in darkness and pouring rain relieved the First Battalion in their waterlogged positions without the French being aware

This dugout would not resist heavy shelling. *Tom Gudmestad*

The main street of Ornes in 1916, with the church on the right. The hill on the skyline is the Butte de Caurières, with the summit and the Vaux Cross just out of sight. *Tom Gudmestad*

of the changeover. At 5.45am on 29 October, German guns and trench mortars opened up and one minute later the assault waves moved off along an 800 metre front. The French barrage came too late to be effective and the attackers were soon upon them. The Vaux Cross position fell swiftly to a flame thrower assault and by 6.30am the whole of the French first and second lines were in German hands, with all companies on their objectives. It was a brilliant success and praise soon followed. Corps Orders referred to the' bold attacking spirit of the regiment, which had repulsed every attempt by the enemy to retake the Vaux Cross', while Crown Prince Wilhelm expressed his gratitude to every participant in the assault and invited a delegation from the regiment to his headquarters at Charleville, where they were personally thanked and decorated.

That action led to a major improvement in the German position but the French were not going to sit back and allow them to remain within 500 metres of their front line. Their first counter attacks were repelled easily enough but the German lines needed serious improvement if Guard Infantry 7 was to retain the Vaux Cross position permanently.

'The heavily shelled and mud filled trenches could scarcely be recognized. In places they were just a series of shell holes linked by footpaths of varying depth. Some parts of the communication trenches had to be dug again. The number of

97

available dugouts – those that were not full of water – was completely insufficient. It all meant work, plenty of work for everyone, in difficult conditions made worse by the continuing bad weather and especially by the systematic enemy shelling of our positions and the hinterland with high explosive and gas.'

After a period in rest, they returned to the sector on 28 November, this time with all three battalions in line and deeply unimpressed by the state of the trenches they took over from the neighbouring division. 'The 46th Division had not over-exerted themselves', was the regimental historian's tart comment. However:

'In the circumstances it was fortunate that the enemy infantry in front of the First Battalion remained entirely quiet. French sentries in the saps thirty to forty metres from the Germans showed themselves unprotected down to waist level and gave signs indicating 'don't run, no one is going to shoot'. The French may have been influenced by the ceasefire negotiations on the Russian front that were broadcast and reported in Army despatches on 3 December, and were possibly hoping for a cessation of hostilities on their own front. At least that is what the white flags on the enemy wire indicated. Our patrols threw fliers into the French trenches with news of the ceasefire negotiations on the Eastern Front.'

German commanders were expecting an imminent French attack and as a result placed great weight on raiding the enemy trenches and bringing in prisoners. Patrols went out regularly but, as the nights were clear and the French sentries on the highest alert, they were unsuccessful. At that time the French regiment facing the Guards was the 83rd Infantry, which had arrived in the sector on 10 November and found conditions to be just as bad as on the other side of the line:

'When the regiment arrived, the sector was 100% active. No organization, nothing stable, shell craters for the forward elements, a few bits of trench for the troops behind, no shelters, no communication trenches, a few footpaths crossing totally destroyed terrain under constant shelling for troops coming into line or being relieved.'

There were no telephones and communication was only possible using runners and earth conduction telegraphy. Food, which was brought from kitchens fourteen kilometres away, always arrived cold and every day

A typical view of the terrain in the Butte de Caurières sector. *Tom Gudmestad*

French troops trying to keep warm in the winter. The man in the foreground is wearing a sheepskin.

men were evacuated with frostbite. Despite the awful conditions, there was no doubt about German determination. On 4 December the 83rd's War Diary noted that:

'The enemy is very vigilant and energetic. The artillery duels are constant; every night, raiding parties and reconnaissance patrols try to get into our lines and capture our sentries, who are just crouching in shell craters'.

By now the niceties of earlier times had been forgotten. During the afternoon of 6 December, sentries from the 83rd saw:

'...soldiers wearing stretcher bearers' armbands and carrying a Red Cross flag leave the enemy lines. On arrival at our lines the NCO in command presented [the lieutenant] with a note written in French by a certain Lieutenant Otten, requesting permission to search for and remove the body of an officer killed the previous night during a reconnaissance. He was the commander of the patrol which had appeared in front of 2 Company ... during the night of 4–5 December. The four men were taken prisoner and sent to the rear.'

Methods of fighting were changing too. During the night of 13-14 December, 3 Company, 83rd Infantry, was holding a salient which was close the German line and weakly organized:

'The enemy had already tried several raids against this point. They tried again on 14 December at 2.30am, arriving in front of two of our sections in four columns of about twenty men each without any artillery preparation and taking advantage of thick fog and driving snow. Thanks to our brave sentries their approach was quickly spotted.'

The trick of raiding with little or no artillery preparation was used again by the Guards the following day, when after only a two minute bombardment the assault troops of three companies fell on the heavily wired craters that formed the French front line in a five minute burst of violent action that took four prisoners and blew up a dugout. Fighting did not even stop at Christmas. After a lightening raid on the French trenches in the late afternoon of 24 December, a major undertaking was planned for 26 December to forestall what was believed to be an imminent French operation. It involved all three regiments of the Guard Ersatz Division, plus detachments from

Sturm-Battalion Rohr, flame thrower troops and pioneers. Facing them were the French 9th, 11th and 98th Infantry Regiments, the latter having just arrived in the sector. According to Guard Infantry 7:

> 'It was a beautiful winter's day, clear and frosty, with snow covering the hills and valleys. At 9am [German time] our guns began shelling the French batteries and rear positions with gas. Shortly before 10am artillery and trench mortars began bombarding the French front lines. A few minutes later the assault troops…broke into the enemy positions south of the Vaux Cross, swept all resistance aside and returned a quarter of an hour later with fifteen prisoners from the 9th Infantry… Soon after 11am the guns fell silent on both sides.'

Right and below: **A German *Granatwerfer* 16 (small bomb thrower) and shell.**
Author's collection

But if the French thought they could relax, they were wrong:

'…at 3.21pm fifty nine batteries, 150 trench mortars and countless *Granatwerfern* [small bomb throwers] launched a hurricane of fire on their first and second lines. Less than two minutes later, the first storm waves from the [two Guard Infantry regiments] broke out, followed by the second and third waves… The front line was only 100 metres away and it was quickly reached. Almost entirely destroyed, unoccupied or evacuated by the enemy, it did not present an obstacle and the attackers streamed boldly on to the strongly held second line, heedless of enemy machine gun and artillery fire. They broke in easily. With the help of well aimed hand grenades and the superbly manipulated flame throwers…the enemy resistance was broken…Some of the enemy surrendered. Where they resisted, they were wiped out. Many fled and were killed by our box barrage. Both the enemy lines were totally destroyed, dugouts and concrete positions for trench mortars and bomb throwers were blown up.'

The 98th's war diary described the afternoon bombardment as 'excessively violent with every calibre of shell and heavy trench mortar bombs' but very short and followed immediately by the German attackers in fifteen columns of roughly twenty five men each accompanied by flame throwers. One hundred and five men became casualties, half of whom were missing.

The violence and brevity of the action was typical of the fighting in the Vaux Cross sector and it continued into 1918. The Guard Infantry was soon withdrawn. They left the sector in which they had spent nine weeks and lost over five hundred men with a feeling of superiority over an enemy whom they:

'had fought victoriously in East and West and now on the Vaux Cross. Guard Infantry 7 left the position in the proud knowledge that they had a place among the battle hardened troops who would lead the assault in the expected German breakthrough battle to come.

But such a breakthrough never came. The monstrous artillery battle continued on the Butte de Caurières but the vital summit position remained in German hands.

The results of the Second Battle of Verdun
The offensive of 20–30 August 1917 involved 420,000 men, or 16.5% of the entire army resources available to the French. Its immediate

result was to remove any danger to the city, which was now eleven kilometres behind the front. As promised by General Pétain, success had been achieved through meticulous planning, the maximum of artillery and the minimum of infantry. Although fighting continued on the Right Bank, French commanders were generally pleased with the result. French losses for 20–25 August amounted to 14,970 men, with a further 6,030 casualties reported between 25-30 August. However, they had tied up twenty five German divisions at a time when Field Marshal Haig was preparing for the Third Battle of Ypres, taken 7,000 prisoners, and seized or destroyed masses of equipment. Most important of all, the success of the August operation had contributed greatly to the restoration of morale after the mutinies of the spring and early summer. The French divisions involved, which had benefited from a long period of rest and physical and psychological training in areas far from the front over ground resembling the sectors to be attacked, had come to the battle with high morale. In his report on the lessons to be drawn from the battle, the commander of XV Corps made the importance of morale quite plain:

'In some of the earlier offensives we prepared everything except the main instrument – the men…In the offensive of 20 August, we were wise enough not to do that. We allowed the attacking divisions a month's rest, during which they were prepared physically and psychologically. Every action was minutely studied by each unit on terrain similar to that to be attacked. Every man, every commander, from the highest to the lowest, knew perfectly what he was supposed to do, both for himself and in liaison with other units. Hearts and spirits were at their highest. The units returned to the front sure of victory and went forward steadily and with confidence….With success achieved and consolidated, they returned to the rear and were justly and generously rewarded. Today, their morale and their physical value are higher than ever.'

In the scathing judgment of the French Official History, the massive German effort at Verdun since February 1916 had been in vain and their position at the end of 1917 'did not add to the prestige of the enemy High Command'.

The relevant volume of the German Official History accepts that the French offensive of August 1917 was a serious defeat and ascribes it to a failure to follow the clearly expressed principle that tactically unfavourable positions should be abandoned when threatened by a major

German troops with the inevitable results of war. *Tom Gudmestad*

enemy offensive; at Verdun, however, the overall military and political situation had meant that such positions could not be abandoned, and the result was not only loss of ground but also great damage to morale. Whether in the end abandoning the sectors which became the focus of such desperate fighting would have made any difference in the sense of allowing the Germans to retire and regroup for a counter offensive in 1918 is impossible to say, although given the state of the German army in 1918 it is unlikely. What can be said, however, is that such a tactical withdrawal would undoubtedly have saved a great many lives.

The Tours

Advice to Tourers

Getting to Verdun: Verdun is easily reached by car and for visitors coming from Paris there is the high speed TGV service from the *Gare de l'Est* to the new Meuse TGV station. This is twenty two kilometres south of Verdun and connected to the city centre by shuttle bus.

Accommodation: The city and surrounding area offer accommodation ranging from three star hotels to self-catering cottages, Airbnb, bed and breakfast and camp sites. For a full list of accommodation, contact the tourist office or check this site: http://www.verdun-tourisme.com

To reach the start of the walking tours: These begin at some distance from the city at places not served by public transport. Car hire is available in Verdun and the *Office de Tourisme* in Verdun has information about bike hire. See the **Useful Addresses** section at the back of this book for contact details.

When to travel: Summer normally brings the best weather but the disadvantages are thick forest and mosquitoes. Autumn and early spring are better, particularly the latter, as by then the organized hunting season is over. Fleury Memorial Museum, the Ossuary, Fort Douaumont and Fort Vaux are closed from the third week of December to early February.

Hunting/Logging: Roughly speaking, hunting takes place on any day of the week between September and the end of February. Hunts can temporarily block access to large areas, including the main historical sites, so be prepared to choose another route if need be. Keep away from foresters using heavy logging machinery. At the time of writing, a plague of Bark Beetle means that the spruce plantations are being cleared and this can make large areas difficult of access.

Firing range restrictions: The walking tours are not affected by firing range restrictions.

Winter weather: Take particular care in snow and icy weather as minor roads are unlikely to be cleared, salted or gritted. This also applies to the roads across the battlefield.

Clothing/footwear: Verdun can be wet and the forest tracks are likely to be muddy all year, especially where there is logging. Bring a rainproof jacket and wear stout, waterproof and non-slip footwear. A walking stick may be useful too. Make sure you have appropriate medical insurance. In summer, bring plenty of mosquito repellent, including mosquito spray for your room. Cover up with long trousers and sleeves to protect against mosquitoes and ticks.

Refreshments/Toilets: These are very limited unless you are close to the main sites on the Right Bank. They are available during opening hours at Fleury Memorial Museum, the Ossuary, and the *Abri des Pèlerins* café/restaurant.

Access for visitors with restricted mobility: The main memorials on the Right Bank may be reached by car but the forest tracks are inaccessible. Apart from Fleury Memorial Museum, which has a level entrance and an internal elevator, the battlefield sites are not well equipped to deal with visitors with restricted mobility. The *Abri des Pèlerins* café/restaurant and the Ossuary have ramps to the entrance.

French War Diaries *(Journaux des marche et opérations)*: These are held at the *Service Historique de la Défense*, Château de Vincennes, Avenue de Paris, F-94306 VINCENNES Cedex
For information see: http://www.servicehistorique.sga.defense.gouv.fr
They may be consulted online at: https://www.memoiredeshommes.sga. defense.gouv.fr/fr/article.php?larub=3&titre=premiere-guerre-mondiale

French regimental histories: *(Historiques régimentaires)*
These are to be found on the website mentioned above and in *Gallica*, the digital document collection at the *Bibliothèque Nationale de France* at this link: http://gallica.bnf.fr/accueil.
While some French regimental histories contain detailed information, many are merely a summary.

List of *Morts pour la France*: This is available on *Mémoire des Hommes* through this link: http://www.memoiredeshommes.sga.defense.gouv.fr/ fr/arkotheque/client/mdh/base_morts_pour_la_france_premiere_guerre/
Inevitably, it is not complete.

French war graves: A searchable database of burial sites is available on *Mémoire des Hommes* under *Sépultures de Guerre* here: http://www. memoiredeshommes.sga.defense.gouv.fr/fr/arkotheque/client/mdh/ sepultures_guerre/
It is not complete and does not include the graves of men whose remains were returned to their families.

German regimental histories are available on CD-Rom via this link: http://www.military-books.de.vu/

A note on time: During the Battle of Verdun German time was normally one hour ahead of French time. Unless otherwise stated, any specific time mentioned is French time.

Separate sections at the end of this book contain information on guidebooks, other places of interest and useful addresses.

Introduction to the Tours

GPS waypoints
These appear as bracketed numbers in the text and as numbers in bold on the maps. The full GPS references are gathered in a section at the end of each tour.

Maps
1. For a driving tour of the area: IGN (Orange Series) Meuse 55.
2. For general interest: *Sites de la Guerre 1914-1918, 1/200.000*, published by Michelin and showing the fronts and French and German sites of interest;
   IGN 1/75.000 Grande Guerre – Bataille de Verdun 1916. Although the lines and unit deployments on the latter relate to the 1916 battle, the map covers the area visited in this book and indicates many sites of interest.
3. For a close study of the areas covered by these tours and for the walking tours the most useful maps are those published by the French *Institut Géographique National* (IGN). The relevant numbers are indicated at the start of each tour.

These maps may be unavailable in Verdun, so buy them before you visit. IGN maps are available from their website on http://www.ign.fr and from various internet outlets. **Note:** the current version of IGN 3112ET does not show the forest block numbers used in Tours 3 and 4 but older versions of the map, which do show them, are to be found on the internet.

A note on heights and spelling
The word Cote is written without a circumflex accent when followed by a number, eg Cote 304, but with a circumflex accent when referring to a named height, eg Côte du Talou. This can result in such apparent incongruities as Cote 265 on the Côte de l'Oie. A number does not necessarily indicate altitude.

Warning: At all times visitors should remain on the paths, stay away from the edges of holes and avoid heavy logging equipment. Current work to clear spruce plantations affected by a plague of Bark Beetle can render affected areas difficult to access, so be prepared to choose another route if work is underway.

Collecting 'souvenirs', digging or using metal detectors are absolutely prohibited and subject to heavy fines. Forts, shelters, dugouts and other positions are dangerous and should not be entered. Live ammunition, shells, grenades and mortar bombs should not be touched under any circumstances.

Light *Minenwerfer* (German trench mortar) shells on Hardaumont Plateau in February 2020. *Author's collection*

Tour No 1

From Chattencourt to Consenvoye via Forges, Regnéville, Samogneux and Haumont

Distance: Roughly twenty kilometres.
Duration: A half day's driving tour
Maps: IGN 3112 ET or IGN Blue Series 3212 Ouest

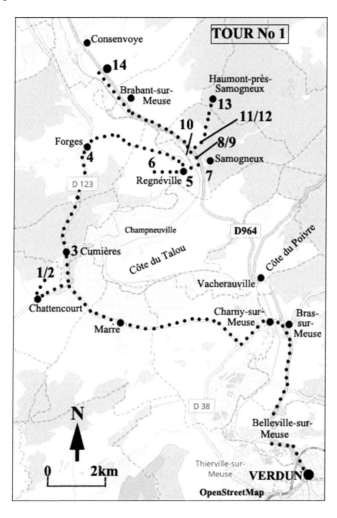

The tour covers sites on the Left and Right Banks of the River Meuse connected with the August 1917 offensive and includes a visit to the destroyed village of Haumont-près-Samogneux. Short walks are available at Forges and Haumont if desired. There is a picnic table on the site of the old village of Forges and several by the Austro-Hungarian memorial at Samogneux. Refreshments and toilets are only available at Bras-sur-Meuse and Marre before the start of the tour and at Consenvoye at the end.

To reach Chattencourt from Verdun, take the D964 (Stenay) road. At Bras-sur-Meuse turn left on the D115, following signs to Charny-sur-Meuse, then drive through Charny and turn right on the D38 towards Marre. Continue through Marre to the crossroads and turn left on the D38 towards Esnes and Varennes-en-Argonne. Continue into Chattencourt. The road bends to the right as it enters the main part of the village and just before it bends left again turn sharp right along the side of a farm to the French military cemetery. This is signposted with *Chattancourt* and a symbol representing a French helmet and cross against a tricolour background. The track runs alongside the farm and turns uphill. The memorial by the track will be visited later, so continue to the cemetery and **stop**.

The cemetery (1)
This is a concentration cemetery and many of the 1726 men buried here were transferred from other cemeteries or individual sites, some of them as late as 1982. They include twenty seven casualties of the

Above and opposite: **Foreign Legion recruits came from all over the world. These men were recruited in French Indochina and Russia.** *Author's collection*

112

Second World War and also two brothers, Joseph and Henri Coraboeuf, gunners in the 51st Field Artillery Regiment, who were killed in fighting on the Right Bank on 30 June 1916 and 2 January 1917 respectively. There is a Muslim section on the eastern side. Being close to the French front line of August 1917, the cemetery contains many burials from that offensive, including a substantial number from the Foreign Legion and a glance at their graves shows how diverse they were: plot 340, Joseph Rachmann, born in 1886 in Russia; plot 346, Jean Mousel born in Luxembourg in 1876; plot 348, Huynh-Va-Day, born in 1895 at Chau Doc, Cochinchina (now Vietnam); plot 349, Jean Joseph Lafaye, born 1888 in Puerto Rico; plot 1828 Corporal Guido (Guy) Agostini, born in 1893 in Spain, according to his French death certificate, but commemorated by the Legion as a Californian. The Legion's list of casualties on 20 August also includes men born in Turkey, the Netherlands, Switzerland, Germany, Austria, Belgium, Syria, Jersey, Romania and Argentina.

Guilland memorial **(2)**

This handsome memorial commemorates twenty five year old Lieutenant Pierre Guilland, an air observer with Escadrille C34, who died of injuries received when his Caudron G4 crashed on 20 August 1917. A law student when mobilized into the 38th Field Artillery Regiment, he was posted to the Moroccan Division (XVI Corps) in February 1917 and served as an observer from 5 March of that year.

The Caudron G4, a twin engine biplane originally designed as a bomber but later relegated to a reconnaissance and artillery direction role because of its slow speed, was attacked by three German fighters over the Mort-Homme and came down just inside French lines. The memorial originally stood in an enclosure on the actual crash site one hundred metres away but it became inconvenient for the farmer and was moved here. Escadrille C34 was based at Osches, near Souilly, south west of Verdun, and on 20 August it comprised one command plane and twelve planes carrying out infantry liaison, artillery direction, surveillance and photographic missions. That was in addition to the two Corps escadrilles of thirteen planes each, two heavy artillery escadrilles of ten planes each, four companies of ten planes each and four balloon companies, each with four balloons, that were also available to XVI Corps.

The inscription on the face of the monument reads: 'Remember before God Pierre Guilland, Knight of the Légion d'Honneur, Croix de Guerre with Palm, Lieutenant in the 38th Field Artillery Regiment, air observer with the Moroccan Division, Escadrille C34. Born at Marseille on 27 August 1892. Aged twenty five, died for France on 20 August 1917 in aerial combat over Chattancourt during preparation of the action to recapture the Mort-Homme'. The side facing the cemetery bears his citation in Army Orders: 'An elite observer who throughout the action demonstrated the highest military qualities. On 20 August, when undertaking an infantry liaison mission under difficult conditions and flying at low altitude, he met a glorious death in unequal combat against three enemy planes.' The inscription at the rear refers to the benediction of the cross on 7 August 1921 by Monseigneur Ginisty, Bishop of Verdun, and accords fifty days' indulgence applicable to the souls of the heroes of Verdun to those who when stopping before the cross repeat the words *Resquiescant in pace*. Another very weathered inscription on the side facing the village refers to Lieutenant Guilland on a stretcher at the crash site receiving the Last Rites from a military chaplain.

The crash also killed the pilot, thirty year old Corporal Thimotée Vila. In commerce when war broke out, Corporal Vila was mobilized in the 12th Infantry and saw combat at Charleroi, Guise, on the Marne

The memorial to Lieutenant Pierre Guilland which stands close to Chattancourt cemetery. *Author's collection*

Corporal Thimotée Vila, pilot, who died in the crash with Lieutenant Guilland.

and elsewhere before acquiring his pilot's licence and joining Escadrille C34. He was posthumously awarded the Croix de Guerre with Bronze Star and cited in Army Orders as a 'Courageous pilot always energetic and conscious of his duty. Met a glorious death on 20 August in unequal combat against three enemy planes.' Both men were buried in Fromeréville-les-Vallons, but as their names do not appear in the current register of French military cemeteries it is reasonable to assume that their remains were returned to their families. Pierre Guilland and his brother, Lieutenant Jacques Guilland, 1st Battalion Chasseurs à pied, who was killed at Aure, Champagne, on 28 September 1918, are commemorated in a stained glass window in the church of Fromeréville-les-Vallons. *For more information on French aviation and a visit to Osches, see Tour No 2.*

German aviators at Verdun

A number of famous German aviators flew at Verdun at various times. In 1915, Hermann Göring was an aerial observer there, notably over the forts and the front lines. One of the greatest air fighters of all, Oswald

The Höhndorf memorial at Iré-le-Sec. *Author's collection*

116

Boelcke, who formalized the rules of aerial combat and died with twenty one confirmed victories, operated from March to July 1916 from the airfield at Sivry-sur-Meuse, which he managed to connect to a front line observation post, thus establishing a tactical air direction centre. Manfred von Richthofen served at Verdun with Kampfgeschwader 2 at the same time. Walter Höhndorf, a pioneer aviator, aeroplane designer and constructor, test pilot and fighter ace credited with twelve victories, was killed in a flying accident on 5 September 1918 at Iré-le-Sec to the north of Verdun. He is commemorated in a remarkable memorial that portrays him as Icarus.

Chattancourt

Return to the village and stop when you reach the road. Chattencourt has existed for centuries. In 1914, most of the 321 people living here were involved in agriculture but there was also a paper mill in a local farm, an oil mill, a cooperative dairy producing local butter and from 1878 the railway, connecting Chattancourt to the outside world. When war broke out, most of the population remained in the village but on 12 February 1916 the beating drum of the *garde champêtre* [a rural official] announced evacuation for the following day. This was soon changed to 'immediate evacuation'. Being so close to one of the main centres of the Battle of Verdun in 1916, Chattancourt, Charny and Marre could not escape destruction and after the war returning inhabitants and workers brought in to clear the battlefields were housed in huts until permanent structures

Peace and quiet in Chattancourt before the First World War. *Author's collection*

could be built. Together with a number of other villages destroyed during the Battle of Verdun, Chattencourt was awarded the Croix de Guerre.

If you wish to visit the *Tranchée de Chattancourt* before continuing the tour, bear right and continue to the road fork a short distance ahead, then take the right fork and stop almost immediately. This reconstructed trench has been rebuilt using original maps, documents and photographs, together with accounts by some of the men who served there. To visit the Mort-Homme memorials, pass the *Tranchée* and follow the road uphill through the fields to the parking area. For more information about the fighting on the Left Bank in 1916, see *Verdun – The Left Bank*.

Cumières-le-Mort-Homme (3)
To continue the tour, return through Chattancourt to the crossroads you passed earlier and turn left on the D123 towards *Cumières village détruit*. After about 200 metres you will cross the French front line of 20 August 1917 in this sector; the tree line ahead roughly marks the German front line of that day. Continue for a little over one kilometre and park on the right by the war memorial. The boards on either side have information about Cumières and the Foreign Legion.

When war broke out, most of the 205 inhabitants of Cumières were involved in agriculture but other trades were also represented, such as smithying, saddlery, carpentry, tailoring and cheese making. Although it

Cumières. – Rue de l'Église.

Cumières in happier times. *Author's collection*

118

was only a small place, Cumières was important, because it commanded this road, the Verdun-Sedan railway line, and river and canal crossings in the Meuse valley. Mobilization orders arrived soon after war was declared and the first men left for the depot at 6am on 4 August 1914; shortly afterwards, French troops arrived in the village, together with refugees from the north of the Department of the Meuse fleeing the German advance.

In September there were several German incursions into Cumières and a report submitted to the Sous-Préfet complained that they had not only helped themselves to what they wanted, destroyed the only telephone line and threatened to kill one of the shopkeepers, but had also arrested the mayor and taken him to Germany as a hostage. A new mayor was appointed but already the inhabitants had begun to leave and the school had closed. In September and October 1914 the fighting was several kilometres to the north of here and Cumières, Chattancourt and Marre functioned as rear bases and depots. Those villagers who had stayed behind got busy organizing convoys of wagons to carry the sick and wounded to the field hospitals further back and used the village school to look after those who could not be transported; they also buried the soldiers and horses killed in the fighting and even carried rations to positions behind the front line. Despite random shelling in 1915, some civilians clung on until general evacuation was ordered in February 1916.

The German assault on the Left Bank began on 6 March 1916 and twenty four hours later Cumières became a target. Heavy shells from guns guided by German spotter planes sent huge plumes of smoke into the air; batteries were demolished, houses collapsed and the road to Chattancourt became jammed as stretcher bearers and medical personnel rushed to move the wounded out of harm's way. Panic stricken defenders poured down from the front lines but desperate officers rounded them up, rearmed them with whatever they could find and led them forward again. Cumières remained in French hands until 24 May 1916 when, in a pre-dawn action preceded by yet another earth shaking bombardment, German infantry, flamethrowers and pioneers stormed out of their lines. Artillery preparation had completely flattened the surrounding trenches and blown up the remaining houses, forcing the defenders, the 5th battalion of the 254th Infantry, to take refuge in the cellars. The battalion commander had been seriously wounded the previous evening and command had passed to Captain René Lisbonne, who recorded the final dramatic moments in his diary:

'23 May: All the command posts had collapsed on the officers and their staffs; a few men were holding on in shell holes. The bombardment was beyond description and not even a hundred

Cumières war memorial. *Author's collection*

120

men were still standing. At midnight a panic stricken man arrived at our post, where we'd been for hours. "Captain, the Germans are just behind us." I got a few men together … and rushed outside while my quartermaster launched flares. We didn't get very far; an exploding grenade knocked me down and wounded me slightly in the legs. Ten Germans were immediately upon me. My poor men were falling and I saw a flamethrower directed at the cellar where the stretcher bearers and wounded were. To save the wounded I had to say the terrible words: "You've got us. At least let my men come out." It was then that I noticed something strange: there was nothing left of the village. Everything had been smashed, including my own shelter.'

The loss of Cumières was a terrible blow to the French because it was the last organized part of the Mort-Homme sector and once it was in German hands there was little to stop them from continuing towards open country. An immediate French counter attack got nowhere but a second attempt two days later was more successful and a little group of men managed to retake the chateau – a substantial building behind the chapel, of which nothing now remains. However, as the new position was very close to the German lines, open to counter attack at any moment and subject to continuous bombardment, it could not be held for long without a major supporting operation and on 30 May 1916 the last men were withdrawn. Cumières remained in German hands until it was recaptured by the Foreign Legion on 20 August 1917, as described in Chapter Four.

After the war
A photo on the information board shows the state of Cumières after the war when returning inhabitants found that not only their houses but also the forests and fields that had provided them with a living were completely destroyed. The task of clearing the area, rebuilding, and returning the land to agriculture and forestry was considered uneconomic and Cumières became part of the Red Zone. This was the name given to former battle areas which could not be restored to pre-war use without excessive expense.

The village and the land belonging to it were purchased by the State and Cumières acquired the status of a village that had died for France; as such, it is managed by a mayor, who is appointed by the Prefect of the Meuse Department, and three councillors. There are nine destroyed villages on the former Verdun battlefield but Cumières is the only one on the Left Bank, and to preserve the name of the battle in which this village was destroyed it is known today as Cumières-le-Mort-Homme. Apart

The memorial to René Lisbonne. *Author's collection*

from the refurbished property at the level crossing over the railway line, the only new constructions are the memorial to the Blessed Jeanne Gérard, a Daughter of Charity of St. Vincent de Paul who was born in Cumières and guillotined for her beliefs in Paris in 1794; the chapel dedicated to Saint Rémi, which stands on the site of the former church, and the war memorial. This commemorates the seventeen men of Cumières who died for France during the war, the heroic defence of the village by the 254th Infantry Regiment and its liberation by the Foreign Legion.

A plaque to the left of the cemetery gate commemorates Captain René Lisbonne, who was mobilized in 1939 with the rank of Lieutenant Colonel and executed by the Germans at Struthof camp in July 1943 for 'acts of resistance'. Louis and André Lavigne whose names are recorded to the right of the gate, were respectively a well known writer and a post war mayor of the destroyed village. Like Chattancourt, Cumières was awarded the Croix de Guerre.

Forges (4)
Now follow the D123 over the Côte de l'Oie to the junction with the D160 and turn left towards Béthincourt and Aubréville. Cross the bridge over Forges stream and stop roughly seventy five metres directly ahead by a small fenced area where there is a picnic table and an information board with photographs and a plan of the pre-war village. The sites of various former buildings are also indicated by photographs on individual wooden posts. Starting by the bridge, a marked path along the stream takes visitors to the site of two mills, one of the original bridges and a German shelter, one of five built on higher ground by the road. This is a gentle twenty minute stroll but it is likely to be fairly wet in winter and may be a bit overgrown in summer.

Forges, with a population of 462 in 1914, commanded a crossroads and two bridges over the fast flowing stream. As such it quickly came under German pressure and changed hands four times between

One of the former German shelters close to Forges Stream, with a second behind it. *Author's collection*

1 September and 4 October 1914. The French then held it until 6 March 1916, when it was captured by Reserve Infantry Regiment 51 after hours of shelling. The German plan for the Battle of Verdun did not include operations on the Left Bank unless they became absolutely necessary; it was only when flanking fire from French batteries massed on this side of the River Meuse brought the Germans advancing on the other side to a standstill that General von Falkenhayn, the Chief of the German General Staff, authorized action on the Left Bank. His aim was to clear the hilltop observatories on this side of the river that provided the French batteries here with outstanding views of both German movements on the other side of the river and of German artillery on this side. The observatories in question were situated on Cote 304, the Mort-Homme and the Côte de l'Oie, and as Forges commanded access to the Côte de l'Oie it immediately became a target.

On 6 March 1916 the village was defended by a mixed group composed of 9 Company, 54th Territorials, and most of the 5th Battalion, 211th Infantry, a reserve regiment which until recently had been labouring in the rear. The Left Bank had been a quiet sector for months and the defenders, who had no experience of intense bombardment, were stunned by the deluge of shells that hit them at 7am that morning. Forges and the Côte de l'Oie fell that day. The Côte de l'Oie was recaptured by the Foreign Legion on 21 August 1917 but Forges itself remained in German hands until cleared by the American 132nd Infantry Regiment on 26 September 1918; by then it was completely destroyed.

A view of old Forges village with destruction well under way. The photo is taken from the junction of the D123 and the D160. The road running uphill past the church goes to Drillancourt. *Tom Gudmestad*

124

One hundred and forty of the inhabitants wished to return but with clearing and draining the site too difficult and expensive the new village was built some distance away.

Regnéville (5)

Now drive through the new village of Forges. At the crossroads approximately 600 metres ahead turn right on the Route de Consenvoye. Take the left fork after 150 metres and at the T-junction 100 metres further on turn left on the D123a and follow the road through the fields to Regnéville, noting how close you are to the Right Bank. At the crossroads in Regnéville, turn left and then immediately right into the Rue de la Chanvre and park on the left by the play area.

In 1914, Regnéville was another place whose importance was much greater than it size because it commanded the Meuse valley, the river and canal crossings and access to the Côte de l'Oie. From 3 March 1916 the village was garrisoned by 18 Company, 211th Infantry, and 10 Company, 54th Territorials, commanded by Captain Aynard. Their task was to keep watch along the River Meuse between Regnéville and Forges; with the Germans only 1000 metres away on the Right Bank and all movement at night forbidden, it was not easy. After a preliminary bombardment lasting

Crossing the Meuse at Regnéville before the First World War. *Author's collection*

several hours, the village was attacked on 6 March by infantry and pioneers from the 22nd Reserve Division, who crossed the river from the Right Bank on pontoons and gangplanks, supported by an armoured train which steamed down the railway line (360 metres uphill from here) and smashed a hole through the massive wire entanglements blocking it. This was quite beyond the experience of the defenders but they fought back as well as they could. However, with the village cut off, no one knew what was happening. Lieutenant Colonel Mollandin, commander of the 211th, reported that Regnéville had been overrun by the enemy but it was not clear whether resistance was continuing. On 6 March, the 54th's war diary reported 'Very lively action from early morning and all day in the region of Regnéville, Forges and further west. No news of the three trench companies. Sealed note attached with more information.' The sealed note dated 7 March 1916 read as follows:

'Confidential and subject to confirmation. No news of 9, 10 and 11 Companies [Third Battalion] detached at Forges, Regnéville and the Côte de l'Oie. According to the few men who returned, on 6 March all three places were shelled with unheard of intensity and very heavy calibre (305mm). Sergeant Martin of 9 Company (in Forges) got back with twelve men and reported that the elements of the 211th infantry that were in front of them were almost entirely wiped out by the bombardment and that 9 Company only just had time to get out of the dugouts and engage the enemy in the village streets, where they must have been surrounded by the enemy. A handful of men from 9 Company were seen wandering around at Cumières. It is rumoured that Regnéville has also been taken (10 Company). There has been nothing from 11 Company on the Côte de l'Oie since this morning. The sergeant who carried the rations to Cumières yesterday evening informs me that he found no one there but the company messengers and that they had no news of their units. Moreover, none of these three companies has collected the rations for 5 March; they are still where the sergeant left them the night before. In sum, unless the day's events have been different from the accounts given by the stragglers, it is to be feared that the three companies and perhaps units from other corps have been taken prisoner after a very unequal struggle.'

By the time the note was received Forges and the Côte de l'Oie were already in German hands but Regnéville held out until 7 March. Those two days cost 9, 10 and 11 Companies, 54th Infantry, ten officers and 460 men, while the 211th lost two thirds of its effectives, including

Like Forges, Regnéville was completely destroyed. Returning inhabitants were housed in huts until permanent accommodation could be built. *Author's collection*

Colonel Mollandin, who was captured. The ranks were filled up with drafts from other regiments but on 14 April the 211th was broken up.

Return to the junction and walk uphill for a little over one hundred metres, pass the church and stop at the Place du Capitaine Aynard **(6)** where there are a number of memorials and information boards. Captain Raymond Aynard, Croix de Guerre, described on the plaque behind the fountain as the regimental commander, in fact commanded 10 Company, 54th Territorials, and died here on 6 March 1916. Aged forty eight in August 1914, a highly successful diplomat with a glittering career and already an Officer of the Légion d'Honneur, he had volunteered for service and received a staff appointment as a second lieutenant. Not being satisfied with that he applied for a command and was posted to the 54th Territorials. The war diary does not mention him but the regimental history reports that he was killed on 6 March when reconnoitring the enemy's movements in the open.

Foreign Legion Memorial
This recently inaugurated memorial commemorates all members of the Legion who died for France and not only those who fell in the offensive of August 1917. Following their success on 20-21 August, General Pétain reviewed the regiment, awarded numerous decorations – including a second Palm to Colonel Rollet's Croix de Guerre – and conferred the crimson lanyard of the Légion d'Honneur on the regimental colours.

The Foreign Legion memorial at Regnéville. *Author's collection*

128

War Memorial
The war memorial, which was inaugurated in November 2007, names the three men of Regnéville who died for France. The civilian victim, Melanie Pigeard, an elderly resident born in 1846, refused to leave her house when ordered to evacuate and was killed when it was shelled on 26 February 1916.

The cemetery
Even though it is not a First World War site, it is worth visiting the cemetery next to the Place du Capitaine Aynard. As is clear from the information board there, the three men killed in the First World War

The 'Christ de l'Orme' in Regnéville Cemetery. *Author's collection*

were not the first sons of Regnéville to die on military service but were following in the footsteps of six men of the village who died serving France on battlefields in Russia, Spain, Lübeck, Algeria and Cochinchina between 1807 and 1873. Before leaving the cemetery, look for the cross tucked between trees to the right of the information board. The head of Jesus is all that is left of the well loved *Christ de l'Orme*, a wayside cross that stood under a spreading elm tree beside the track from Regnéville to the Côte de l'Oie roughly 800 metres uphill from where you are standing. The tree, which provided exceptional views over the Meuse valley, functioned as a signalling station until it was destroyed during the war. A small grove of trees with a new cross now stands on the same site. It is worth a walk up to the cross to get an idea of the importance of the position at that time.

Return to your car and look across the valley at the Right Bank, which is only a short distance away. The hills directly ahead form the western edge of the Meuse Heights, which rise gently from the river and run east for roughly five kilometres before dropping sharply to the Woëvre Plain. The village opposite is Samogneux and the hill behind it is Cote 344, the scene of such desperate fighting between September–November 1917. It was with Samogneux that the Foreign Legion established telephone liaison on 21 August 1917, thereby linking up French troops on both sides of the river. Standing here it is easy to see how French artillery and machine guns on this side of the river could obstruct troops advancing towards Verdun on the other side.

Samogneux **(7)**
To continue the tour, return to the junction, turn right and drive across the valley to Samogneux. Park in the main street and face uphill. In 1914 the village stood along the D964 and the current village is mostly on a new site. The information boards by the playground refer to Gaston Thiébaut, an eminent son of Samogneux and post war mayor of Verdun, who was one of the eighty four members of parliament who refused to vote full powers to Marshal Pétain in July 1940.

Lines of defence on the Right Bank and the capture of Samogneux in 1916
When the Battle of Verdun began there were theoretically four lines of defence on the Right Bank. The first, which ran eastwards across the Meuse Heights roughly two kilometres north of where you are standing, was composed of four reasonably well developed of centres of resistance based on hilltops and forests, whereas the second line, which included Samogneux and Cote 344, was just a number of unconnected and

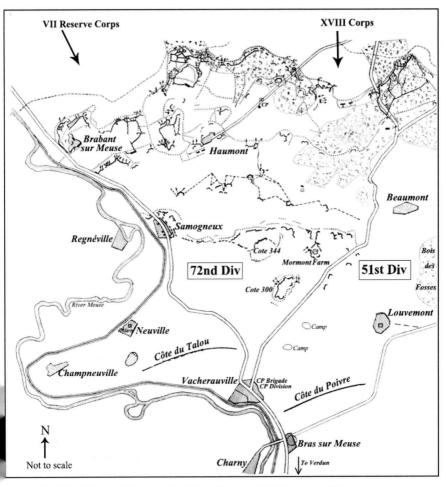

72nd Division positions on the Right Bank on 21 February 1916.

A typical defence work in the Samogneux-Haumont sector in February 1916. *Tom Gudmestad*

incomplete works. The third line comprised the Côte du Talou and the Côte du Poivre but it was barely sketched out and could not offer an effective defence, while the fourth was the main line of resistance and included many of the forts. Defending them from the assault of three German army corps on 21 February 1916 were two infantry divisions, the 51st and 72nd, and about 270 guns of various calibres.

Samogneux and Cote 344 were in the sector held by the 72nd Division, a formation then comprising one active and three reserve regiments, two light infantry battalions and one battalion of territorials withdrawn from guarding roads and railways. Although strong and reliable men, mostly from the Department of the Meuse, the 72nd's opportunities for regular training had been few and their experience of warfare was that of 1914. The force of the assault by units of VII Reserve Corps and XVIII Corps on 21 February 1916 was overwhelming to these brave but inexperienced men and the result was terrible. Writing after the war in the *Revue Militaire Française*, Lieutenant Colonel Grasset, a former serving officer and well known military historian, described the effect on the 72nd Division of the first thirty six hours of the Battle of Verdun:

'A half company of Chasseurs [light infantry], two and a half battalions of the 165th, one and a half battalions of the 351st and two and a half companies of the 44th Territorials. That, in sum, was all that remained in the evening of 22 February of those units of the 72nd Division who had been in action since the morning of the 21st.'

By then half of the first line of defence had fallen and the attackers were pouring through the gap. On 23 February, Brabant – a strongly organized village two kilometres to the north of Samogneux which anchored the first line of defence to the River Meuse – was in danger of encirclement and the commander of the 72nd Division, General Bapst, ordered it to be evacuated. As evacuation was contrary to orders, he was instructed to retake Brabant without delay but it was impossible; Samogneux was now in the front line. With no let-up in the bombardment, casualties reaching critical levels and a complete absence of information about what was happening elsewhere, the local commander, Lieutenant Colonel Bernard, 351st Infantry, placed his troops as best he could. It did not amount to much – a handful of companies from various regiments, some machine gunners and a few elements of the 44th Territorials, all out of touch with the neighbouring units and generally not knowing where they were. An infantry officer sent up to report described the situation he found:

'Amid the moving wreckage of Samogneux, with houses blowing up and collapsing all around them, it was difficult to find Colonel Bernard's command post. They finally found it, cut off from everything and everybody. The telephone lines to the rear had been cut; the horses used by the mounted patrols had been killed; the bicycles were out of action; the runners ran out into the bombardment and never returned. Any house still standing was on fire. All the dugouts had been demolished except for those along the road which had been mined deep into the hillside under twenty metres of earth… In addition, almost half of the officers had been killed'.

Just before midnight on 23 February, General Kühne, commander of the 13th Reserve Division, VII Reserve Corps, was ordered to take Samogneux without further ado. Reserve Infantry Regiment 57 was given the task and, accompanied by a staff officer from the Fifth Army, infantry, pioneers and flame thrower squads moved forward carefully over the broken ground. French guns were firing from the Côte du Talou and men were falling as they advanced but by midnight they were a short distance from Samogneux and waiting for the signal. Fifteen minutes later heavy shells began to crash into the village and to the horror of the defenders they were French. A general lack of information, confusion as to the whereabouts of the front line, and contradictory reports from men

Oberstleutnant von Abercron, a pioneer of balloon flight and commander of Reserve Infantry Regiment 57 at the assault on Samogneux.

returning from the front, had led French commanders to believe that Samogneux had already fallen and the 155mm turret guns of Fort Vacherauville was ordered to crush it. After a moment of panic, signallers began firing rockets to tell the fort to stop but it took a long time for the message to get through and by the time the Germans advanced the village was a smoking ruin. An attempt to recapture it the next day came to nothing and Samogneux remained in German hands until 21 August 1917. (*See Tour No 3 for its recapture*)

Only 173 people lived in Samogneux before the war and at first the French authorities decided that it was not worth rebuilding. However, this was contested by two determined families and by a wealthy American woman, Mrs Horace Gray, who had served as a nurse in France during the war.

In 1926, Mrs Gray visited Verdun and was touched by a fictitious account of the lives of refugees from the Meuse as written by 'Père Barnabé' of Samogneux. She asked the author, Henri Frémont, for permission to have the work translated and sold in America to raise money to rebuild the village. A Franco-American committee was formed to receive donations and receipts and with the illustrious name of the President of France, Raymond Poincaré, attaching to it money flooded in. By August 1927 Mrs Grey had raised $25,000 towards the rebuilding of the village and in 1935 she was the guest of honour at a grand fête to inaugurate the Mairie [town hall], the school, the church and a new bridge over the Meuse. Mrs Grey also financed a statue of Père Barnabé and contributed to the war memorial, which was inaugurated on 1933. To visit both of these sites, walk uphill to the main road (D964) and stop. A cast of the statue of Père Barnabé is to your right front on the other side of the road, while a new sculpture is to the left below the war memorial.

Samogneux War Memorial **(8)**
It is better to visit the war memorial on foot as it is not easy to park on the roadside. Turn left along the D964 for a little over 200 metres and you will see it above road level on the right, accessed by a short grassy track. It stands above the site of the old village church. The striking sculpture by Gaston Broquet entitled 'Gas Alert!' represents a young French infantryman rushing to pull on his gas mask; his rifle is a fairly recent replacement as the original one was, alas, stolen some years ago. The war memorial lists the military and civilian victims of Samogneux in two world wars, while to the left a modern memorial commemorates Captain Batailler, 5th Battalion, 259th Infantry, and machine gunner Daniel Charles, 362nd Infantry.

On 22 February the 362nd was defending Haumont, which you will visit later, and the actions of the day are described there. Oddly, Daniel Charles' name does not appear in the regimental history's list of men killed or missing and the war diary comes to an end in November 1915, so does not cover the relevant period. In addition, the name does not appear in the list of men who died for France, although he may be listed under another name. Forty nine year old Captain Emile Batailler, a holder of the Légion d'Honneur and the Order of St. Anne of Russia, Third Class, died in the Haumont sector on 1 September 1914. That morning the 259th, a reserve regiment of two battalions, passed through Haumont on their way to attack German positions in nearby woodland and it was at that time that Captain Batailler was killed. His military death certificate mentions Samogneux as the place of death, so his body may have been brought back to a field hospital here. The 259th's war diary mentions no overall casualty figure for 1 September although the regimental history records that 'On this day on which 600 men remained on the field, the men of the 259th surpassed themselves in courage and heroism.'

Samogneux War Memorial. *Author's collection*

135

Père Barnabé. *Author's collection*

Père Barnabé **(9)**

The new sculpture of Père Barnabé, who is portrayed returning to his village and sadly surveying the ruins, stands by the roadside at the foot of the war memorial and in front of the remains of the pre-war church. It is a recent addition to the village and the existence of two has left many people scratching their heads.

Austro-Hungarian Memorial **(10)**

Return to your car and drive a short distance past the war memorial, then turn right into a parking and picnic area. The memorial to the men of the Austro-Hungarian army who fell fighting on the Western Front was inaugurated in 2014.

Although Austro-Hungarian heavy howitzer batteries had supported German troops in the early months of the war, it was not until June 1918 that the Austro-Hungarian High Command agreed to send infantry and heavy artillery to the Western Front. Russian prisoners of war were also sent there to work as labourers. In return, the German authorities agreed to deliver flour to Austria as soon as possible to make up the shortfall caused by a poor early harvest. The first troops to arrive were the Imperial and Royal [usually abbreviated to KuK] 1st and 35th Infantry Divisions, which together numbered almost 19,000 men and comprised, in addition to infantry, storm troops, sappers, field artillery, hussars and Jägers (light infantry). While the 35th Division was made up of men from Transylvania, with a majority of Romanians and Hungarians, the 1st Division spanned the entire Empire and included ethnic Germans, Hungarians, Romanians, Czechs, Croatians, Bohemians and Poles. Together with two balloon companies and 15,000 Russian prisoners of war, they arrived on the Western Front in the middle of July 1918.

Field Marshal von Hindenburg, however, wished for more troops and at the end of August the 106th Landsturm Infantry Division was also despatched to France. The last Austro-Hungarian formation to arrive was the 37th Honved Infantry Division, which numbered over 15,000 officers and men and was sent in reserve to a sector south of Strasburg. The 35th Division entered the line south east of Verdun and saw action during the American assault on the St Mihiel Salient on 12-13 September, where hard fighting cost them ninety nine officers and 3,268 men. While General Ludendorff was not satisfied with their performance, the Fifth Army despatch referred to them favourably. The 1st Division, which took over a seven kilometre section of the German line in the Consenvoye sector just to the north of here, saw serious action from the start of the Meuse-Argonne offensive. Their fighting qualities achieved favourable notice and the commander of Infantry Regiment 5, Oberstleutnant

The Austro-Hungarian memorial at Samogneux. *Author's collection*

Austro-Hungarian prisoners of war at Vacherauville. *US Signal Corps*

Rudolf Popelka, received the 'Pour le Mérite', Germany's highest award for bravery; he was the only Austro-Hungarian officer to do so for action in the field. Although the five days of fighting in the Consenvoye sector cost the 1st Division well over 5,000 officers and men, they remained at the front until 3 November 1918, when the armistice signed between Austria-Hungary and Italy brought their part in the war to an end. They had only served on the Western Front for a few weeks but in that time over 10,000 Austro-Hungarians had become casualties. Those who did not return home are to be found in many German cemeteries, including at Consenvoye, which you will visit later.

Grave of Captain Juanahandy **(11 and 12)**
To visit the next two sites, leave the parking area following the sign for the destroyed village of Haumont-près-Samogneux. On the right a short distance ahead and roughly in line with the red roofed barn on the hillside to the left there is a low wooden crossing over the ditch **(11)** and a worn sign pointing uphill between the trees. A pathway has been cut but it is still a steep scramble to the grave of forty one year old Captain Pierre

MORT POUR LA FRANCE

SOUVENEZ VOUS DEVANT DIEU
DE
PIERRE **JUANAHANDY**
CAPITAINE ADJUDANT-MAJOR AU 1ᵉʳ BATAILLON
DU 55ᵉ RÉGIMENT D'INFANTERIE
Décoré de la Légion d'Honneur,
de la Croix de Guerre avec 4 citations,
de la Médaille de Chine, de la Médaille du Maroc,
Chevalier du Mérite Agricole,
du Dragon de l'Anam, de l'Aouissa Hafidien
et du Nicham-Iftikhar,
Tombé glorieusement devant Samogneux,
à Verdun, le 21 Août 1917,
à l'âge de 41 ans.

Above and left: Captain Juanahandy's grave and memorial card. *Author's collection*

Juanahandy, 55th Infantry, a native of Mendives, south west France, who was killed on 21 August 1917 in the successful recapture of Samogneux. Before that offensive began, Captain Juanahandy had expressed the wish to be buried where he fell if he did not survive the day and he died in this area. His wife visited the grave every year until 1977 but after her death it became overgrown and it was some years before the trees were sufficiently cleared for visitors to pay their respects. The enamel medallion on the grave used to show Captain Juanahandy in his dress uniform but sadly time and the weather has effaced the image.

When it was proposed to put up a memorial to Austro-Hungarian troops, there was a feeling locally that the money would be better spent on maintaining this and other field memorials in the area, as well as French memorials and cemeteries, but the authorities went ahead anyway.

Destroyed village of Haumont-près-Samogneux (13)
Return to your car and continue along the road which winds uphill through the forest to the destroyed village (a little over two kilometres). There is parking space and information about the village by the chapel, so park there and face uphill. Haumont is an ancient site. A well watered and sunny spot – its pre-war name was Haumont-le-Soleil – there has been a settlement here since at least Gallo-Roman times and the remains of a Roman altar have been found nearby. The fact that people lived here for almost 2000 years is commemorated on the rear of the war

An observation post in the main street at Haumont. *Author's collection*

memorial, which refers to Haumont and a number of outlying farms and dependencies as having existed from the first century AD until 1914.

One hundred and thirty one people lived in Haumont when war was declared and their lives and occupations are described along the discovery path. Between October 1914 and February 1916 the German front line was several kilometres north of here and Haumont functioned as a command post and depot; the two bunkers you see on the main street were built at that time.

At the beginning of November 1915, the 362nd Infantry, a reserve regiment of two battalions (5th and 6th), took over the Haumont position, which was one of four centres of resistance in the first line of defence on the Right Bank. Each centre had its own garrison and command post and included trenches, dugouts and machine gun emplacements, backed in certain areas by concrete redoubts. The Haumont centre of resistance, which was based on the extensive Bois d'Haumont to the north of the village, covered the hilltop and blocked the road ahead. It comprised three defensive positions: the outpost line, the support line and redoubts.

The outpost line was a series of small positions linked by shallow trenches and intended to meet and break the enemy assault; it was connected by communication trenches to the support line. This was a series of earth and timber positions, including two substantial fieldworks known as *Grand'gardes*, which housed a platoon or more of men and functioned as the company command posts for each sector. Tree felling provided clear sight lines and fields of fire and the resulting gaps were covered by wire and secondary defences.

On 21 February 1916 the 5th Battalion had two companies in Bois d'Haumont and two in the village, while the 6th Battalion was in reserve. The German bombardment began at 7.16am that morning and within minutes the companies in Bois d'Haumont were reporting very heavy calibre shelling of the outpost and support lines. The regimental commander, Lieutenant Colonel Bonviolle, was based in Samogneux; but when the news came through he moved up to Haumont with his staff. The telephone links to the outpost line were soon cut and from 10am no runners could get through, so nothing came back from the front lines until almost 6pm, when a straggler arrived with a runner to say that they were being violently attacked but that the defenders were fighting back. Captain Richard was holding *Grand'garde II*:

'By systematic bombardment the enemy completely destroyed our front line trenches and the few shelters that resisted had their exits blocked up, imprisoning the men inside who owed their lives to the German medical dogs which found them there some

142

French defences at the top of the main street before the German assault of 21 February 1916.

twelve hours after the enemy had passed. *Ouvrage S³*, which looked like a formidable position, was violently shelled with very heavy calibre and that concrete shelter, which we regarded as the strongest in the whole line of defence of Bois d'Haumont, was reduced to rubble, burying some of the occupants, who, when they were dug out, had to withdraw to another concrete shelter … which was shelled so hard that it shook continuously.'

The German infantry assault began in the late afternoon of 21 February and by 7.30pm it was clear that reinforcements were needed. At 8pm patrols reported that the Germans – elements of Infantry Regiment 159 – had reached the southern edge of Bois d'Haumont and set up machine guns. A counter attack planned for 6am the following morning was postponed until reinforcements arrived but the Germans were shelling the village so hard that no one could get in or out. By 10am everything was in ruins; a concrete redoubt collapsed, killing the eighty men inside, ammunition dumps blew up and casualties rose.

At 5pm on 22 February, the Germans attacked Haumont from three sides, overwhelmed the remaining defenders and reached the main street. The few machine guns still firing were soon captured and anyone who could do so fled to newly dug trenches outside the village. Hoping to capture Colonel Bonviolle, the attackers directed flame throwers into

Germans in the main street at Haumont shortly after capture.

A postcard view of the ruins of Haumont in 1918. *Author's collection*

his underground command post, but he and handful of the staff managed to break out and report to Samogneux. When, later that day, he returned to Haumont to gather up the remains of his regiment, hardly anyone was left. Between 7am on 21 February and 6pm on 22 February, the 362nd lost thirty-two officers and 1,625 men; only sixty men escaped death or captivity. Between March and June 1916 the regiment was reconstituted and returned to the line but it was disbanded in January 1917 and the colours returned to the depot.

Haumont was not a French objective in August 1917 and it was recaptured by the 68th Battalion of Senegalese Tirailleurs (18th Division) on 8 October 1918 in the course of the Meuse-Argonne offensive. The level of destruction was so great that, like Cumières, it became part of the Red Zone and it is administered in the same way. The only post war constructions are the war memorial, which bears the names of the ten men of Haumont who died for France, including two from the same family, and the chapel. This stands on the site of the destroyed church of St Nicholas and was built in the early 1930s. Mass is said on the annual saint's day, when a fête is organized to remember the village and the families who lived there before 1916. One can only wonder what Melanie Pigeard, the elderly resident of Regnéville who refused to leave her home in the face of the German assault and who was born here, would have made of it all.

Consenvoye German Military Cemetery (14)
Now return to the D964, turn right and continue to the military cemetery which is on the right of the main road just before you reach the village of Consenvoye (just under four kilometres). This concentration cemetery

The German military cemetery at Consenvoye. *Author's collection*

was laid out by the French authorities in 1920 and it is one of the biggest German cemeteries in the Verdun area. Transfers from war time burials all over the Verdun sector began in 1922 and continued until 1943, when the German authorities brought the remains of 6,000 men here from cemeteries in the Argonne Forest. The 11,146 burials include 8,609 identified men in individual and group plots and a mass grave containing both unknowns and identified remains; the latter include a nurse, Johanna Gabriel, who died on 30 October 1916, possibly as a result of bombing or long range shelling. There were nurses in the field hospital at Sivry-sur-Meuse five kilometres north of here and the German cemetery was cleared and the remains transferred to Consenvoye in 1943. On 22 September 1984, President François Mitterand of France and Federal Chancellor Helmut Kohl met here in reconciliation and laid wreaths in memory of the dead of both World Wars. The meeting, which was the first time that a French President had visited a German military cemetery, is recorded by a plaque in front of the mass grave. The gesture was repeated in 2016, when President François Hollande and Chancellor Angela Merkel represented their countries during the centenary commemorations.

Return to Verdun

The quickest way back to Verdun is by the D964. However, for anyone needing refreshment the other possibility is to continue to the centre of Consenvoye and turn left downhill on the D19. There is a café/restaurant just before the canal. From there, continue straight ahead over the bridge to the other side of the valley and at the T-junction with the D123 turn left to Forges. Drive through the village and follow the signs to Chattancourt and Verdun.

GPS Waypoints Tour No 1

1. N49°13.361' E005°16.309'
2. N49°13.329' E005°16.337'
3. N49°13.883' E005°16.835'
4. N49°15.451' E005°17.151'
5. N49°15.190' E005°19.591'
6. N49°15.178' E005°19.492'
7. N49°15.263' E005°20.268'
8. N49°15.387' E005°20.260'
9. N49°15.382' E005°20.246'
10. N49°15.496' E005°20.114'

11. N49°15.577' E005°20.242'
12. N49°15.533' E005°20.282'
13. N49°16.337' E005°21.075'
14. N49°16.785' E005°17.788'

Other Waypoints connected with the tour:
Walter Höhndorf Memorial N49°27.939' E005°24.007'
This is south of Iré le Sec, on the D643 and very close to the junction with the D905. Parking is a bit difficult. Iré-le-Sec is six kilometres south of Montmédy, where the Vauban citadel is not to be missed.

Tour No 2

Glorieux Military Cemetery, Voie Sacrée Memorial, Vadelaincourt, Osches, Souilly, Clermont-en-Argonne

Distance: A circular driving tour of approximately seventy-eight kilometres beginning in Verdun at the French military cemetery at Glorieux and visiting sites connected with the medical and ambulance services, logistics and the air war.

This tour uses two maps: Map A covers sites between Verdun and Souilly; Map B covers sites between Souilly and Clermont-en-Argonne and indicates the return to Verdun.

Duration: A whole day's tour, allowing time for photos and a picnic.

Maps: IGN 3112 ET, IGN Blue Series 3113 Ouest and 3113 Est

Once you leave Glorieux refreshment and toilet stops will be few and far between. Fuel stations are also rare so make sure you have enough before you set off. There is a picnic table under the trees above the Voie Sacrée memorial car park and by the belvedere at Osches, a bakery in Souilly and another, with cafés, restaurants, fuel stations and a supermarket, in Clermont-en-Argonne at the end of the tour. There is also a roadside café at Dombasle-en-Argonne on the return journey.

Map A: Collège St. Jean (1)
This tour begins at Glorieux Military Cemetery on the Left Bank of the River Meuse. To reach the start of the tour from Verdun, take the D603 from the city centre and follow the signs for the A4 motorway. At the roundabout after the railway bridge take the third exit, then stay on the D603 and after 470 metres fork right on the Rue de Blamont at the sign for *Collège St. Jean* and Glorieux. At the next two roundabouts (immediately after one another) continue ahead for approximately 360 metres and **stop** at the *Collège St. Jean*, which is on the left.

This building belonged to the Diocese of Verdun until 1905, when it was taken over by the army. From 3 August 1914 until

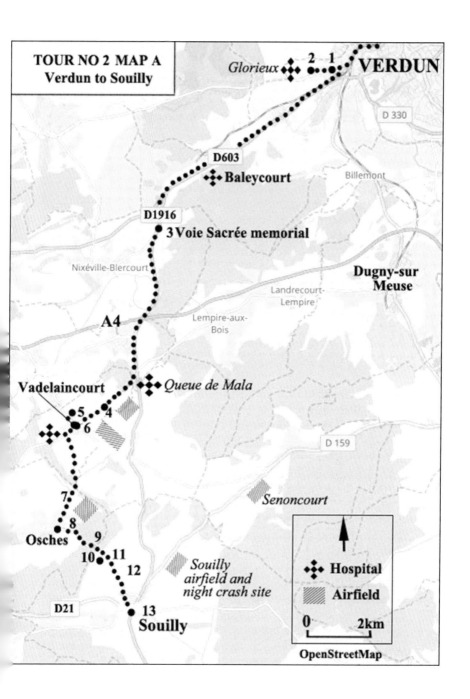

TOUR NO 2 MAP A
Verdun to Souilly

Glorieux 2 1 VERDUN

D 330

D603

Baleycourt

Billemont

D1916

3 Voie Sacrée memorial

Nixéville-Blercourt

Dugny-sur Meuse

Landrecourt-Lempire

A4

Lempire-aux-Bois

Vadelaincourt

Queue de Mala

5 4

6

D 159

7

Senoncourt

8

Osches 9

10 11

12

Souilly
airfield and
night crash site

D21 13

Souilly

Hospital

Airfield

0   2km

OpenStreetMap

A postcard view of Glorieux Cemetery, with the barracks in the background.
Author's collection

evacuation in February 1916, it operated as Temporary Hospital 7 and thereafter it formed a triage centre with Evacuation Hospital 13 described below.

Glorieux Cemetery **(2)**
From here continue ahead for a little over 500 metres, then fork right on the Allée des Hayevaux and **stop** at the cemetery. There are two entrance gates; parking is easier by the second gate but the cemetery register is in the first gate. This cemetery was created in 1916 but it has been much extended by the transfer of remains from elsewhere, the latest being in 1983. Old photographs show American burials in the lower left hand side but they have all been transferred. The 4,733 men buried here include two famous French rugby players, Jean Aimé (Léon) Larribau and Félix Hau in plots 2816 and 804, and two British soldiers in plots 3942 and 3943.

Sergeant Léon Larribau, 12th Infantry, born in 1899 in Anglet, Department of Pyrénées-Orientales, was a cobbler by trade. Only 1.60m in height but strongly built and renowned for his long passes, he played scrum half for Club Athlétique Périgeux until 1912 before joining Biarritz Olympique, where he captained the team until war broke out, being capped six times for France between 1912 and 1914 and scoring a try against Wales in March 1912. His last selection was for the match against England in the Five Nations Tournament of 1914.

Mobilized in the 12th Infantry, he saw action on various parts of the front before serving in the Cote 304 sector of the Left Bank in the summer of 1916. In the offensive of December of that year his regiment took over a disorganized part of the Côte du Poivre sector and set about creating order, but shelling, bombing and persistent rain undid their work as fast as it was done. On 30 December, Larribau's battalion was providing the working and carrying parties needed to organize and maintain the position against the elements and it was in the course of those duties that he was killed. He is listed in the war diary as having died on 31 December 1916 but according to his military service record he died here at the hospital on 2 January 1917.

He was awarded a Croix de Guerre with the following citation: 'At the front from the beginning of hostilities in the most difficult circumstances, always perfectly indifferent to danger when ensuring liaison between the regiment and the rear.' In November 1954, his former stadium in Biarritz was renamed the Stade Léon Larribau.

Above and left: **Rugby enthusiasts have not forgotten Captain Félix Hau.**

Captain Adjutant-Major Félix Hau, 12th Infantry, Légion d'Honneur and Croix de Guerre, captained Club Athlétique Bègles before the war and was cited twice for his conduct in the Cote 304 sector in May 1916. He died in August 1917 during the assault on Cote 344 'falling gloriously when, having broken the enemy's resistance, he was positioning his battalion on the conquered objective'. His military death certificate states that he died on 20 August but the plaque here gives the date as 23 August 1917.

Private J.Brown, 12th (Service) Battalion the Royal Scots,
9th (Scottish) Division
The division was withdrawn for rest in late October 1918 and was still in billets at the Armistice when it was selected to advance to the Rhine as part of the occupation force, crossing into Germany on 4 December. The place of Private Brown's death from sickness on 25 December 1918 is not mentioned in the Graves Registration Report but he may have been suffering from Spanish flu and remained behind at a hospital in France when the division moved on.

Private T. Downie, 1/6th Battalion Durham Light Infantry,
39th Division
On 16 August 1918 the 1/6th Battalion transferred to the 39th Division and took part in training newly arrived units of the American Expeditionary Force at Varangéville, Lorraine. With no details of the cause or place of death available, one can only assume that Private Downie also contracted Spanish flu and died at one of the French military hospitals in that town.

French medical services in the Verdun sector
For the first two years of the war the aim of the French Medical Service was to remove wounded men from the front as soon as possible. First aid was provided at divisional field hospitals, where most of the doctors were mobilized general practitioners untrained in war medicine and surgery. Their role was limited to disinfecting entry and exit wounds and applying a protective dressing, so that patients could be evacuated to the surgical teams at hospitals in the interior. As the dressings were not changed until hospital was reached, and during that time the wounded lay on stretchers or straw in trains that took anything from two to five days to reach their destinations, the result was fearful levels of mortality and urgent calls for surgical teams to work close to the front. Systems were changed and improvements made; but in the Verdun Fortified Region, which was quiet for much of 1915, a lack of time and resources meant that a plan to create major hospitals and treatment centres outside the town was not implemented.

A relaxed French medical detachment wearing a mixture of uniforms. *Tom Gudmestad*

On 1 February 1916, the medical services of the Verdun Fortified Region were placed under the authority of Dr Mignon, senior medical officer of the Third Army and director of the Army medical services training school. He toured the medical facilities of the Fortified Region and the Zone of Supply and found hospitals empty or serving as troop accommodation, operating theatres unused, contagious patients treated side by side with wounded, and barely enough resources to cover a single day's fighting. He reported that 'the atmosphere was one of absolute calm, indifference and lethargy, with no sign whatever that anyone was aware that circumstances might change'. But change they did. Nine days later, the governor of the Fortified Region, General Herr, ordered Dr Mignon to evacuate every patient in the Verdun hospitals within a week; and if violent snowstorms had not prevented the German assault on Verdun from starting on 12 February as planned, the evacuation would not have been concluded. As it was, the ten days of bad weather that delayed the start of the Battle of Verdun allowed Dr Mignon to begin the colossal task of reorganising the medical services at the front and in the Zone of Supply. The Verdun hospitals were emptied of all patients except a handful of non-transportable men and a group with typhoid and dysentery, who remained at the contagious diseases hospital on the hillside to the right of this cemetery.

Evacuation hospital 13

Glorieux barracks, some of which is still in use, was built on what was then an isolated site outside the city walls. It originally housed the 165th Infantry Regiment but from the outbreak of war until shortly after the start of the Battle of Verdun it accommodated a hospital for contagious diseases. Here, in a collection of wooden huts on the hillside, the patients were cared for by Dr Nicole Mangin, one of the few woman doctors in France and the only one to serve at the front and in the Zone of Supply. Mobilized by error on 2 August 1914, she could have remained at her post in Paris but preferred to report as ordered, to the consternation of the doctor in charge of the hospital to which she had been posted and who would have preferred to get rid of her. Being short of doctors, the medical authorities left the decision to her and she stayed, accepting the jacket and cap worn by women doctors in the British Army as there was no corresponding French uniform available.

Some weeks later she was sent to the Rheims area and then transferred to Verdun – at the time a quiet sector. Still meeting the same dismissive attitude, she served with several formations in the Verdun area before being posted to Temporary Hospital 7. At first the doctor in charge refused to let her enter the wards on the ground that her 'feminine condition' would be disturbing to the patients; but her capacity for work and her accommodating manner won respect and after several weeks she was transferred here.

Between November 1914 and February 1916, Dr Mangin and her team of one sergeant and a dozen nurses successfully treated over 750 men. When evacuation was ordered in February 1916, most of the patients were transferred to nearby Evacuation Hospital 6 at Baleycourt, although with only one ambulance available and the road jammed

Dr Nicole Mangin with her dog, Dun. Mobilized in error in 914, she served at the front until the end of 1916 before taking up an appointment as Director of the Edith Cavell Nursing Training School in Paris. In June 1919, she was found dead, aged forty one. The only French woman doctor to have served at the front during the First World War, she was met with suspicion everywhere but proved her worth wherever she served. She received no decoration for her service.

with trucks, ambulances, horse drawn vehicles and convoys of every description, it took many journeys to transfer them all. In any case, as fast as they were evacuated, other wounded arrived, filling the rooms and corridors and taking whatever space they could find, even ignoring warnings not to use the recently-evacuated beds of contagious patients. When a second evacuation order was issued on 25 February there were still nine men who could not be moved; and amid general chaos, surrounded by troops moving up and artillery taking position nearby, assisted by two volunteer nurses but without dressings and sometimes without electricity, Dr Mangin remained at her post doing what she could with whatever resources she could get her hands on, sure that in the end they would all be captured.

Twenty four hours later another evacuation order arrived and this one was absolutely final. Shelling had put the main railway line out of action, so five delirious patients and two nurses were embarked in an ambulance –and never seen again – while Dr Mangin and her driver set off with the remaining four for Clermont-en-Argonne some thirty kilometres away. The main road was so blocked that it took sometimes two hours to go a single kilometre, so they took a rough country road which was quieter because it was within range of German guns. It also brought them close to the railway line where they saw why it could not be used: a locomotive had plunged into a shell crater so deep that only the rear wheels were visible, putting it out of action on the first day of the German offensive. It was hours later, with shell splintered windows front and back (and in Dr Mangin's case, a cut face), that they arrived at Clermont to find a massive influx of wounded and no space for dying contagious patients.

They set off again and another hospital in a peaceful country chateau seven kilometres away took them in. Here, with the war temporarily a distant memory, Dr Mangin had her first hot drink for several days before getting back into the ambulance to report to Bar-le Duc – another forty kilometres along jammed roads. The following day she was posted to the Evacuation Hospital at Vadelaincourt, which will be visited later.

With the contagious patients gone, the buildings at Glorieux were taken over by two field hospitals and for the next fortnight doctors and medical staff worked round the clock in helmets and with gas masks within reach, treating in all 1,800 wounded and carrying out thirty to forty major operations every day. Shelled on 1 March, gassed a week later, damaged by a shell exploding half a metre from a room full of wounded, always crammed full, and with enough work for a month on any single day, this site soon became too dangerous for field hospitals and on 12 March 1916 they were transferred to Evacuation Hospital 6 at

The Germans also had isolation hospitals. This is the contagious diseases hospital at Inor, in the north of the Department of the Meuse. *Tom Gudmestad*

Baleycourt on the main road out of Verdun. Thereafter the hospital here functioned with Temporary Hospital 7 as a triage centre and cantonment, and American and British ambulance units were based here. Their task was to pick up the wounded from the forward aid posts, bring them to Glorieux for triage and then transport them to various hospitals in the Zone of Supply. Ernest R. Schoen, a driver with Section Eighteen of the American Field Service, described it in May 1917:

'At Glorieux we relieved Section Eight…Our cantonment was about one mile from the citadel of Verdun on the southwest side, and was located on the slope of a hill from the crest of which a large portion of the defences to the north of Verdun could be seen. It was made up of several stone hospital buildings and numerous long frame barracks. The *bâtiment* [building] which Section Eight evacuated the morning of our arrival … was a commodious one and we were able to fix ourselves up very comfortably, indeed, these quarters being considered among the most comfortable at the front. In an adjoining *bâtiment* was an English section … attached to the French Army [also Section Eighteen]. They did evacuation work alternately with us and the two groups were thrown close together and became very firm friends.'

After a period of rest, Section Eighteen returned to Glorieux in time for the August offensive but:

'...this time we did not have the commodious quarters that we formerly occupied. Indeed, we were restricted to three rooms and the remainder of the building was given over to a French divisional stretcher bearer transport squad and our English friends of SSA Eighteen, who arrived soon after we did, and who had to be partly quartered in tents. What had been barracks before had now to be converted into hospital wards. But otherwise things had not changed much since our departure. The cemeteries had grown a bit, some temporary structures had been erected and there was an observation balloon station nearby that interested us mightily.'

The first aid post served by the British and American ambulances during the August 1917 offensive was at Bras-sur-Meuse, almost nine kilometres from here along a road fraught with danger (the D698 from Verdun to Bras-sur-Meuse driven in Tour No 1). On the night of 20 August 1917:

'The approach to Bras...was a scene of bewildering confusion. The road was choked with horses and vehicles of every description seemingly mixed in inextricable chaos...batteries roared and flashed

BRITISH AMBULANCE SHATTERED BY SHELL-FIRE AT THE FRENCH (VERDUN) FRONT.

A badly damaged ambulance belonging to SSA (Section Sanitaire Anglaise) 2. This section had four drivers killed at Verdun and was awarded eight individual Croix de Guerre and a Médaille Militaire for its service. *Author's collection*

in every direction, while shells whistled overhead continuously…A short while after midnight, gas shells began to come over and then the confusion became worse and the difficulties for us increased – for as the breath soon condenses on the lenses of the gas mask, to see through it at night is well-nigh an impossibility. Horses affected by the gas pranced all over the road…In the meantime, the traffic assumed more and more a condition of turmoil, and finally everything had to be halted until the worst had passed, while those of us at the *poste* were compelled to enter the [shelter] … But as soon as there was a lull in the gas attack, the ambulances were loaded and started on their way. Most of them, however, did little more than start, for soon the gas was as thick as ever, and again the traffic became badly congested and everything had to halt. With our gas masks on, we waited, wedged in the mass, while on one side fell the gas shells, on the other the high explosives, and overhead occasionally burst shrapnel. Sometimes a shell would find its billet, and the screams of horses and shouts of men would add to the hideousness of the scene. After what seemed an interminable time, the gas let up, the road was partially cleared, and, though still hampered with gas masks, we crawled and felt our way toward Verdun, where we deposited our burdens at the triage with a feeling of relief no words can describe.'

The next day:

'…the little Fords went up and down the Bras road like so many mechanical toys…the wounded were being brought into the *triage* so rapidly that its facilities were overwhelmed, and the drivers had to act as their own *brancardiers* [stretcher bearers], deposit the wounded in the open courtyard until room could be made inside the building. Finally we even had all to turn in and evacuate them to the railroad station at Souilly, where they were transported to hospitals in cars of other sections.'

Before leaving the cemetery, spare a thought for twenty eight year old Private Napoléon Lempereur, 161st Infantry, killed in action on the Left Bank in April 1916, who lies in plot 2655. One wonders whether he might have preferred a less remarkable name.

Voie Sacrée Memorial **(3)**
To continue the tour, return to the Rue de Blamont and turn left. Pass the Collège St. Jean and continue to the roundabout, then take the first exit. At

the next roundabout one hundred metres further on, take the first exit on the D603 (signposted A4 Paris) and continue ahead, passing the extensive industrial area of Baleycourt. This covers the site of the evacuation hospital mentioned above and of the two 400mm railway howitzers which bombarded Forts Douaumont and Vaux in the run up to the French offensive of 24 October 1916. Continue ahead for six kilometres. At the roundabout after the industrial area take the second exit on the D1916 and after 400 metres turn left into a parking area and **stop**. Just before the turn you will see a blue sign pointing left and reading *'Codecom Meuse Voie Sacrée'* beside one of the kilometre stones that mark the route of the Voie Sacrée between Verdun and Bar-le-Duc. In the parking area there is information in three languages about the Voie Sacrée and its importance during the Battle of Verdun and you can walk or drive up to the memorial, where there is an orientation table. Note the memorial to Captain Doumenc, the remarkable French transport officer who is commemorated here as the organizer of the Voie Sacrée. If you wish to photograph the kilometre stone, **take great care when crossing the road.**

In August 1914, Verdun was a *Place forte* [fortress] and the northernmost bulwark in the heavily fortified eastern frontier of France. Until then it had been served by two standard gauge railway lines but during the Battle of the Marne in September 1914 the German attempt to pinch out the fortress cut one of the lines and left the other – the western line from Sainte Ménéhould to Verdun – within range of German artillery. Thereafter, Verdun depended on two weak supply routes: a narrow gauge railway line named the *Petit Meusien* and the road you have just driven, which links Verdun with Bar-le-Duc. Known today as the Voie Sacrée, or Sacred Way, this road became the most famous of the supply routes used during the Battle of Verdun. Originally less than six metres wide, it was widened in 1915 to allow two vehicles to pass; but as long as the Verdun sector remained quiet further measures to develop it were deemed unnecessary, and at the beginning of 1916 it remained winding and poorly surfaced. Once it became clear that an assault on Verdun was imminent, the question of supply became more pressing, and the Army's *Service Automobile* took steps to improve the situation.

The *Service Automobile* had come a long way since the beginning of the war when it depended on requisitioning privately owned cars and trucks to fulfil military needs. At the time the system had worked well and in the first month of the war it provided the army with 9,000–10,000 motor vehicles, but the Battle of the Marne showed that many more would be needed. Further experience in 1915 also showed the need for a proper regulatory structure to cover not only the movement of convoys but also of problems outside their control, such as slow horse drawn

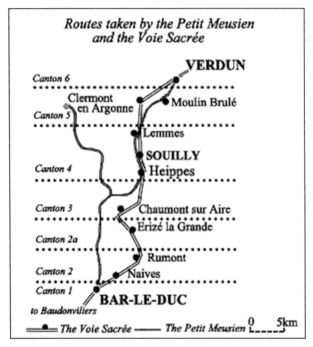

Routes taken by the Petit Meusien and the Voie Sacrée

Left: Routes taken by the Petit Meusien and the Voie Sacrée.

Below: Trucks on the Voie Sacrée. Note the driver in the middle of the road wearing a fur coat. This was needed to keep warm in an unheated truck. *BDIC_VAL_179_014 https://argonnaute.parisnanterre.fr*

vehicles on the road, jams at crossroads, obstructions, and other convoys unilaterally deciding to take priority. The *Service Automobile* was already considering the creation of such a regulatory body when on 18 February 1916 it was ordered to prepare without delay for a major German assault on the Meuse front.

Captain Doumenc, who at that time was assistant to the director of the *Service Automobile* at General Headquarters, was immediately sent to Bar-le-Duc, where over the next two days he and other transport officers considered the resources of the whole region. It was immediately clear that the transportation problem was overwhelming. Captain Doumenc would have to ensure the daily supply of 2,000 tonnes of ammunition to the Verdun region in addition to the 100 tonnes of subsistence and other supplies needed by each of the fifteen to twenty divisions at the front. Then there were reinforcements and reliefs to be moved in and out, amounting to 15,000 to 20,000 men each day, the evacuation of the sick and wounded and the movement of vast quantities of salvaged material to the rear.

The only way to solve the problem was to use the remaining standard gauge railway line where possible, the *Petit Meusien* to transport subsistence supplies and some of the ammunition, and motor vehicles to carry troops, engineer material, the bulk of the ammunition and such subsistence supplies as the *Petit Meusien* could not carry. As the maximum capacity of the *Petit Meusien* was some 800 tonnes per day, trucks would have to carry the rest; but even adding the resources of the Third Army in the Argonne sector, the Fortified Region could only muster 720 trucks – enough to carry 1,250 tonnes daily but far from the 6,000 tonnes daily that would be needed.

On 20 February 1916, it was agreed that the road should be exclusively reserved for military purposes if the standard gauge line became unusable and that evening a regulatory commission was established. Captain Doumenc divided the seventy five kilometres between the start of the Voie Sacrée and the advanced depots in the forts south of Verdun into six administrative units, with each one under the control of an officer with responsibility for signage, keeping the

Captain Aimé Doumenc, who devised the plan for supplying the Verdun front by road and rail.

traffic moving and the road repaired at all times. Security was ensured by military police, cavalry units and fighter planes.

Within hours of the start of the German artillery bombardment on 21 February 1916 the standard gauge line was out of commission and at midday on 22 February control of the road was handed over to the *Direction des Services Automobiles*. Four hours later it had been cleared of all civilian traffic; troops and supplies began to flow along it and artillery convoys and horse drawn vehicles had to use other routes. At first the weather was icy but after several days a thaw set in and, to prevent the road from breaking up, quarries were opened nearby and territorial battalions brought in to break the stone and shovel it under the wheels as the trucks passed. It was an unending task. Army transport reserves provided the extra vehicles and men required and throughout the Battle of Verdun almost 9,000 vehicles were used to carry men and supplies to and from the front. Vehicles – buses, two ton trucks carrying troops and three ton trucks carrying ammunition and engineering supplies – travelled in organized convoys; they were forbidden to stop and any that broke down were ditched. Only ambulances and staff cars on official business were allowed to overtake. Troops bound for Verdun disembarked in this area and made the rest of the journey on foot, while supplies were offloaded at dedicated stores dumps along the road. An example of the type of truck that made the journey is to be seen in Fleury Memorial Museum.

Frank Hoyt Gailor spent two months driving an ambulance at the start of the Battle of Verdun and got to know the road very well.

'The picture of the attack that will stay with me always is that of the Grande Route north from Bar-le-Duc, covered with the snow and ice of the last days of February. The road was always filled with two columns of trucks, one going north and the other coming south. The trucks, loaded with troops, shells, and bread, rolled and bobbled back and forth…It was almost impossible to steer them on the icy roads. Many of them fell by the wayside, overturned, burned up, or were left apparently unnoticed in the ceaseless tide of traffic that never seemed to hurry or to stop… Soon the roads began to wear out. Trucks brought stones …and sprinkled them in the ruts and holes; soldiers, dodging in and out of the moving cars, broke and packed the stones or sprinkled sand on the ice-covered hillsides. But the traffic was never stopped for any of these things…At night, on the main road, I have watched for hours the dimmed lights of the *camions*, winding away north and south like the coils of some giant and luminous snake which never stopped and never ended…Behind each light was a unit, the driver, whose momentary negligence might throw the whole line into confusion…He must be continually awake to avoid any one of a thousand possible mis-chances. The holes and ice on the road, his skidding car, the cars passing in the same and opposite directions, the cars in front and behind, the cars broken down on the other sides of the road – all these and many other things he had to consider before using brake or throttle in making his way along. Often snow and sleet storms were added to make driving more difficult. Objects six feet away were completely invisible, and it was only by watching the trees along the side of the road that one could attempt to steer.'

The Voie Sacrée was busy throughout the Battle of Verdun and until a new standard gauge railway line was built it formed the main access and supply route to the front. Every day thousands of vehicles ground their way forward whatever the weather. Traffic jams were frequent and drivers worked for days without a break, often sleeping in the back of the truck between shifts. The trucks passed given points at the rate of one every fourteen seconds in 'normal' times, with one every five seconds during particularly desperate times. Between March and June 1916, when a new standard gauge line began to take the pressure off the Voie Sacrée, monthly traffic on the road exceeded half a million tonnes of supplies and 400,000 troops. This was in addition to the 200,000 wounded evacuated by ambulance.

The new line, numbered 6*bis*, linked the rail hub of Nettancourt, northwest of Bar-le-Duc, with Dugny-sur-Meuse, six kilometres south of Verdun. Part of it was double tracked and two branch lines linked it to the Sainte Ménéhould–Verdun line on either side of the section under German guns. Work on the new line began at each end almost immediately and when fully operational in June – just in time to meet the demands of the last major German offensive – it allowed for the daily movement of sixty trains with a capacity ten times greater than the *Petit Meusien* and three times greater than the Voie Sacrée.

By December 1916 almost two and a half million men had passed along this road and 700,000 tonnes of broken stone had been thrown on the road bed. While German aerial attacks had, to a degree, succeeded in interfering with the railway, they were practically powerless against the motor transport system. Direct hits on vehicles on the Voie Sacrée were extremely rare; and while an occasional bomb or shell stuck the road, the crater formed was repaired in a very short time. Throughout the First World War no other single route on the Western Front carried as

163

Labour gangs excavating a cutting for Line 6*bis*.

The Voie Sacrée Memorial. *Author's collection*

much traffic for as long a period as did the Voie Sacrée; and the lessons learnt here were later applied to the Somme and elsewhere. It was the overwhelming importance of this road and its place in the experience of so many Frenchmen that led the writer Maurice Barrès to name it the Voie Sacrée, after the sacred processional road of ancient Rome. The name stuck and after the war each kilometre of the road was marked by a red and white stone, surmounted by a bronze helmet. The original helmets have all been stolen and the current marker stones, still one kilometre apart, have resin helmets.

The memorial panels commemorate the massive effort to supply Verdun by road, rail and horse drawn vehicle. The winged wheel on the central pillar is the emblem of the logistics branch of the French army, while the little locomotive is of the type that ran on the *Petit Meusien* railway. This seventy eight kilometre line had been completed before 1914 and when the battle began it was being extended and improved. As the company that ran it did not have sufficient rolling stock to meet the needs of a major battle, an appeal was launched for narrow gauge stock from other parts of France, which swiftly brought more locomotives and wagons. Its main task was to carry rations and evacuate wounded and at the beginning of March, with 800 wagons already available, twenty two trains were running every day with supplies for over 430,000 officers and men and 136,000 horses and mules. During that month the *Petit Meusien* carried 54,000 tonnes of supplies and over 14,000 men, while in June this had risen to 70,000 tonnes and almost 75,000 men. Although much less than the tonnages carried by road, it was nevertheless a remarkable effort.

Aviation, logistics and medical services
The area you will visit next is situated behind the middle of the Verdun front and with easy communications to both Right and Left Banks, which made it an obvious logistical centre. The sites visited represent only a small part of the enormous effort involved in organizing, supplying and supporting the battles of 1916 and 1917 and dealing with their human consequences.

Queue de Mala (4)
Return to the D1916, turn left and continue ahead for four and a half kilometres; pass under the A4 motorway and turn right on the D20 in the direction of Vadelaincourt, then drive through the wood. On reaching open ground, continue for roughly 600 metres until you see a level dirt track on both sides of the road with signs reading *Sauf ayants droits*. The track is actually the embankment for the Petit Meusien railway which

N

**Department of the Meuse
Principal airfields 1914–1918**

German airfields in italics

Zone of combat

● Mouzon

● Montmédy

● Stenay

Marville ●

Jametz

● Aincreville

● Longuyon

● Cunel

● Sivry-surMeuse

Verdun

Clermont-en Argonne ●   Brocourt ●

Julvécourt

Vadelaincourt

Froidos ●   Lemmes   ● Ancemont

Osches ●   ● Senoncourt

Antrécourt ●   ● Souilly

Foucaucourt   Beauzée/Aire

Senard   ● Issoncourt

Pretz   ● Courcelles/Aire

Sommeilles
Nettancourt   ● Rembercourt/Erize

● Noyers

● Isle/Barrois   ● Belrain

Bellefontaine

Rancourt ●   Brabant le Roi   ● Rumont

● Remenaucourt   ● Vavincourt   ● Commercy

● Bar-le-Duc
Béhonne

● Combles   Ourches ●

● Maulan   Vaucouleurs

● Delouze Rosières

● Epiez
● Amanty

166

served airfields and hospitals in this area. Pull off the road, **stop** and face the fields on the other side.

On 28 February 1916 Evacuation Hospital 6 at Baleycourt was closed and the wounded were transferred elsewhere. The doctors were first placed in reserve and then transferred to an existing facility for lightly wounded men known as *la Queue de Mala*, which was situated on the windy hilltop to your left front. It was not long before more space was needed and soon there were twenty eight large tents in which men were triaged and received urgent care before being evacuated either by road or by the *Petit Meusien*. Serious surgical cases and very sick men were evacuated to Hospital 12 at Vadelaincourt, where there were surgical teams. In September 1916 this hospital was transferred to Vadelaincourt and much extended.

Vadelaincourt and Lemmes airfields
When the war began the only equipped airfields in the Department of the Meuse were at Bar-le-Duc, Commercy and Verdun; the latter also had a balloon field outside the city. By early 1916 the air resources had increased to one fighter escadrille and three escadrilles carrying out aerial photography, reconnaissance and artillery direction; but when aerial photographs taken on 17 and 20 February 1916 showed an increase in enemy batteries, it was clear that urgent reinforcements were needed. Two more escadrilles arrived and the existing two balloon companies were also reinforced, but the German opening bombardment on 21 February created a barrier which French reconnaissance and fighter planes could not penetrate and within hours of the start of the battle German mastery of the air was complete.

On 28 February, with the aeronautical branch completely overwhelmed and artillery observation reduced to terrestrial views, General Pétain, commander of the Second Army, who had taken over at Verdun two days earlier, invited Commandant Charles de Tricornot de Rose, the pioneer of organized aerial combat, to his headquarters at Souilly and gave him the freedom to organise fighter escadrilles as he thought best.

Dozens of fighters flew in from other parts of the front with two missions: to prevent German incursions and to attack the enemy lines. De Rose's method was based on two principles: using planes in mass formation and keeping them in the sky at all times. Fighters flew in groups of three, six and finally nine planes, while the patrols, which operated one above the other at three levels, were rotated every three hours so that the sky was never empty. The situation was so rapidly re-established that de Roses's combat group was dissolved in March 1916 and the fighter escadrilles dispersed into other sectors, but the Germans reasserted

ICI A REPOSÉ
DU 28 DÉCEMBRE 1916
AU 11 JUILLET 1921

PIERRE VIOLET
NÉ À THUIR LE 3 OCTOBRE 1894
ADJUDANT PILOTE AVIATEUR
CHEVALIER DE LA LÉGION D'HONNEUR
MÉDAILLE MILITAIRE FRANÇAISE
CROIX DE GUERRE
5 PALMES 1 ÉTOILE D'OR
MÉDAILLE MILITAIRE ANGLAISE
MORT POUR LA FRANCE
EN COMBAT AÉRIEN
À ORNES FRONT DE VERDUN
LE 27 DÉCEMBRE 1916

Adjutant Pilot Pierre Violet was killed in aerial combat at Ornes on 27 December 1916 and buried by the Germans at Nouillonpont the following day. His decorations include the Légion d'Honneur, the Médaille Militaire, the Croix de Guerre with five Palms and Gold Star and the British Military Medal. His remains were returned to his family in 1921 but the memorial remains in the village cemetery at Nouillonpont. *Author's collection*

themselves and it had to be reconstituted. Captain Le Révérend, another believer in mass offensive action, took over, and by the end of May French fighters again ruled the skies.

Among the famous aces flying at Verdun was Jean Navarre, whose victory over a German Aviatik C, shot down over Avocourt on the Left Bank in May 1916, made him the first Allied ace to have ten confirmed victories. The same month saw the arrival on the Verdun front of the 'Lafayette Escadrille', formerly Escadrille N124, composed of American volunteer pilots who quickly became famous. Charles Nungesser, a French ace who ended 1916 with twenty one confirmed victories, served with the Lafayette Escadrille during 1916 and it was probably during the Battle of Verdun that his personal insignia was first painted on the side of his Nieuport 17: a skull and crossbones surmounted by a coffin and two candles against a black background.

While Commandant de Rose organized the fighter escadrilles, it was Lieutenant Colonel Barès, commander of Military Aeronautics, who was responsible for the reconnaissance, photographic and surveillance escadrilles, bombers and balloon companies. He organized a centralized service to collect and disseminate all the information brought in by planes and balloons and brought laboratory trucks into the airfields so that the glass plates brought back by the observers could be developed without delay. This, together with information from planes flying low enough to identify the movement of friendly or enemy units, made continuous surveillance of the lines possible. Bombing such objectives as railway hubs, troop concentrations, camps, command centres and ammunition depots at first took place in daylight but casualties were so high that from April 1916 they were carried out at night.

Almost one hundred airfields were established in the course of the war, with many of them in this area. Between January 1916 and the Armistice, two of them were here: **Lemmes field** to your left front and **Vadelaincourt field** in front of you. Their construction began in January 1916 and within days of the start of the German offensive the escadrilles formerly based at the Verdun field (today the site of Desandrouins hospital) were evacuated here. From then on, Vadelaincourt field was the home of several famous escadrilles, including N3 – the celebrated fighter group that included such aces as Antonin Brocard, Jules Vedrines, Georges Guynemer and Albert Deullin and later became known as *les Cygognes* – and bomber squadron MF25. This squadron had already spent months bombing ammunition depots, billets, camps and troop assembly points but the arrival of several other bomber formations during March 1916 enabled it to increase the number of targets.

A crashed Nieuport at Lemmes field. *BDIC_VAL_202_071 /Lapeyre https://argonnaute.parisnanterre.fr,*

Trümmer eines französischen Flugzeuges Differdingen am 10. Fe

Not all bombing raids were successful. This French plane crashed on 3 February 1917 at Differdingen (Differdange), Luxembourg, in the heart of the steel making area. *Author's collection*

Daylight bombing gave way to night time raids, which continued with previous targets and added more distant objectives, such as major rail hubs as far away as Montmédy and Charleville-Mezières, factories, blast furnaces, forges, steel mills and power stations on the Franco-Luxembourg border, metal working factories at Thionville in annexed Lorraine and even German general headquarters in the St Mihiel Salient. A raid on the German city of Trier, a distance of roughly 120 kilometres, started multiple fires and caused thousands of marks worth of damage to private property, including a bank and a power station; blast furnaces and sheet metal works were also destroyed in the German city of Dillingen, where a thousand men became casualties. In 1917, bombing raids in massive air strength concentrated on vital German airfields and railway hubs to the north and east of Verdun and further afield. These expeditions were not without casualties and invited retribution.

Vadelaincourt village was a tiny place and, faced with a lack of facilities for refreshment and entertainment, the crews made themselves at home on the airfield, where they were quartered in double-walled fibre-cement barracks. The aircraft were in Bessoneau hangars. There were gardens, a vegetable patch, a henhouse, a duck pond and lots of rabbits, in addition – of course – to a well stocked bar, pianos, a stage and various animal mascots.

Visitors were frequent and included the doctors from the nearby hospitals, who equally frequently had to repair the aviators. At night, the airfield was illuminated for take off and landing, while a powerful

The hangars at Lemmes field, with a Farman in the foreground. *BDIC_VAL_202_089 https://argonnaute.parisnanterre.fr*

searchlight guided planes home and banks of red lights outlined the limits of the field and any damaged areas; but once German bomber crews found it, all lights were extinguished. Although attacked by three German planes in April 1917, the first major bombing raid came during the night of 20-21 August 1917, when the airfield, hospitals and surrounding area were bombed for hours, resulting in extensive damage and many casualties. German bomber crews returned on several more nights in September and thereafter MF25 added the German bomber airfields to their long list of targets.

The military cemetery **(5)**
Now continue to the crossroads ahead, then turn right uphill on the D204 towards Souhesme-la-Grande and after roughly 200 metres **stop** at the military cemetery. The memorial on the left just before the entrance

Lieutenant Pilot Yves Garnier du Plessis (or Plessix), Légion d'Honneur, Croix de Guerre with 4 Palms and four citations. Detached from the 66th Infantry to the 2nd Groupe d'aviation, he was killed over the Ravin du Helly, Douaumont sector, on 22 August 1917, aged twenty-five. He is buried in plot 652 in Vadelaincourt Military Cemetery.

commemorates nineteen year old Jules de Langlade, a volunteer with the 22nd *Section d'Infirmiers Militaires*, who was wounded in the hospital bombing of 4 September 1917 and died the following day. This cemetery was opened in February 1916, five days into the Battle of Verdun, and at the height of the conflict the hospital chaplain reported burying fifty men every day. Today it holds the remains of 1,726 French soldiers and aviators and two Russians, the Muslim soldiers originally buried here having been transferred to an ossuary in 1966.

Being so close to a number of airfields, many aviators were buried here but over the years most have been transferred elsewhere. However, some remain: twenty two year old Sergeant Marcel Gilbert, *1ᵉ Groupe d'aviation*, who was injured when his Farman plane crashed into a hangar and died at the hospital on 16 July 1916, still lies in plot 1627. Clément Voltz, a Sergeant Observer, also with the same group, who was wounded in action when his observation balloon was attacked by Fokkers firing incendiary bullets and died several days later, lies in plot 1611. Captain Augustin Hubert and Brigadier Marie Chabert, observer and pilot with the *2ᵉ Groupe d'aviation*, were wounded in aerial combat on 20 August 1917 and died at Hospital 12 the same day and were buried alongside one another. Captain Hubert remains in plot 650 but Brigadier Chabert's remains have been reclaimed. Other aviators are buried in plots 1102, 549, 530 and 652.

The memorial at the top of the cemetery dedicated to the heroes of Verdun was sculpted by Corporal Julien Domont, 216th Infantry, and raised by subscriptions from officers of the medical service. The German victims of the hospital bombings were buried in a separate cemetery by the Ippécourt road and together with other German burials in this area transferred to the German cemetery at Consenvoye in 1922.

Evacuation Hospitals 6 and 12 **(6)**

To visit the site of the hospitals, return to the crossroads and turn right along the D20 in the direction of Ippécourt. Follow the road around the curve and after 270 metres **stop** on the right at the entrance to the *Chemin de l'hôpital*. As you face the information board, which has a contemporary aerial view of the formations and another superimposed on a modern view, Hospital 12 was across the road on the left, while Hospital 6, a surgical field hospital transferred here from Les Islettes in the Argonne and later extended by using the dismantled huts from *la Queue de Mala*, was on the right. The information board stands at the entrance to Hospital 6 and the *Chemin de l'hôpital* was specially laid to allow ambulance access. According to May Guinness, who was nursing at Hospital 6 with the Red Cross in 1917, it was a model formation with

The memorial to the heroes of the Army of Verdun in Vadelaincourt Cemetery. *Author's collection*

800 beds in wooden huts linked by a covered gallery offering direct access from the railway line to the medical units. There were lodgings for the medical staff and officers, a pharmacy, kitchens, offices, store rooms, sanitary facilities and a laundry. The road between the hospitals, no wider then than it is now, became so busy that a wooden footbridge had to be built to allow staff to pass from one side to the other – something difficult to imagine today.

Hospital 12 had been transferred here from Verdun in 1915 when German long range naval guns began to bombard the city. The site was chosen because it was out of artillery range, served by the *Petit Meusien* and at the junction of four metalled roads. At first unoccupied premises, such as houses, barns, stables and lofts, were taken over for the patients, while the medical service staff moved into an abandoned chateau; but later huts were built and at the end of 1915 the patients were moved in. When the Battle of Verdun began in February 1916, Hospital 12 was just a small facility with a dozen huts and sixteen hundred beds but within days it was full to the doors and the wounded crowded everywhere.

By the following May the number of huts had grown to thirty, with a pharmacy, surgical teams operating night and day, a sterilization room, an electricity generator and a mobile X-ray unit. Dr. Mangin joined the teams here on 7 March 1916, working 'without stopping, day and night, for weeks, until one falls exhausted on a stretcher to sleep for a few minutes'. During her service here she finally managed to achieve recognition of her status as a military doctor with the appropriate level of pay.

During the first four months of the battle, Hospital 12 treated and evacuated almost 11,000 seriously wounded men; but the completion of the new railway line 6*bis* increased the evacuation rate and in the French offensive of December 1916 almost 8,000 were evacuated in five days, a massive operation requiring four to five sanitary trains per day over several days. The capacity of the new line put Vadelaincourt at the head of the evacuation chain.

20 August 1917

Bombs had been dropped in this general area several times during the summer of 1917 but they were occasional and nothing to compare with what happened late in the evening of 20 August, when the hospitals were overflowing with French and German casualties from the Mort-Homme and Cote 304 sectors. Two hundred and fifty wounded had been received that day and the operating theatres were fully occupied. Robert Randolph Ball, an American ambulance driver with Section Sixty Eight, who had been sent there to help evacuate the many wounded, was sitting outside

Ward huts after the bombing of 20-21 August 1917.

with other drivers enjoying the evening when a German plane flew over and bombed a nearby airfield. At 10.30pm:

> '...we heard the same roar again, and in an instant three crashes hurled showers of earth and missiles upon our hospital, caused every light in the place to go out, and everybody, including ourselves, fell flat on the floor...Things were becoming really serious, so the *Chef* ordered us to look for an *abri*. But alas! Before we could do this six more bombs fell all around us...By this time there were several planes above us, and one of their bombs had hit its mark, for the section of the hospital across the road was now a mass of roaring flames, and the whole place was as bright as day. The screams of the wounded were drowned by the crashes of the bombs and, to add to the horror, the gas signal was flashed...we all thought our time had come, for the bombs were now raining in all directions, and the whole village was aglow from the burning hospital...We had to crank our cars and stand by them so as to be ready to rush the wounded away as soon as they could be brought from the burning buildings. But presently another bomb burst still closer to us, when we were all ordered to fly to an *abri* at once... After this bomb had fallen, there seemed to be a little lull. So ...we all hurried back to our cars. The hospital was still burning furiously but the fire had not reached across the road where we were. The lull was only for a moment; another lot of planes now flashed over our heads

strewing incendiary and gas bombs in all direction. The work was now too serious for us to leave our cars, for the wounded were being rapidly loaded into them…It seemed to us as if the *brancardiers* took months to load our car, while every moment the flying machines increased in number…I never felt so happy in all my life as I did when the signal was given for us to pull out, when we passed right beside the burning buildings and could see many of the poor, helpless wounded trying to drag themselves out…As this hospital was filled with seriously wounded patients, none of them had the slightest chance of escaping…Strange to say, the majority of cases were Germans, and most of those lost were Boche wounded…Needless to say, the part of the hospital which was hit was totally destroyed, but the part on the other side of the road was not harmed.'

Hospital 12 was the target and here bombs falling on the huts caused violent fires that spread rapidly. Doctors and nurses, officers, drivers, mechanics and visitors all rushed to help. The bombing went on for

Huts damaged in the second bombing of 4-5 September 1917.

hours and the noise was tremendous, with shouting and screaming, planes circling low and machine gunning the buildings, anti-aircraft guns firing, buildings collapsing, and a nearby ammunition dump blowing up. In the morning, four of the wards had been burnt to the foundations, leaving only the twisted bed frames amid piles of ash and debris.

Hospital 6 had suffered little material damage but there were still almost fifty casualties among the patients, stretcher bearers, staff and German prisoners of war undergoing treatment. Bombs also caused devastation among the vehicles in a nearby artillery park and a quarry, and so many bombs fell on Souilly that the Second Army staff had to move into an underground command post. The hospital victims were buried in a common grave on 23 August in the presence of an enormous crowd. But that was not the end. German planes returned here and to other nearby sites almost every night for the next fortnight, and with bombs dropping all around the hospital, shelter trenches were dug and some of the nursing orderlies took to sleeping in the woods at night. The medical director, Dr. Morin, who wished to evacuate the hospital, was told to keep it going, but on 4 September there was another terrible bombardment during which a bomb fell into a triage ward and sent wounded and debris flying in all directions. Some of it smashed into the nearby operating theatre, wounding the surgeon, who was in the throes of an operation, and also Dr Morin, who had just entered. Both doctors died. Altogether, twenty nine people were victims of the bombing of 4 September, most of them nurses or nursing orderlies. The entire hospital was evacuated the next day and the remaining huts were later dismantled.

The only visible trace of these two hospitals is the *Chemin de l'hôpital*, which was laid by French engineers using limestone quarried locally, and a short stretch of the embankment for railway line 6*bis* in the trees to the left of the *Chemin*.

Osches (7)

To continue the tour, drive ahead for a little under 200 metres and turn left on an unnumbered road. At the junction 1200 metres ahead keep straight on towards the wind turbines and at the top of the ridge **stop** by the water tower on the left, which is now a belvedere. There is parking by the tower or at the entrance to the wood on the right. The belvedere provides wide views over the area and general information about the Voie Sacrée, the Battles of Verdun and the Marne and the history of wind turbines. There is also information about the airfield, the escadrilles based here and Captain Albert Deullin, a highly decorated pilot with

Captain Albert Deullin. He survived the war and became a pioneer of commercial aviation, dying in a flying accident in 1923.

twenty confirmed victories who commanded Spa73 here from February 1917. The airfield was established in July 1916 and at the height of the fighting in August 1917 it was used by five escadrilles, including C34; it was from here that Lieutenant Pierre Guilland flew to his death over the Mort-Homme on 20 August 1917. The airfield's infrastructure was seriously damaged by a German bombing raid on 29 September 1917 that destroyed hangars, trucks and trailers and a mess hut with furniture and equipment.

Between Osches and Souilly
Continue into Osches and take the first right turn on the D21b in the direction of Souilly. Continue for roughly 550 metres and **stop** by the first of a series of information panels between here and Souilly **(8)**. This is a quiet road and it is normally possible to pull in to read the panel but be careful nevertheless. This first panel deals with the quarries that provided stone for roads and railways in the area. They were worked by French territorials – elderly men and fathers with five children who were normally exempt from front line service – colonial labourers and prisoners of war, and they also suffered in the August and September bombings.

Three hundred and fifty metres ahead **(9)**, another panel commemorates Halifax bomber JD406 EY-P, 78 Squadron, which was shot down and crashed in the forest near Osches on 28 August 1943. It had taken off from RAF Breighton the previous evening as part of a force of 673 aircraft tasked with destroying the Siemens-Schukert works, Nuremberg, which built diesel engines for submarines. The raid was successful, despite the loss of thirty three planes, 178 men killed and forty nine captured. Two aircraft did not return to Breighton: one exploded over the target, while this one was shot down on the return flight by a German night fighter ace named Reinhard Kollak. It was his twenty ninth victory. The only survivor was the mid-upper gunner, Sergeant William Dunleavy, Canadian Royal Air Force, who was captured but returned to Canada at the end of the war. The remaining crew members are buried in the cemetery behind the church at Souilly. Ten days earlier the same crew had taken part in the Peenemunde Raid on the experimental rocket centre.

179

Follow the road through the wood into open fields, pass a dirt road lined with trees on the left and two hundred metres further on **stop** on the right **(10)** at a panel showing American soldiers in huts along this road. Preparation for the Meuse-Argonne offensive of September – November 1918 brought thousands of Americans to this area. Like the other villages in the area, Vadelaincourt was entirely taken over by the Americans, who brought unimaginable tons of guns, equipment and supplies of all kinds. Onésime Lemaire, a teacher who had been in Vadelaincourt since 1915 and wrote an account of life there during the war, was particularly impressed by:

> 'those monster guns pulled by machines we had never seen before: they had tracks and moved like tanks. We counted seventy five of them in twenty four hours. But what a noise, what a deafening racket when those monstrous engines of war… ground up the hill past the school, which shook frightfully.'

He was not just impressed by the guns: the young Americans were well built, strong, healthy, energetic and adventurous. And then there was:

Company B, 317th Infantry, 80th Division, in Osches Woods, September 1918. *US Signal Corps 24782*

'...American tobacco, which the soldiers have in abundance: little white packets with a yellow thread and a cardboard medal containing fine cut tobacco the colour and scent of honey. Cigarette packets in every pocket! The Americans are generous. They take pleasure in offering their hosts packets of scented tobacco and cartons of luxury cigarettes. There is no shortage of cigars either. After that, no one wants French tobacco; everyone smokes 'honey tobacco'.

To civilians worn out by four years of shortages and war, such largesse was nothing short of miraculous.

Continue to the top of the next rise and **stop** when you reach another dirt road on the left **(11)**. Souilly airfield, which is described on this panel, was actually situated on the D159 road from Souilly to Senoncourt-les-Maujouy but it is easier to view from here than from the D159. The actual site – the field with the wind turbines in front of the trees on the horizon – was chosen in March 1916 because it was close to the Voie Sacrée and out of German artillery range. It was used by various escadrilles carrying out fighter patrols, reconnaissance and surveillance tasks and bombing; and as at Vadelaincourt the aircraft were in Bessoneau hangars, while wooden huts provided accommodation for flight and ground crews and for storage. Activity was intense and by the end of the war eighteen French and American escadrilles had used this field, with the famous N23 being based here for over two years. Notable aviators included Maxime Lenoir, with eleven confirmed victories, Eugène Gilbert, a famous pre-war pioneer racing pilot with five victories, Jean Casale, one of the few to survive throughout the war, with thirteen victories, and the extraordinarily decorated Arnaud Pinsard, Légion d'Honneur, Croix de Guerre with nineteen palms, with twenty seven victories. François de Rochechouart, Marquis de Mortemart and Prince de Tonnay-Charente, with seven victories, was also based here. Killed in aerial combat on 16 March 1918, his remarkable memorial is to be seen on the D964 a little to the south of Dun-sur-Meuse. The waypoints for his memorial and for the information panel at the site of Souilly airfield on the D159 are given at the end of this tour.

The next panel stands on the left opposite a farmyard **(12)**. In this area there were German prisoner of war camps housing thousands of men. After arriving from the front, a journey that could take several days, prisoners were examined by a doctor and interrogated; the sick went to hospital, the officers were separated from the men, and everyone was quarantined for two weeks. They were then evacuated to camps in the interior of France or kept in the Zone of the Armies as labourers.

The memorial to Lieutenant François de Rochechouart near Dun-sur-
Meuse. Transferred from the 7th Chasseurs à Cheval to the aeronautical
service in August 1915, he became a bombardier observer before obtaining
his pilot's licence in June 1916 and joining Escadrille N23 six months later.
He was killed in aerial combat on 16 March 1918. *Author's collection*

French prisoners of war unloading trench mortar bombs. On the rear of the photo, a handwritten note in German states that 'In reprisal for the French use of German prisoners of war close behind the front, our French prisoners carry mortar bombs towards the front line'. *Tom Gudmestad*

The conditions of detention here did not respect the Hague Convention of 1907 that France had signed. This required prisoners of war to be 'humanely treated', which meant that any labour should not be excessive and should have no connection with war operations. However, prisoners in these camps were required to work eleven hour days on such tasks as unloading war supplies and excavating dugouts, cutting stone and building railways, all within thirty kilometres of the front. The Germans complained but they had used French prisoners in the same way both before and during the Battle of Verdun. The prison camps also suffered in the bombing raid of 20 August.

Among the 5,000 prisoners taken in the French offensive of December 1916 was one referred to in the history of Infantry Regiment 155 as *Kammerad Pfannkuche*. He spent some days behind barbed wire in a Verdun market place where:

'There was neither roof nor straw. Without food, we stood shivering under open skies. From Verdun we marched to Souilly... The punishment camp lay behind the village. For twelve days we stood there in the cold amid deep mud. Rations for four men were a single loaf and dirty water from a gutter. At night they crammed more than a thousand of us into a hut scarcely big enough for

200. There was no room to move. The air was thick and many men collapsed. This is where we also spent Christmas. We were strictly forbidden to sing our beautiful old Christmas carols but we did anyway…On New Year's Day we were deloused. A boiler stood in a room with no windows. We had to take off all our clothes and rub ourselves with kerosene. As we had not been able to wash since capture, our bodies were covered with a thick layer of dirt. Then we marched naked through sleet across a field to the so-called baths. For eight men, a single bucket of water was poured in a funnel. As there was no shower head, it came out in a thick stream and the kerosene and dirt just stayed on the skin. Then we ran naked back to the boiler and got our clothes. That was the first day we could write to our families. We also got our first warm food…The next day we marched to a quarry. It poured for fourteen days without stopping. By 9am our boots were soaked through. In the evenings we marched in step back to the camp. Every man had to bring a big stone with him. Soaked to the skin, 12,000 men crawled on to the straw, which was never changed and worse than manure. I soon got dysentery.'

Souilly **(13)**
At the road junction a short distance ahead do not turn left but continue to the T-junction with the Voie Sacrée, then cross over the road and park behind the detached building opposite with the handsome external staircase. Unlike the other villages in the area, Souilly, a town which stands where the ancient road from Verdun to Bar-Le Duc crossed two east-west routes linking Champagne with the Meuse valley, had been an important judicial and administrative centre for centuries and had plenty of spacious buildings to offer the staff and services of the Second Army.

This building, originally the Mairie (town hall) of Souilly, was chosen by General Pétain on 26 February 1916 to be the headquarters of the Second Army during the Battle of Verdun. His arrival was not the first time that the people of Souilly had seen the war: the German advance in August and September 1914 had brought their troops to within four kilometres of Souilly. Fighting in the nearby woods caused hundreds of casualties among the regiments covering the French right flank during the Battle of the Marne and it was only the order for a general German withdrawal that saved Souilly from capture. Two casualties of those engagements between Osches and Ippécourt are buried in the cemetery behind the church. As in Vadelaincourt and Osches, some civilians remained in Souilly during the war, particularly those who had something to sell. One of the complaints made by Onésime Lemaire in

The Mairie (town hall) at Souilly, headquarters of the Second Army. *Author's collection*

his memoir was the rise in the cost of living caused by local producers preferring to sell to the richer new arrivals, and the problems that rising prices caused for the villagers.

Between 26 February 1916 and September 1918 Souilly was the nerve centre of Second Army operations, which were commanded by Generals Pétain, Nivelle, Guillaumat and Hirschauer respectively. A village with a pre-war population of just over 500 became a town of over 10,000, with two stations, vast railway yards, an airfield, hospitals, the Second Army medical directorate and all the necessary administrative services, including a strong military police department to enforce regulations.

On 21 September 1918 the Mairie became the headquarters of the American First Army, commanded by General John Pershing. George C. Marshall, then a colonel on General Pershing's staff and later the man behind the Marshall Plan, was here during the Meuse-Argonne campaign of autumn 1918 and described Souilly as a depressing village and not improved by almost constant rain. Apart from the cars and telegraph poles, this street has changed little and looking downhill it is easy to imagine the scene during the Battle of Verdun, when a constant stream of trucks and cars rumbled along the road. Inside the Mairie an impressive and very well illustrated exhibition provides information

185

about Souilly before and during the war, as well as the Voie Sacrée, the airfield, medical services, prison camps, colonial labourers, evacuation routes, refugees and much more, including an explanation of how the headquarters operated throughout the day. Be sure not to miss General Pétain's office on the upper floor. Two plaques on the wall outside the Mairie record that the building functioned as both the headquarters of the French Second Army and of the American First Army, and to keep up the American connection Souilly has been twinned with General Pershing's birthplace in Laclede, Missouri. The opening hours are given in the Useful Addresses section of this book.

If you wish to visit the graves of the Halifax bomber crew referred to earlier, walk up to the church and you will find them among the graves at the back.

MAP B: Souilly hospital and main railway station **(14)**
To continue the tour, leave the Mairie, turn left downhill and take the first right on the D21towards Ippécourt and Clermont-en-Argonne. After several twists and turns the road runs straight, with a long field rising to the forest on the right (one kilometre from Souilly). **Stop** on the roadside just beyond a little tree and face the forest.

Between 1916 and the Armistice this quiet valley was the site of hospitals, huge railway yards, sidings and workshops. When huts originally intended for the evacuation hospital at Souilly were taken over by the staff of the Second Army in February 1916, a new hospital had to be built and it was logical to place it close to the new railway line, the 6*bis*. The only trace of the line here today is a section of the receiving and despatching platform, long enough to accommodate an entire hospital train, which crosses the field in front of you from left to right about half way between the road and the forest.

The hospital was spread out along the hillside between the platform and the forest. There were thirty huts altogether, fourteen reserved for evacuation patients close to the railway line and a further sixteen for patients needing hospital care without evacuation. Although incomplete when the French launched their first major counter offensive on 24 October 1916, the hospital was able to offer 225 beds and 500 places for seated wounded awaiting evacuation; between 24–30 October over 7,000 wounded and sick were treated here, with twenty one hospital trains needed to evacuate them.

By the start of the December offensive there was a radiology department, extra surgical teams, and the number of beds had doubled, but that did not prevent the triage wards from being so overrun that

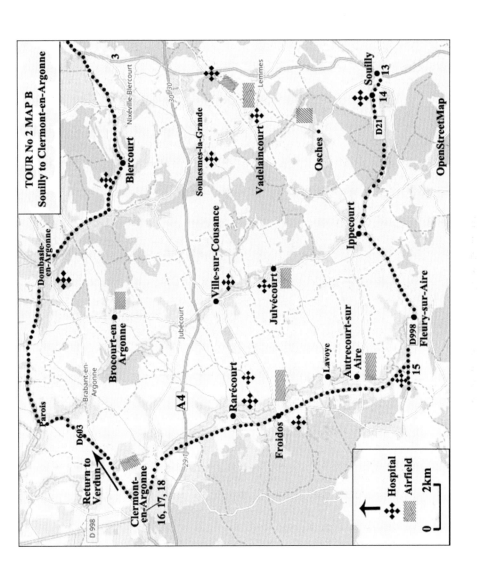

TOUR No 2 MAP B
Souilly to Clermont-en-Argonne

Nixéville-Blercourt

3

Blercourt

Lemmes

Souilly

13

14

D21

Oches

Vadelaincourt

Souhesmes-la-Grande

Ippecourt

OpenStreetMap

Dombasle-en-Argonne

Ville-sur-Cousance

Julvécourt

Fleury-sur-Aire

Brocourt-en-Argonne

Jubécourt

Brabant-en-Argonne

Autrecourt-sur-Aire

D998

15

Parois

A4

Rarécourt

Lavoye

D603

Return to Verdun

Froidos

Clermont-en-Argonne

16, 17, 18

D 998

Hospital

Airfield

0   2km

187

The evacuation hospital at Souilly.

additional teams had to be brought in. From April 1917 this hospital specialized in gas cases and, like Vadelaincourt and the surrounding area, it was frequently bombed. In August 1918, the whole facility was handed over to the American medical service and became American Evacuation Hospital 7; Hospital 6 at Vadelaincourt was transferred here at the same time with practically all its equipment. Hospital 7 had the north end of the site and Hospital 6 the south end and, while the receiving station was common to both, they operated independently. Passageways between the buildings were floored and roofed and for protection there were concrete shelters rather than dugouts.

Patients arriving here were divided into seriously wounded, lightly wounded and medical; men who could be evacuated quickly were rapidly dealt with in a separate area, while seriously wounded patients were undressed, bathed, X-rayed and prepared for operation, only transferring to a ward once these procedures had been completed. Although the two hospitals were in operation in late August 1918 with 2,200 beds available,

The huge railway yards operated by the (American) 13th Engineers (Railway). The receiving and despatching platform and the hospital huts are on the left of the picture. The railwaymen of the 13th Engineers were the first American troops to arrive in France in 1917 and they were attached to the French Second Army from arrival to the Armistice in 1918. *US Signal Corps 48953*

there were few patients until the start of the St Mihiel Salient offensive on 12 September 1918 when they quickly became very busy. The Meuse-Argonne offensive launched on 26 September 1918 coincided with the Spanish flu which was caught by 25% of American soldiers, many of whom were treated here. It is hard to imagine today just how much activity there was in this quiet valley.

Fleury-sur-Aire **(15)**
Continue along the D21 to Ippécourt (just under five kilometres). At the crossroads in the middle of Ippécourt fork left on the D20 towards Fleury-sur-Aire. At the roundabout in the centre of Fleury take the first exit on the D998 towards Froidos and Clermont-en-Argonne and continue for one kilometre to the junction of the D998. **Stop** at the memorial by the road fork. Care is needed here; there is a stopping place in front of the memorial but it tends to be overgrown.

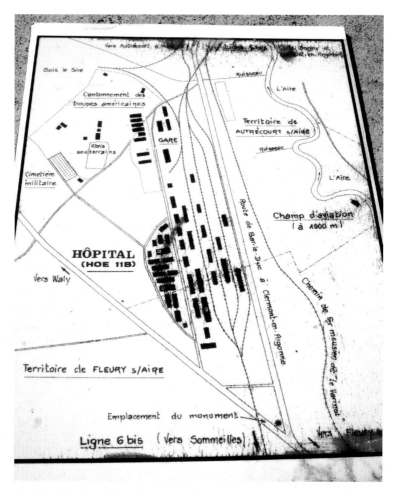

A plan of the hospital at Fleury-sur-Aire during the war. *Author's collection*

The open fields between the D20 and the D998 were the site of one of the most important hospitals in the Verdun region, Evacuation Hospital 11B. It was inaugurated shortly after completion of the first section of Line 6*bis* in May 1916 and when fully operational had 1,220 beds. As well as receiving wounded and sick men from both the Left and Right Banks and the Argonne, it received the overflow from several other hospitals and was always very busy.

The offensive of 20 August 1917 brought in 7,000 wounded in three days and during its thirty months of operation 116,000 wounded men were treated here. There were eight parallel railway lines, one of which

190

was reserved for evacuation trains stopping along the lengthy reception and dispatching platform, and a vast station with a water tower, coal yard, turntable and sidings. The evacuation huts (630 places) were situated along the reception platform; behind them stood the hospitalization huts, surgical and radiological units and, further back, staff accommodation, workshops, laundries, kitchens, the pharmacy, a sterilization unit, ice machines, garages, shelters, cemetery and the morgue. The *Petit Meusien* light railway ran on the far side of the D998. None of it remains today but for several months after the war the huts remained in place and served the local civil population. Among the many eminent personalities on the staff was Infirmière-major Mme Jacquemaire-Clemenceau (whose name sometimes appears as Clemenceau-Jacquemaire), daughter of the Prime Minister, Georges Clemenceau.

On 18 September 1918, this hospital was transferred to the American Red Cross and thereafter it dealt mostly with American wounded; the

Memorial to the wounded soldiers and medical services of France and America. *Author's collection*

191

memorial by the roadside commemorates the wounded soldiers and medical services of France and America. The rough hewn monument inaugurated in 1999 represents a doctor and nurse at the bedside of a wounded soldier and refers to the meeting here of a wounded American ambulance driver, John Verplanck Newlin, and Mme Jacquemaire-Clemenceau. During the summer of 1917, nineteen year old Newlin, a well educated Pennsylvanian, was attached to Ambulance Section 29 which was evacuating troops from first aid posts on the Left Bank to this and another hospital. On the night of 3 August a shell exploding near the entrance to the drivers' dugout wounded him severely just as he was about to start his ambulance. He was rushed to the nearest hospital and then transferred here in a critical condition and operated on twenty four hours later. The next day he rallied sufficiently to see some of his fellow drivers and receive his citation, Médaille Militaire and Croix de Guerre, but he died soon afterwards. Mme Jacquemaire-Clemenceau wrote to his mother to say that her son had died without suffering and had received his decorations with deep joy. After the war Newlin's body was transferred from the cemetery here to the Meuse-Argonne American Cemetery at Romagne-sous-Montfaucon. He lies in Plot A, Row 32, Grave 19.

Another American ambulance driver is buried only a few kilometres away. Twenty-two year old Harmon Craig died of wounds received when loading his ambulance at Dombasle-en-Argonne, a town on your return route to Verdun. An operation to amputate his leg was carried out at the field hospital at Ville-sur-Cousances but he died a few hours later. He lies today in plot 814 in the nearby French military cemetery.

Clermont-en-Argonne (**16**)
The tour returns to Verdun via Clermont-en-Argonne. Return to the D998 and continue for twelve kilometres into the centre of the town and park near the Place de la République. This little town, situated at a crossroads on the ancient road from Paris to the east of France and once fortified, was heavily damaged in September 1914 during the Battle of the Marne. When the Germans arrived in the town on 4 September, there were already many wounded being treated at the hospital run by the Sisters of Saint Vincent de Paul. Sister Gabrielle, the head of the community, had been unable to evacuate her patients because of the shelling and had moved everyone to the cellars. Despite threats to her life, she remained with her patients throughout the fourteen day occupation of the town; and after the German retreat she continued to care for the sick and wounded, as long range shelling gradually reduced the town to ruins. In December 1914 Sister Gabrielle was awarded the

Sister Gabrielle's hospital at Clermont-en-Argonne. *Author's collection*

Croix de Guerre and cited in Third Army orders. She died in September 1927 and is buried in the cemetery on the Rue Basse **(17)**. Her hospital, which is now apartments, stands at the corner of the D603 and the Rue Gaston Lelorain **(18)**, 160 metres from the Place de la République, and in the adjoining chapel a commemorative plaque and several stained glass windows recall her devotion to the French wounded.

The sculpture in front of the Mairie in the Place de la République commemorates the seventy two men of Clermont who were deported in July 1944 and died in captivity, while the nearby war memorial bears the names of military and civilian victims of the First and Second World Wars. In the church of St. Didier, which is at the top of the steep hill above the Place de la République, there are several interesting memorial windows and a plaque in honour of Sister Gabrielle.

To return to Verdun, follow the D603 back to Moulin Brulé and continue into the city.

GPS Waypoints Tour No 2

1. N49°09.445' E005°21.524'
2. N49°09.428' E005°20.859'
3. N49°07.410' E005°17.722'
4. N49°04.603' E005°16.476'

5. N49°04.362' E005°15.692'
6. N49°04.237' E005°15.668'
7. N49°03.311' E005°15.683'
8. N49°02.733 E005°15.772'
9. N49°02.577' E005°15.963'
10. N49°02.294' E005°16.587'
11. N49°02.105' E005°16.771'
12. N49°01.951' E005°16.888'
13. N49°01.683' E005°17.164'
14. N49°01.746' E005°16.031'
15. N49°01.077' E005°08.719'
16. N49°06.307' E005°04.174'
17. N49°06.135' E005°04.187'
18. N49°06.353' E005°04.306'

Other waypoints connected with this tour

Site of former Souilly airfield and information panel:
N49°02.623' E005°18.204'
Nearby night crash memorial: N49°02.573' E005°18.142'
Mortemart memorial: N49°21.968' E 005°11.584'

Tour No 3

Ravin de Vacherauville, Cote 300, Cote 344, Ouvrage du Buffle, Côte du Talou

Distance: A walking tour of approximately thirteen kilometres covering sites involved in the French offensives of 1917 on the Right Bank.

Duration: A three quarter day's tour, allowing time for stops, photographs and a picnic.

NB: For a short tour to look at the view from the Côte du Talou and inspect the remains of the well preserved German front line, allow one hour (under three kilometres). Park at **(17)** and follow the track up to **(16)**. For a view along the Meuse valley in both directions and of the Left Bank, continue to the top of the hill.

Maps: IGN 3112ET or IGN Blue Series 3212 Ouest

There are several steep stretches on this tour and a walking stick may be useful. There are no refreshments or toilets after you leave Vacherauville and you are unlikely to meet other walkers, so charge your phone and make sure you have everything you need. There are no organized picnic sites and the only benches are close to Vacherauville cemetery at the end of the tour.

Warning: when walking this sector, visitors should stay on the paths and keep away from the edges of holes. Do not attempt to enter old dugouts.

To reach the start of the tour, take the D964 (Stenay) road out of Verdun. Continue through Bras-sur-Meuse to Vacherauville and at the roundabout take the fourth exit into the Rue du Colonel Driant which has a hotel and restaurant on the corner.**(1)** Park and walk back to the roundabout, then cross over to the D905 which is signposted Ville-devant-Chaumont and Damvillers. The first part of the tour follows this road, so be careful to keep to the verge and face the oncoming traffic. After one kilometre **(2)** turn left on a sandy track between fields and walk straight ahead

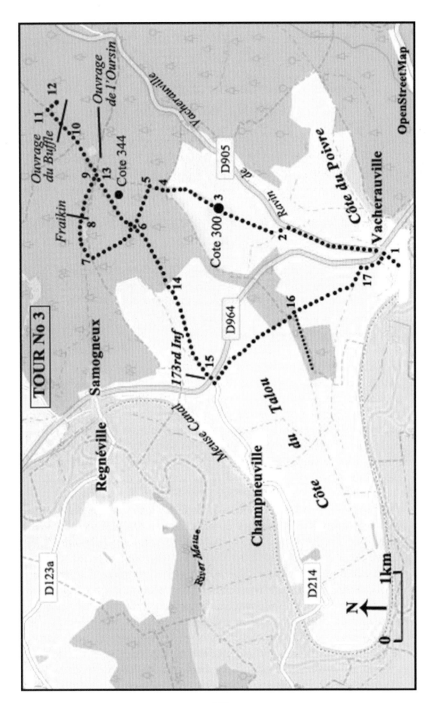

TOUR No 3

Ouvrage du Buffle
Ouvrage de l'Oursin
Fraikin
Cote 344
Vacherauville
Samogneux
Regnéville
Meuse Canal
River Meuse
D123a
Champneuville
Côte du Talou
D214
Côte du Poivre
Vacherauville
Cote 300
Ravin de
D905
D964
173rd Inf
OpenStreetMap

N
0   1km

196

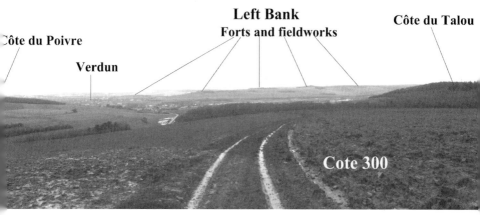

The view towards Verdun from Cote 300. *Author's collection*

for 150 metres, then take the right fork; continue to the top of the hill, then **stop (3)** and face ahead along the track. This is Cote 300. If you imagine a clock face, the summit of Cote 344 is at 10 o'clock. Bois le Fays and Beaumont, attacked on 26 August 1917, are at 2 o'clock. Now turn and look back the way you have come. To your left the forested hills and ridges of the Left Bank conceal a line of French forts, fieldworks and batteries which communicated directly with positions on the Right Bank and facilitated the observation and bombardment of German lines during the Battle of Verdun. The valley below you on the left is Ravin de Vacherauville and the wooded hill to your left front with new houses on the lower slopes is the Côte du Poivre. The pine covered hill to your right front with a phone mast on the top is the Côte du Talou, which you will visit later. Note that Verdun can be seen from here.

On 20 August 1917 this sector was attacked by two divisions of XV Corps, the 126th on the left and the 123rd on the right. They were facing Reserve Infantry Divisions Nos 28 and 25, neither of which was in good condition. The 28th had been serving in the sector since February 1917, while the 25th, which had suffered heavy losses in the French attack on the Chemin des Dames the previous May, had returned to Verdun after hasty reorganization involving 1,100 replacements, 25% of which came from the 1918 class. Both divisions had been recently weakened by an epidemic of dysentery.

The first obstacle facing the attackers that morning was a line of German fieldworks which ran from the Côte du Talou across this hilltop to Mormont Farm, a powerful redoubt overlooking the Ravin de Vacherauville one kilometre from here. On 20 August 1917, the French

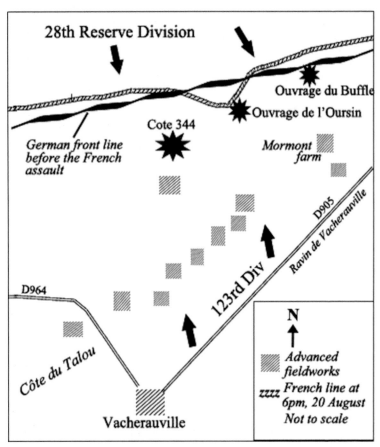

German defences in the Cote 344 sector on 20 August 1917.

front line was on the opposite side of the Ravin de Vacherauville, which had to be crossed in the first minutes of the assault. German guns were targetting the ravine but fortunately for the attackers thick fog and smoke before zero hour allowed them to get across without too many casualties and take cover at the foot of the hill. Then, at 4.40am, advancing by the compass and using hand signals because the noise was too great to hear voice commands, the assault battalions moved off. However, for tactical reasons the Germans had evacuated the fieldworks on 15 August 1917 and retired to the main line of resistance on Cote 344, so it did not take very long to clear them – sixteen minutes, according to the 173rd Infantry (126th Division) – and, leaving occupying troops in possession, the attackers moved on. In fact, there must have been some

One of the casualties of the assault on Mormont Farm on 20 August 1917 was another French international rugby player, Captain Marc Pierre Giacardy, 6th Infantry. Born in 1881, he played for Stade Bordelais before the war, captained the team in 1909, represented France against Wales in 1907 and refereed the French rugby club final in 1912. Mobilized with the rank of sergeant, he had an illustrious military career, being cited four times and awarded the Croix de Guerre with Palm and Stars. Today the only legible part of the inscription on his grave reads ' …leading his men in the assault …' *Author's collection*

Germans in position because the message from the 126th Division at 6.45am reporting the capture of the fieldworks stated 'Many Germans killed. No quarter given to the survivors.'

Now continue along the track, entering the forest with block 221 on the right and 230 on the left **(4)** and after 300 metres turn left between blocks 224 and 230 **(5)**. Continue for 500 metres until you reach a five-way junction, then **stop (6)**. The summit of Cote 344 is to your right.

Cote 344

When the Battle of Verdun began the French second position on the Right Bank was based on Samogneux, Cote 344, Cote 300 and the Mormont Farm redoubt. However, it was far from strong, being basically a number of individual and incomplete flanking works situated on rear slopes and surrounded by wire. Cote 344 was the highest point and, with views encompassing both the Left and Right Banks and stretching south to Verdun, the Germans regarded it as the key to the city. When Samogneux fell, the Cote 344 sector – a sizeable area which stretched to the Meuse and included the Côte du Talou – was defended by a mixed bag of units from several divisions. On 24 February 1916, the local commander reported the troops available to him as: 1st and 3rd Battalions, 60th Infantry, fractions of the 324th Infantry (numbers unknown), three companies of the 351st Infantry, two companies of elderly men from the 44th Territorials and fifteen machine guns. One company stood between Cote 344 and Samogneux, a little over two kilometres as the crow flies. An 11am report on the situation from Major Falconnet, commander of the 3rd Battalion, 60th Infantry, pulled no punches:

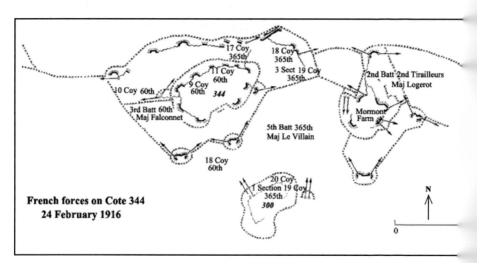

**French forces on Cote 344
24 February 1916**

200

The memorial to the 44th Territorials, a Verdun regiment, stands close to the Ossuary. *Author's collection*

'The incessant bombardment of Cote 344 has led 21 Company to abandon its position, which has become untenable. The trenches shown on the plan could not be used because they led towards the Germans. Trenches should have been prepared on the rear slope. As a result there will be a gap between Cote 344 and [the 1st] Battalion, whose whereabouts are unknown to me. The hillside between Cote 344 and the Meuse is untenable and we are unsupported by the artillery...I no longer know who is on my left. I do not know if I am still protected in front; I have no idea who is behind me. I am in contact with ...the 365th on my right. What is to be done?'

Having received no reply, he tried again one hour later:

'I am informed by Major Le Villain of the 365th that the Germans are attacking Cote 344 from the north and the west. I have positioned two companies in a skirmish line on the left of Cote 344, with one machine gun section on each flank, the third company in reserve and another in the redoubts on Cote 344 with two machine gun sections. I fear for my left flank, which does not stretch to the main road [the D964].'

In addition, there was a battalion of Tirailleurs at Mormont Farm and some scanty remnants of two other infantry regiments 'all in the last stages of exhaustion and needing urgent replacement'.

Once the Germans had captured Samogneux the way to Cote 344 was open and by the time Major Falconnet's second report was received aerial observers were reporting large numbers of German troops massing in the ravines in preparation for an assault. The plan called for a combined operation by units from XVIII Corps and VII Reserve Corps, with nine battalions available between Samogneux and Mormont Farm – a distance of less than three kilometres. At 2pm the movement, described by one French observer as a great grinding machine, began to overwhelm the scattered and dazed defenders. French artillery on the Left Bank and machine gunners on the Côte du Talou firing over open

sights could see the attackers falling but the hours of preparatory bombardment with superheavy guns and mortars had done its work. With drums beating, horns blowing and shouts of Hurrah!, the attackers swept to the top of Cote 344, where some began to dig in; others attempted to continue towards the Côte du Talou but were driven back by French artillery. It was all over very quickly. In the words of *Schlachten des Weltkrieges*, the German narrative history of the war, it was a:

Lieutenant Colonel d'Auzac de Lamartinie holds the colours of the 2nd Tirailleurs, which are decorated with the Légion d'Honneur and the Croix de Guerre. Note that his left sleeve is empty.

'parade ground assault, such as occurs in modern warfare when the artillery has so crushed the enemy that there is no life left in him. The waves went forward almost erect with the prescribed distance between them. Here, the infantry plucked the fruits of the gunners' work'.

To continue the tour cross over the junction and take the track opposite with block 225 on the right and 231 on the left. Continue straight ahead; **do not turn left** where a track joins after 120 metres but follow the track downhill between blocks 225 and 226. In August 1917 there were only scattered areas of woodland here and the German lines – a series of strongly organized trenches running across this hillside from left to right – would have been clearly visible. Some trench remains can still be seen here in winter. Continue downhill to a T-junction with a wide driveable track **(7)**, then **turn right** and walk ahead with an open field on the right.

Private Albert Fraikin **(8)**
The field memorial of twenty-six year old Private Albert Fraikin, 412th Infantry, is about fifty metres from the track on the right hand side and not far beyond the end of the open field. Recent forestry clearance has left debris on the hillside but at the time of writing (February 2020) the white painted cross was clearly visible.

Twenty seven year old *Private Albert Fraikin* was born in Avesnes, Department of the Nord, on 6 December 1890. On 20 August 1917 the 412th was tasked with capturing a major section of the German main line of resistance in this sector which included the Tranchée de Trèves and the Ouvrage de l'Oursin - a commanding fieldwork roughly 500 metres ahead. They took casualties when crossing Ravin de Vacherauville but got through the advanced fieldworks, only to be held up when the 3rd Battalion was hit by friendly fire; as a result, the 412th was too far behind the rolling barrage when they reached the German front line. There they found that the artillery bombardment had not achieved the planned level of destruction and this, combined with machine gun fire, forced them to pull back short of their final objective. They managed to dig in but everyone was exhausted and their position was weak. Private Fraikin died on 20 August when he was hit by shell splinters and his body was never found. The 412th's war diary gives no final casualty figure for that day, reporting only that twenty officers were out of action and that losses were particularly high in the 3rd Battalion, which may have been Private Fraikin's battalion. The original, very simple, memorial placed here by Private

Above left: **The very simple memorial to Private Albert Fraikin, 412th Infantry, who died on 20 August 1917 almost on the final objective.** *Author's collection*

Above right: **The modern memorial.** *Author's collection*

Fraikin's brother, has recently been improved by the addition of this cross.

Now **return** to the main track and continue for seven hundred metres until you reach an open space where six tracks meet **(9)**. When you reach it, the track immediately to your left, which descends steeply between blocks 212 and 213, leads into Ravin Desserieux, which the Germans called the *Hindenburg-Schlucht*. This was the main German supply and shelter ravine for the Cote 344 sector and it was from there that the raid on the 2nd Zouaves was launched on 23 November. In winter a short walk down the track will give you an idea of how steep and sheltered it was but in summer it is too overgrown to see much. The Ouvrage de l'Oursin, the German strongpoint which commanded access to this ridge via ravines on both sides, was sited nearby. It covers the gap between Cote 344 and the Ouvrage du Buffle on Cote 326.

Ouvrage du Buffle, Private Raymond Lavielle, 42nd Infantry, and Private Baptiste Chieze, 169th Infantry **(10,11,12)**
If you wish to visit these sites, follow the directions below and then return here. It will add two kilometres to the overall tour. To inspect the remains of the Ouvrage du Buffle – shallow trenches and shell craters – cross diagonally over the open space and take the grassy track between blocks 219 and 210. Do not take the hard drivable track next to it on the right. Where the track forks by an open field after 200 metres, take the **left fork** between 203 and 210 and walk ahead. Entrenchments begin after about 400 metres **(10)** but the whole area is heavily shelled and shapeless. Roughly three hundred metres further on a wide opening **(11)** in the trees on the right leads to two small memorials **(12)**. *NB. If you are walking without a GPS and reach a track on the left between blocks 204 and 210 you have gone too far, so turn back for a short distance and look to your left for a white cross.*

The Ouvrage du Buffle, a network of strong trenches and wire on Cote 326 commanding access to this ridge from both sides, formed a salient in the French lines and was connected to the Ouvrage de l'Oursin by the Tranchée de Jutland. The German assault on the Ouvrage du Buffle of 23 October 1917 referred to in Chapter 4 was an attempt to outflank Cote 344 following a long series of unsuccessful direct assaults on that position. A violent barrage at 4.30am that day, combined with a heavy fog, allowed the Germans to penetrate the Ouvrage du Buffle and although they got no further it was enough for their machine guns to play havoc with the French lines. Two counter attacks by the 42nd Infantry launched later that morning failed with high casualties and another was ordered for the late afternoon. The war diary described the result:

'At 4.35pm, ten minutes' destructive fire. The men moved off at 4.45pm protected by a box barrage extending one hundred metres to the north of the salient …With officers in the lead the valiant troops moved forward. Captain Dubert, 5 Company, hit in the foot by shell splinters, continued to lead his men. Lieutenant Frossard received a bullet wound but kept command of 6 Company. The NCOs kept the ranks moving. The heavy calibre bombardment was intense between [the new French front line] and Cote 326.
Our units crossed the southern edge of the ouvrage, which had been completely smashed by our artillery, was strewn with French and German corpses, and covered with equipment, weapons and grenades. The counter attack flooded over Cote 326 and continued downhill to the German front line, where the enemy resisted weakly with hand grenades…Groups of Germans

Left: Until recently, the memorials to Private Raymond Lavielle, 42nd Infantry, and Private Baptiste Chieze, 169th Infantry, were combined, with the plaque covering the reference to Private Chieze. *Author's collection*

Below: The plaque recording Private Lavielle's death in the assault on the Ouvrage du Buffle on 23 October 1917. *Author's collection*

were fleeing from shell hole to shell hole towards Anglemont Farm [a flanking position to the east]. At 5.05pm Major Andriot [the battalion commander] was in command of the salient, which he reorganized. A Maxim gun taken that morning in the Tranchée de Jutland ... four French machine guns and seven gunners from the 3rd Machine Gun Section came back into our hands.'

Casualties were very high; the operation lasted only twenty minute operation but it cost the 42nd twelve officers and 311 men. As the war diary only names the officers, we cannot know whether twenty two year old Private Raymond Lavielle was killed in this area, died of wounds or simply disappeared in the action. His body was never found and he is commemorated on the war memorial of Villiers-Adam, Department of Val d'Oise.

Twenty two year old Private Baptiste Chieze was born on 16 March 1895 in Argentat, Department of Corrèze, and died in the Samogneux sector on 25 November 1917 in the last major action in the sector until the start of the Meuse-Argonne offensive in September 1918. On 25 November 1917, the 2nd Battalion, 169th Infantry, was supporting the assault battalions of the 168th Infantry by manning the front line trenches after the 168th had moved off and escorting prisoners. The aim of the assault that day was to clear the main German line of resistance once and for all, destroy their underground barracks, force the Germans to evacuate the ravines and establish a new outpost line sufficiently far ahead to

The restored memorial to Private Baptiste Chieze, 169th Infantry, who was killed supporting the 168th Infantry in the offensive of 25 November 1917. *Author's collection*

prevent them from launching any more surprise attacks. The 168th was facing Infantry Regiment 112 (29th Division), who reported that the French artillery preparation had completely flattened the trenches and that violent shelling of their barracks had blocked up three of the entrances. Their regimental history reports that at 12.20pm:

'The enemy assault waves advanced close behind the wall of shells. Weakened by their losses, the shattered defenders of the front line could only resist weakly. A few men ran to the barracks to warn the garrison. [Two companies] were ordered to counter attack. The enemy was approaching the barracks from all sides; some had already pushed past it and continued down into [the valley]. The first thing was to defend the entrances. The French were already aiming a flamethrower at Entrance 7. Calm and well aimed fire by Vizefeldwebel Kuentz put it out of action'.

Forty minutes later French observers on the Left Bank reported that the assault battalions appeared to have reached their objectives; but Infantry Regiment112 was not giving up:

'Once the immediate threat to the barracks had been dealt with, the counter attack could begin. Step by step the enemy was pushed back, a line was established some fifty metres in front of the old front line trench and held despite numerous attempts to drive the garrison out'.

Further along the hillside two other barracks also came under attack; a machine gun was set up to cover the entrances and grenades were thrown inside:

'The only thing to do was to get out. Vizefeldwebel Schneider, who was wounded, managed to set up a light machine gun and when another one fired from the other side of the valley the enemy became uncertain and gradually the attack weakened. We even managed to push the enemy back as far as the company commander's dugout.'

Unable to hold the new positions, the 168th had to retire to the main line of resistance and the 1st Battalion of the 169th was sent forward in support. In the end they were not needed to resist a counter attack but were kept busy escorting prisoners to the rear. The 169th's casualties – all unnamed – were thirty four wounded, five killed and one missing.

A view inside the Landwehr Barracks. *Wim Degrande*

Given that the name Baptiste Chieze does not appear in the French military graves list, it is possible that he was the missing man. He is commemorated on the war memorial in his home town of Argentat.

To continue the tour return to the main path and retrace your steps to the open space where the six paths meet, cross over to the track directly opposite **(13)** and walk ahead with block 225 on the right and 224 on the left. This will take you over the summit of Cote 344. Continue straight ahead for 1500 metres and **stop** when you leave the forest and enter open ground **(14)**.

The hills on the Left Bank that saw so much bloody fighting in 1916 were, from west to east, Cote 304, the Mort-Homme and the Côte de l'Oie. They are directly ahead on the other side of the River Meuse. The Côte du Talou is to your left front and Samogneux is over the hillside to your right. The low wooded hill on the distant horizon to your right front is Montfaucon d'Argonne. Sharp eyed visitors may be able to make out what appears to be a small tower on the top; this is the American memorial to the Meuse-Argonne campaign and far from being small; it is over sixty metres high. Seeing the extent of the area covered by French artillery and machine guns on the Côte du Talou, as well as along the River

Côte du Talou

River Meuse

Cote 304   Mort-Hom

The view from Cote 344 to the Left Bank of the Meuse. *Author's collection*

Meuse and on the Left Bank, it is easy to see why the German advance on this side of the river was not as swift as had been planned and was a great deal more bloody than anticipated. It would have been bloodier still had the Côte du Talou not been evacuated on 25 February 1916. It makes it all the more surprising that General von Falkenhayn, the chief of the German General Staff, should have decided only to attack on the Right Bank.

173rd Infantry Regiment Memorial **(15)**
Continue downhill to the road (D964) and **stop**. The little memorial by the roadside commemorates the 173rd Infantry Regiment (126th Division), a Corsican regiment, which lost almost 3,500 men during the First World War, a considerable number for such a small population. Their exploits won them the *fourragère* (lanyard) in the colours of the Médaille Militaire and four citations in Army Orders, including one for their actions on the Côte du Poivre in December 1916 and another for

210

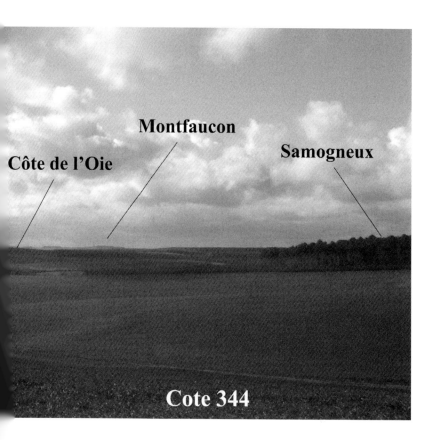

Côte de l'Oie   Montfaucon   Samogneux

Cote 344

their exploits on the western flanks of Cote 344 on 20-21 August 1917, where they were on the right of the 126th Division.

On 20 August the division's assault regiments reached their final objectives more quickly than expected and within a short time two of them, the 173rd and the 55th, were ordered to continue the operation in order to capture the objectives originally fixed for the following day. Having made ready, the Third Battalion of the 173rd began to move off but the 55th, which was on their right, did not; and to avoid being outflanked the Third Battalion was forced to retire, suffering considerable casualties from friendly fire from the Left Bank as they did so. The operation was first postponed until 7pm and then postponed again until 5am the following day, and during the hours of waiting the 173rd resisted several counter attacks and suffered a heavy artillery bombardment which caused even more casualties. By the end of the day their war diary notes that the regiment's ranks had been reduced by 400 officers and men but 'without morale being affected in any way'.

« Ici, le 20 août 1917,
le 173ᵉᵐᵉ R.I. de Corse
a conquis la côte 344
obtenant ainsi la deuxième
de ses quatre citations
à l'Ordre de l'Armée. »

Plaque dévoilée le Dimanche 9 Novembre 2008
en présence de Representants des Communes
de CHAMPNEUVILLE (Meuse) et de CAURO (Corse).

The memorial to
the actions of the
173rd Infantry
Regiment in the
Cote 344 sector.
Author's collection

The plan for 21 August was for two companies of the 173rd's 2nd Battalion, supported by what was left of the 3rd Battalion, to capture the strong German positions between the western flank of Cote 344 and Samogneux, and at 5am they moved off. Although the long artillery preparation had not knocked out all the German machine guns, the 173rd advanced steadily, capturing most of their objectives but only overcoming the last German resistance towards midnight. Recompense followed immediately, with the award in the field of three Légions d'Honneur, four Médailles Militaires and numerous citations in Army Orders. The Germans responded with 'a hellish shower of projectiles of every calibre and with poisonous gas…[but] Thanks to our masks, these only caused light casualties'. Be that as it may, the 173rd's losses in the two day operation were so great that the 2nd and 3rd Battalions were amalgamated. This memorial marks the regiment's jump off line on 21 August.

Côte du Talou
Now cross the D964 and turn immediately left uphill along a stony track. The hill in front of you is the Côte du Talou. Continue over the top and **stop** when you can see down the other side but do not go beyond the wood.

On 24 February 1916 the 72nd Division, which had been holding this sector since 21 February and was effectively destroyed, was withdrawn and replaced by the 37th Division. Fearing that they could be outflanked, on 25 February the 37th's commander, General de Bonneval, ordered a general withdrawal to Belleville Ridge, a distance of more than six kilometres as the crow flies. The withdrawal allowed the Germans to establish themselves here and on the Côte du Poivre, both prominent positions offering excellent observation. The German positions on the Côte du Talou, which formed part of the same defence line as the fieldworks on Cote 300, were evacuated in the run-up to the French offensive of August 1917, so on 20 August the attacking regiments met little opposition. To inspect what remains of the old German front line in this sector, turn right into the wood along a grassy track with block 235 on the right **(16)**. *NB There are two possibilities here: do not take the first right turn into the wood at the top of the hill. The second turn is further downhill and at the time of writing it is marked by a red painted stone.* This well preserved section of the German line, which the French called the *Tranchée de Mackensen*, runs for a considerable distance under the trees on the left of the path.

General de Bonneval was replaced on 26 February 1916, the day after the withdrawal order was given.

Vacherauville Cemetery **(17)**

Return to the track and continue downhill to Vacherauville Cemetery. The little memorial by the cemetery wall commemorates the 56th and 59th Battalions of Chasseurs à pied commanded by Lieutenant Colonel Emile Driant, which were holding advanced lines in Bois des Caures, eight kilometres from here, when the German attacked on 21 February 1916. The Chasseurs had been there for over a year and to ensure honoured burial for any man who died on duty Colonel Driant had a cemetery laid out at his own expense not far from where you are standing. It featured a wooden cross almost six metres high and a statue of a young woman imploring the God of France to grant her victory in exchange for the lives which had been sacrificed. The statue was destroyed during the war

Looking south from the Côte du Talou to Belleville Ridge and Verdun. *Author's collection*

Vacherauville

Belleville Ridge

Côte du Poivre

Ouvrage de Froideterre

Fort Belleville

Verdun

Côte du Talou

A section of the German front line captured on 20 August 1917 by the 112th Infantry. *Author's collection*

but a copy of it was recently placed in front of Vacherauville church, where there is also a commemorative stained glass window. The little memorial here replaces an earlier one which stood close to the road. For information about the fighting in Bois des Caures see *Walking in the Footsteps of the Fallen*. From here return to your car.

GPS Waypoints Tour No 3

1. N49°13.365' E005°21.736'
2. N49°13.999' E005°21.961'
3. N49°14.531' E005°22.245'
4. N49°14.800' E005°22.344'
5. N49°14.941' E005°22.374'
6. N49°15.027' E005°21.946'
7. N49°15.348' E005°21.841'
8. N49°15.341' E005°22.033'
9. N49°15.274' E005°22.416'
10. N49°15.419' E005°22.861'
11. N49°15.546' E005°23.106'
12. N49°15.531' E005°23.125'
13. N49°15.266' E005°22.406'
14. N49°14.793' E005°21.394'
15. N49°14.500' E005°20.512'
16. N49°13.967' E005°21.111'
17. N49°13.505' E005°21.574'

Tour No 4

Vaux-devant-Damloup, Ravin de la Fausse-Côte, Hardaumont Plateau, Ouvrage de Bezonvaux, Bezonvaux, Ravin des Grands Houyers

Distance: A walking tour of approximately twelve kilometres beginning and ending at the village of Vaux-devant-Damloup and covering sites involved in the successful French offensive of December 1916.

Duration: A whole day's tour, including time for photos and a picnic.

Maps: IGN 3112 ET or IGN Blue Series 3212 Ouest

There are several steep stretches on this tour and a walking stick may be useful. There are no refreshments or toilets and you are unlikely to meet many people, so make sure that your phone is charged and you have everything you need. There is a picnic bench and table close to the chapel at the destroyed village of Bezonvaux.

Warning: when walking this sector visitors should stay on the paths and keep away from the edges of holes. Do not attempt to enter old dugouts, the battery shelters in Ravin de la Fausse-Côte or the Ouvrage de Bezonvaux.

Vaux-devant-Damloup **(1)**
The tour begins at Vaux-devant-Damloup. To reach the start of the walk from Verdun, take the D603 to Étain. The road crosses the Meuse Heights and drops down to the Woëvre Plain at a roundabout close to the village of Eix. At the roundabout take the third exit on the D24 towards Damloup. Drive straight through Damloup and at the crossroads one kilometre further on turn left on the D112 towards Verdun. Continue until you see a cemetery on the right hand side and turn right immediately beyond it at the sign reading *Vaux village détruit*. As you drive towards the chapel ahead, note the monument on the right commemorating the destroyed village of Vaux standing just before you cross a stream.

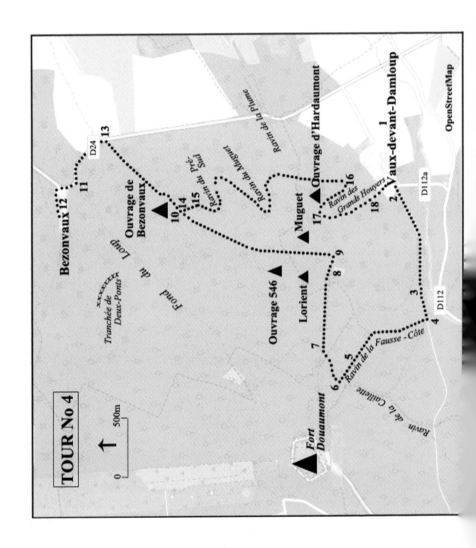

TOUR No 4

0   500m

TOUR No 4

Bezonvaux 12
11
D24
13
Ouvrage de Bezonvaux
10 14
15
Ravin du Pré-Sud
Ravin du Abbinal
Ravin de la Plume
Ouvrage d'Hardaumont
16
17
Muguet
Ravin des Grands Houyers
18
1
Vaux-devant-Damloup
2
D112a
Ouvrage 546
Lorient
9
8
3
D112
4
7
5
6
Ravin de la Fausse - Côte
Ravin de la Caillette
Fort Douaumont
Tranchée de Deux-Ponts
Fond du Loup

Park by the chapel and look back the way you have come. The current village stands on a new site. The old village, which stood by the banks of the stream you have just crossed, was completely destroyed during the Battle of Verdun and the site was included in the Red Zone; this was the name given to former battle areas which could not be restored to pre-war use without excessive expense. However, the embankment for the *Petit Meusien* light railway, which passed through Vaux, had not been destroyed and after the war the lines were relaid to help with battlefield clearance. Temporary accommodation was built and little by little a new village grew up just outside the Red Zone. The water tower by the chapel served the station and a terrace of small houses was built to accommodate workers clearing the battlefields. There is information about the fighting in this area on the information board close to the car park.

Now walk along the railway embankment from the clock tower following the sign to *Monument aux Morts de Vaux*. Pass the village war memorial on the right **(2)** and continue to the orientation table approximately one kilometre ahead **(3)**. The table has an interesting sketch of the area as seen by German balloon observers on the Woëvre Plain before the assault of 21 February 1916. Look across the valley to the other side. Below is the *Etang de Vaux,* the former village millpond. The original village stood in the trees to your left front.

Although it was only a small place, Vaux was important for two reasons.

The war memorial at Vaux-devant-Damloup. *Author's collection*

217

First, it commanded this valley (Ravin de Bazil), which offered easy access from the Woëvre Plain to the inner fortress line and thus to the heart of the French defences. Second, it blocked access to Fort Vaux, which was one of the German objectives in February 1916. It was for these reasons that the fighting here was so vicious. The fort stands at the top of the hill on the opposite side of the valley. In 1916 the valley sides were largely unforested and the Germans attacking down into the Ravin de Bazil from the hillside behind you as they attempted to reach Fort Vaux were fully visible to French defenders on this side, on the flanks and across the valley. The result was slow progress and massive casualties; but German commanders, lulled perhaps by the French confusion of the first days of the battle and the easy capture of Fort Douaumont, did not expect that when the attacks began.

A la mémoire de
LANGEVIN Noë
Caporal au 24ᵉ RI
Mort pour la France
le 17 avril 1916

The orders for the first attempt on Fort Vaux, issued on 27 February 1916, involved attackers sweeping down into the valley at 3pm from the top of the hill behind you, crossing to the other side and capturing the hillside, thus clearing the way for a second wave to move past them and attack Fort Vaux. Rising levels of French artillery fire and an unexpected assault on German positions before the attack was launched showed that the French had recovered from the confusion of the early days of the battle but the orders were maintained. However, at zero hour, French fire was so heavy that only one battalion managed to move off

Corporal Noë Langevin, 24th Infantry, was killed on 17 April 1916, a victim of the prolonged fighting to gain control of the hillside between the war memorial and the orientation table. *Author's collection*

and it was quickly pinned down; a counter attack then inflicted such casualties that the whole operation was called off. A second attempt four days later ran into such determined resistance, supported by strong artillery and machine gun fire, that they were driven back to their starting point with more heavy losses.

This pattern was repeated for weeks. It was 31 March 1916 before the old village was entirely in German hands and it took until 1 June for them to gain full control of the hillside behind you, the mill dam (at the bottom of the steps in front of you) and the dangerous flanking positions that had prevented them for so long from launching a successful attack on Fort Vaux. The memorial by the orientation table records the actions of 116 officers and men of the 1st Battalion of Chasseurs à pied (light infantry) who died resisting one of the many unsuccessful German attempts to gain control of the dam, which was the only firm route across the valley.

Ravin de la Fausse-Côte
Continue ahead for a little under 200 metres and turn right along a level track with forest block 361 on the right and 362 on the left **(4)**. *NB There are two possibilities here; be careful not to take the steep path on the left.* The valley ahead is Ravin de la Fausse-Côte, one of three valleys offering sheltered access between Ravin de Bazil and the Fort Douaumont sector and therefore of great importance during the Battle of Verdun and the scene of bloody fighting. Continue ahead until you reach a sign pointing right and indicating *Batterie du Ravin de la Fausse-Côte* **(5)**. If you are visiting in summer and want to see something of the battery when it is more overgrown, it might be better to carry on past this sign and stop at the next one, as the beaten path from there will take you to a former shelter that is not quite so damaged as the rest of it and will provide a better idea of what it looked like.

Constructed in 1912, this concrete artillery battery was one of several which covered the gap between Fort Douaumont and Fort Vaux. In addition to four gun platforms, there were ammunition niches, magazines and two shelters, each with seating for twenty men. When war broke out it was armed with four short barrelled 155mm guns but during the general transfer of resources from Verdun to other fronts in 1915 it was disarmed and thereafter served as a shelter, dump and command post.

A second battery, which stood on the hillside seventy metres away, must have been rearmed at some time because when a small group from Infantry Regiment 120 reached it on 27 February 1915 four 155mm guns were in situ. The price of their boldness was to be ahead of the general advance and they found themselves cut off in an exposed position that

***Above and below*:** Two of the heavily damaged shelters of the battery in Ravin de la Fausse-Côte. *Author's collection*

could only be resupplied at night. It took until 2 March for the rest of 120th to clear the upper part of this ravine and relieve the little group still grimly holding on.

The thick forest cover makes it impossible to imagine today what it was like here in 1916 but the historian of Reserve Jäger Battalion 4 remembered it clearly:

'This death strewn valley was a frightful sight and it requires an effort to bring the gruesome place to mind again. The rear slope of the valley and the strongly built concrete shelters were subject to such a cascade of iron every day that the ground was churned up two to three metres deep time and time again. There was more or less nothing left of the battery, the old French guns or the forest that once grew here. Fire and iron had turned it all to dust and ashes. As far as the eye could see, all the hillsides and valleys in the Fort Vaux and Fort Douaumont sectors were just as cursed. Apart from us, the fighters, there was no life, no green thing, just a ghastly grey kingdom of death. Our shallow dugouts did not even give us a semblance of protection against the enemy shells.'

The relative shelter offered by this steeply sided ravine meant that it was under constant fire. The machine gunners of Reserve Infantry Regiment 72 were in the front line here in June 1916, which meant suffering day after day:

'...hellish unbroken artillery fire. The sides of the ravine were swamped by the heaviest calibres and the explosions sent shocks far and wide. The whole surface of the ravine was turned over practically every day. We were just in little scrapes; there were only a few properly supported *Stollen* [deep mined dugouts]. Protection against a direct hit was non-existent. The doctors were particularly challenged. The first aid post was a short, low-ceilinged tunnel with space for four to five wounded. It was impossible to dress their wounds inside, so the doctors had to work outside in showers of stones and shell splinters. The stream of wounded hardly ever stopped. As soon as their wounds were dressed the stretcher bearers, who performed an almost superhuman service, carried them away...along the so-called Sanitätsweg [stretcher-bearer path]...It was impossible to maintain a telephone connection and pigeons were used to save the runners.'

Stretcher bearers on the Sanitätsweg between this ravine and a dressing station in a quarry near Fort Douaumont operated under the protection of a Red Cross flag but the machine gunners complained that the flag did not stop French infantry and artillery from firing on them.

It was June before dangerous flanking positions were completely cleared and pioneers could start to excavate the deep dugouts needed to

221

The remains of a stretcher found near the Ouvrage d'Hardaumont. *Author's collection*

house reserves, medical personnel, staff officers, message relay stations, aid posts and dumps of one sort and another. The ravine was crowded and every available inch had to be used, even if that meant excavating under a former French mass grave. 'The stink in this shelter during hot weather can

A German heavy trench mortar in action.
Tom Gudmestad

scarcely be imagined', wrote Hauptmann Spiess, Minenwerfer Company 5, in his contribution to the German pioneers' post-war memoir. The pioneers also excavated a line of trench mortar positions in the steep slopes at the top of the ravine that caused so much devastation that the French brought a mortar battery to Fort Tavannes specifically to deal with it. However, the mortars and their ammunition dumps were so deeply dug into the hillside that the new battery achieved little apart from causing substantial casualties.

When the French launched the offensive of 24 October 1916, this part of the ravine was held by two companies from the 1st Battalion, Infantry Regiment 154. Early that morning, the furious bombardment, which included gas, reached 'insane levels' and by the time the French jumped off German resistance was seriously weakened. Anyone able to get out of the bombardment took refuge underground until the shelling eased but when they emerged they saw French soldiers everywhere. Machine gunners did their best and signal rockets by the boxful called for artillery support but there was little response and finally everyone was ordered to withdraw. 'Now began a race with death' wrote the historian of Infantry Regiment 154, and continued:

> 'Soon the only communication trench …was either shelled flat or blocked by wounded and dead men. To make matters worse, it crossed a steep slope which was under rifle and machine gun fire and that turned our valiant defenders into the sort of target that rarely comes twice. Machine gun fire from enemy planes added to our crushing losses. Hardly anyone came through it unharmed.'

Anyone who did not manage to withdraw in time was rounded up. They included two doctors and the entire medical staff of the 1st Battalion, who had simply continued with their tasks until the French were inside the dressing station.

December 1916
Units from the 133rd Infantry Division had captured this ravine on 24 October 1916 and during the night of 14-15 December they returned here for the second part of the operation. Lined up and ready to go at zero hour on the eastern (right) side of the ravine from the bottom to the top were three Chasseur and four infantry battalions, with four more battalions in the second line. Every formation had undergone specialized training and morale was high despite fierce cold and snow; but the French preparatory bombardment, which ended with the German lines being plastered with 'toads' (French trench mortar shells), provoked a violent reaction that destroyed guns and caused substantial casualties even before they moved off.

General Grüber, commander of the 39th Bavarian Reserve Division on 15 December 1916, who was dismissed by Field Marshal von Hindenburg two days later.

223

The 133rd was facing the 39th Bavarian Reserve Division, which had been transferred to Verdun from the Vosges. During their time in the mountains their losses had been replaced by men aged thirty-five to forty, while a big detachment of young men withdrawn for the Romanian campaign had been replaced by Landsturm – men aged between forty and forty seven, most of whom had never been under fire. While that was acceptable on a quiet front, it was far from experienced enough for Verdun and the four weeks of extra training that they were allowed could not bring them up to scratch.

Private Henri Lacombe
Thirty-three year old Private Henri Lacombe, who disappeared in this area on 15 December 1916, served in 6 Company, 2nd Battalion, 401st Infantry. On 24 October 1916 this ravine was the 401st's final objective and for a while this battery served as the regimental command post. The 401st was made up of men from divisional depots, former wounded and new classes of men from the occupied regions, who between them had received 620 citations for their part in the October offensive. With the October losses made up by a draft of 500 new men from the 1917 class, the regiment had undergone extensive training about which the war diary goes into extravagant detail:

'Rifle and grenade ranges were provided for each battalion. Every man was taught to fire, assemble and disassemble the automatic rifle, the skirmishers acquainted themselves with grenades and thorough training was given to all the specialized units. The regiment received a relief map of the Verdun region and each battalion carried out daily exercises in terrain similar to the coming offensive, which involved incidents requiring officers and NCOs to resolve various problems. An area was found nearby that sufficiently resembled Hardaumont and the ravines to be recaptured and several times the whole regiment rehearsed the planned operation; same order of attack, same distances, same front, enemy trenches and positions clearly represented. Officers and NCOs applied all their intelligence…and the level of training was such that the loss of half or even two thirds of them would not prevent the advance. It can be said without any false modesty that no troops were ever better prepared either physically or as regards training and equipment than the 401st on 10 December'.

Morale was also very high. After taking 1,000 prisoners on 24 October for the loss of only 120 men:

In Memoriam
Henri LACOMBE.
Mort pour la France.
Originaire de la Dordogne,
soldat de la ⬛⬛⬛ compagnie du
401ème R⬛⬛⬛⬛⬛ d'infanterie,
tué à l'enne⬛⬛⬛⬛⬛ disparu le15
décembre 19⬛⬛⬛⬛ le ravin de la
Fausse Côte-sous-Douaumont,
il avait 33 ans.
Sa famille se souvient
11 novembre 2011

The simple family memorial to Private Henri Lacombe, 401st Infantry, who disappeared in this area on 15 December 1916. *Author's collection*

'The Regiment had been cited in Army Orders. The President of the Republic had come in person to attach the Croix de Guerre to the colours. All the Generals had said that the 401st was the finest regiment ever. Our men and our officers agreed…'.

On 15 December 1916, brimming with confidence and fully intending that this operation would bring them the fourragère [lanyard] to add to their Croix de Guerre, the 401st moved off a few minutes before 10am, with the 2nd and 3rd Battalions in the front line. They were heavily laden; in addition to ammunition of various types, flares, rockets, signal cartridges, spades, pickaxes and empty sand bags, they carried five days' reserve rations, two two-litre canteens (for wine and water), entrenching tools, groundsheets, a little bottle of eau-de-vie and a small tin of whale oil (used against frostbite). On that day the casualty list ran to 240 names, with forty four men missing. This simple family memorial was placed here on Armistice Day, 2011.

Hardaumont Plateau
From the battery, continue uphill to the T-junction with the Chemin d'Hardaumont and turn right between blocks 358 and 359 **(6)**. Walk ahead

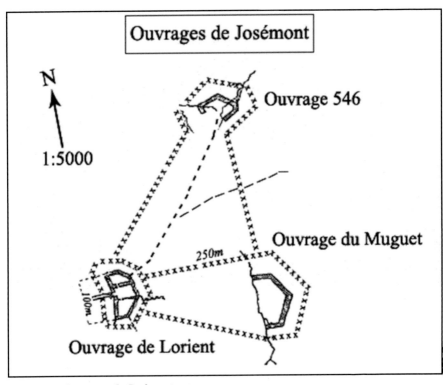

The Ouvrages de Josémont.

for a little over 300 metres until you reach a crossroads in the tracks, then turn right, and walk ahead along a wide grassy ride (the Chemin de la Plume) **(7)**. You are on top of the Meuse Heights, which drop steeply to the Woëvre Plain roughly two kilometres ahead. Continue for just under 700 metres, noting the extensive signs of digging on the left, and **stop** when you reach an open field on the right **(8)**. Stand with your back to the field and face ahead.

The prominent mound at the edge of the opposite side of the track was a French water tower built before the war and used by both sides as an observation post. On 15 December 1916, the 133rd Division's objectives were the five fieldworks on this plateau, the German camps in the sheltered ravines at the edge of the plateau to your right and the ruined village of Bezonvaux some three kilometres away as the crow flies. The most important fieldworks were the Ouvrage de Bezonvaux, which you will visit later, and the inaccessible Ouvrage d'Hardaumont to your right front. There were five fieldworks in all. The Ouvrage

A wartime view of the water tower used by the Germans as an observation post. *Author's collection*

de Bezonvaux and the Ouvrage d'Hardaumont consisted of strong concrete shelters behind earth ramparts protected by a network of wire, while the other three were merely earthworks. Named Lorient, Muguet and Ouvrage 546 but collectively known as the Ouvrages de Josémont, they were constructed in 1913 as a training exercise by a unit of the 9th Génie and comprised earth banks and mined dugouts roofed with heavy logs. Ouvrage 546 was also reinforced with steel bars. On 25 February 1916 German units advancing towards Fort Douaumont found them unmanned and hurriedly garrisoned them before the French could return. The Ouvrage de Bezonvaux will be visited later but the Ouvrage d'Hardaumont is inaccessible.

Ouvrage d'Hardaumont: its capture on 26 February 1916
In February 1916 this plateau was mostly forested but clearings around the Ouvrage d'Hardaumont provided views far and wide. Like the Ouvrage de Bezonvaux, this small work, which was built between 1887–1893 at a total cost of just under 100,000 francs, was a defence against infantry assaults in the direction of Forts Douaumont and Vaux. Smaller than the Ouvrage de Bezonvaux but of very similar design, it had two infantry shelters behind a parapet protected by a field of wire. A water cistern was added in 1903 but a later plan to add a revolving

227

Fort Vaux

Ravin de Bazil

An example of the clear views offered by Hardaumont Plateau. *Tom Gudmestad*

turret for two 75mm guns, two heavy steel observation turrets, a strong concrete barracks with accommodation for infantry and gunners and a double concrete caponier to flank a redesigned ditch was never implemented. In August 1914, the nominal garrison was seventy six infantry, nine sappers, two officers and a telegraphist; the armament was two machine guns model 1907. Both fieldworks were disarmed in 1915 with orders to destroy the wire and the infantry parapet if an enemy approached, so as to remove any obstacles that might prevent its recapture.

It was captured on 26 February 1916 by an assault detachment of infantry, pioneers and machine gunners from Reserve Infantry Regiment 98 and Infantry Regiment 155. Having already captured the Ouvrage de Bezonvaux, they began to work their way forward through the woods, which they described as tangled, trackless and crisscrossed with trenches. They met plenty of resistance but eventually reached the clearing and began to advance towards the fieldwork. As Infantry Regiment 155 soon found out, this made them an easy target, According to their regimental history:

> The companies worked their way forward until they were
> one hundred metres from the Ouvrage d'Hardaumont and the

Above and below: One of the two shelters of the Ouvrage d'Hardaumont remains standing but the other is completely destroyed. *Author's collection*

many other small positions …The Ouvrage was surrounded by an undamaged wire network forty metres wide. That meant we needed artillery support if we were to succeed. But our heavy artillery was silent … The position was critical. Our firing line lay right in front of the enemy work and was completely exposed to fire from positions hidden behind the undamaged wire….There was only one solution: if this hell was to end, the enemy had be cleared out…The First Company lost all its officers in short order; three were killed and the company commander was wounded. There was no time to lose. If necessary, the assault would just have to go ahead without artillery support'.

A machine gun section was ordered forward and opened fire but before the general order to advance could be given:

'A single round from a 210mm mortar smashed in front of the Hardaumont work, leaving a great crater and solving the problem. At a shout from Major Balthasar, everyone rushed wildly forward. Unfortunately, that was the moment that the enemy chose to fire shrapnel with horrible accuracy and the gaps in the ranks increased… As Hauptmann Schön led the 1st and 2nd Battalions through the wire and into the work…some of the garrison left it with their hands up. An officer and 120 men were captured, along with three machine guns. At 3.30pm the German flag was raised on the Ouvrage'.

The flag belonged to an NCO who had carried it since the Kaiser's birthday celebrations in 1914 and frequently expressed the wish to see it flying on a captured French work. His wish was fulfilled at the cost of over 400 casualties. Throughout the Battle of Verdun this plateau offered exceptional observation but no natural cover, so the shelters were reinforced with logs and sandbags but by December 1916 they were destroyed.

Recapture in December 1916
On 15 December 1916 the orders were for the 401st Infantry to clear Muguet and the Ouvrage d'Hardaumont, while the 102nd Chasseurs dealt with Lorient and Ouvrage 546. Jump off was at 10am but four minutes before zero hour somebody shouted 'They're off!' and not wanting to be left behind the first wave of the 401st scrambled forward,

Steel reinforcement in Ouvrage 546. *Author's collection*

A general view of the Ouvrage du Muguet. *Author's collection*

231

to be followed by the second wave and then the 102nd. They reached the rolling barrage two minutes later and bunched up behind it, first and second waves packed together with the rolling barrage in front and German shells falling behind, until the barrage moved on. Smoke and fog meant they had to advance by the compass but sticking close to the line of falling shells they passed through the German front lines, finding only small pockets of resistance. It only took twenty minutes for the 102nd to reach Lorient and round up several hundred prisoners.

Then, changing direction 'as if on the parade ground', they moved on towards Ouvrage 546, charged it at 11am and captured even more prisoners. The battalion commander moved in with his staff and everyone prepared for the next step. On their right the 401st swept through Muguet and the Ouvrage d'Hardaumont, leaving grenadiers

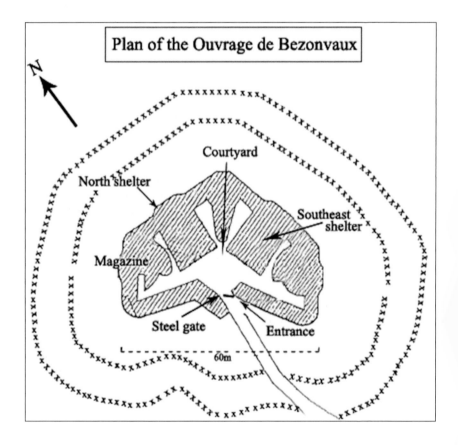

Plan of the Ouvrage de Bezonvaux

Courtyard

North shelter

Southeast shelter

Magazine

Steel gate

Entrance

60m

and light infantry to mop up any resistance and pressed on to their next task, clearing the German camps. So far it had been a great success. Casualties were light, runners were carrying messages in all directions, the telephone lines had not been cut and rations and supplies were arriving.

Now walk ahead for approximately 150 metres, then **turn left (9)** between blocks 351 and 352 and continue for 1500 metres until you reach the signposted entrance to the Ouvrage de Bezonvaux. This is a cleared site and safe to enter provided you exercise normal care.

Ouvrage de Bezonvaux **(10)**
Follow the short track into the centre of the ouvrage and **stop**. Like the Ouvrage d'Hardaumont, this fieldwork stood in a clearing with very extensive views over the Woëvre Plain and the pre-1914 German border, which was less than thirty kilometres to the east. It is the most northerly of all the pre-war permanent works at Verdun and, together with the Ouvrage d'Hardaumont and the three small fieldworks referred to earlier, it formed a centre of resistance and an 'alarm bell' in front of Fort Douaumont and the main line of resistance around Verdun.

Construction began in 1900 after expropriation of the land needed – not only for this site but also the access road and various areas of woodland that blocked necessary sight lines – with many of the labourers lodging in Bezonvaux. It was of roughly triangular shape and comprised an open courtyard protected by an earth rampart forming an infantry parapet and a wide network of wire. In the courtyard, two shelters, each twelve metres long, five metres high and three and a half metres wide, roofed with a thick layer of *'béton spécial'* and several metres of earth, offered accommodation for forty four men lying or 144 sitting. (*Béton spécial* was a specially developed type of concrete reinforced with pebbles which was first used on Fort Douaumont and proved resistant to even the heaviest shelling if used in a thick enough layer.) A third, smaller shelter functioned as a magazine and a water cistern was added in 1903. There was a reinforced entrance with a gate and sentry post but no fixed machine gun position or observation post. The total cost of its construction was 78,299 francs.

When war broke out the nominal garrison was one infantry officer, sixty two men, one telegraphist and two machine guns but, like the other forts and fieldworks at Verdun, it was disarmed in 1915 and thereafter not permanently manned. Like the Ouvrage d'Hardaumont, the infantry parapet and the wire were to be destroyed if the enemy approached.

Magazine   Rampart   Destroyed shelter

Courtyard

The Ouvrage de Bezonvaux. *Author's collection*

A section of the original steel gate lies in the grass on the right as you walk into the former courtyard. Shelling has completely destroyed the entrance, the magazine and one of the shelters; you should not try to access the remaining one.

Capture on 26 February 1916
There was spasmodic shelling here in 1915 but as it occurred at regular hours it did not disturb the garrison's routine; and apart from protecting the entrance and the shelters with tree trunks, planks and sandbags, little changed here until the Battle of Verdun began. Having capturing Bezonvaux village on 25 February 1916, the next step was to clear the fieldworks forming an obstacle to the German advance and, after a night of shelling, the task was given to the assault detachment from Reserve Infantry Regiment 98 and Infantry Regiment 155 that later went on to capture the Ouvrage d'Hardaumont. At 6am on 26 February they moved off quietly, unhindered by French fire from the hillside. The 155th's regimental history described what happened:

'The enemy had not expected the assault but had fled from their commanding and excellently developed positions. What would have happened if a determined enemy had held these

Shelter

almost impregnable positions? The small but dominant and well constructed fieldwork was protected by [wire, blockhouses and trenches]. The assault was such a surprise as to be almost bloodless. The few sentries left behind…were quickly overcome. At 6.45am the fieldwork was in our hands'.

Staff officers moved in immediately, a first aid post was set up and the ouvrage became a relay station for troops moving to or from the front, with a reserve company stationed inside and others in dugouts outside. Every corner was occupied. There was a signalling station, a pioneer park, a ration dump with 6,000 rations and in March 1916 fourteen mounted despatch riders with sixteen horses. Although offering shelter, a hot drink and time for a cigarette before moving on, the ouvrage was not particularly pleasant as the cramped space quickly overflowed; and by mid-April 1916 it was so jammed with staff and liaison officers, runners, telephonists, orderlies, and others as to hinder the passage of orders and the smooth movement of troops. Matters were quickly improved by a Grenadier officer who divided up the available space and got the pioneers to build sheds. The stream of stretcher bearers was continuous and when there was not enough room for them inside the shelters they waited outside and hoped to survive.

A German medical detachment practises for the real thing. Compare the shape of the middle stretcher with the one found near the Ouvrage d'Hardaumont. *Tom Gudmestad*

Father Veidt, a priest serving with Reserve Division 21, experienced a gas bombardment here during the summer of 1916:

'The whole courtyard …was full of wounded. The explosions of the enemy shells were coming nearer. Splinters whistled through the air. Anyone who did not need to be outside sought shelter inside. The doctors allowed everyone to pack in but there was not space for everyone. Some of the wounded had to remain outside. We covered them as well as we could but the courtyard was a frightening place [and] secretly we asked ourselves what would happen if a shell landed in it? We came within a hair of it dozens of times…Fortunately, it was not long before an ambulance took some of our wounded away. But half an hour later it was full again.'

The dead were buried in a little cemetery nearby. As the historian of Infantry Regiment 364 wrote:

'All the misery of the battlefield accumulated in the Ouvrage de Bezonvaux. Anyone emerging bruised and battered from the almighty fury of the front ended up here.…'

The ouvrage offered a short period of rest from that fury and when time was up it was not easy to find the courage to brave the bombardment again.

236

Recapture in December 1916

On 15 December 1916 the Ouvrage de Bezonvaux was defended by elements of the 39th Bavarian Infantry Division. The task of recapturing it had fallen to the 116th Chasseurs and despite the difficulties of advancing over snow covered and heavily shelled ground, through torn wire and metal picket posts, they made good progress. Shortly after jump off they reached the top of the plateau and, drawing level with Lorient, deployed along a 500 metre front. At 11.20am, with a heavy barrage clearing the way ahead of them, all three companies advanced towards this ouvrage. While 1 Company dealt with positions on the right of the ouvrage, including a camp in a nearby ravine, 2 Company attacked the ouvrage itself. The war diary reported that:

> 'The fort had been much damaged by our artillery but it had not been destroyed. Some shelters were still intact in the centre, including a strong arched one. The garrison had taken refuge there and put up lively resistance. Incendiary grenades put an end to it. The defenders surrendered in great number'.

Fearing a counter attack, the new occupants placed machine guns on the parapet, dug hasty trenches and burned all relevant papers. As night fell several groups of Germans tried to slip past the ouvrage but machine guns and rifle grenades held them off and the position remained in French hands until the Armistice.

The thickness of the concrete in the remaining shelter gives an idea of its original strength and also of the power of the shelling. *Author's collection*

Although damaged, it was still useful. The remaining shelter offered protection against light calibre shelling, a tunnel excavated by the Germans to provide external access away from the main gate was still usable, the parapet was not entirely destroyed and the wire was still partially intact. Trenches and external positions were also in reasonable condition and with repair they again formed a centre of

Bezonvaux War Memorial. *Author's collection*

resistance. The Germans were aware of its importance and on at least two occasions managed to get small groups of men up to the wire but were driven off.

Bezonvaux War Memorial (11)
Now return to the track and turn left downhill, noting the enormous extent of the view. The extensive forests on the plain ahead provided the Germans with camouflage and space for barracks, dumps, railways, command posts, sawmills, kitchens, stables, workshops, cinemas and anything else they might need. Continue downhill to the D24, where there is an information board about the Ouvrage de Bezonvaux, then turn left, walk along the road for just under 500 metres and **stop** at the war memorial. This was inaugurated in September 1932 and commemorates the destroyed village, the men of Bezonvaux who died in the war, civilian victims, and men from elsewhere who fell in the area. The central plaque shows a view of the old main street and replaces the original bronze plaque which was, alas, stolen some years ago. A plaque on the left side records the names of the men who died here on 14-15 June 1940. The small granite marker stone at the roadside topped with a French helmet was one of ninety six similar markers erected after the war on important sites along the old front line. This one was the gift of then French colony of Senegal and it marks the French front line at the start of the Meuse-Argonne offensive of September 1918.

Fond du Loup
Between the war memorial and the granite marker is the Fond du Loup, a wide valley of enormous importance to the Germans because it offered access towards the Fort Douaumont sector. It was commanded by the Ouvrage de Bezonvaux on the left and the Tranchée de Deux-Ponts on the right, and it was the latter which held up the 321st Infantry on 15 December 1916. The idea of attacking a strongly held position at night in December and starting from the other side of the valley, as described in Chapter 1, must have seemed unlikely to succeed; but perhaps its very unexpectedness is the reason why it did.

Bezonvaux (12)
With the granite marker on your left, follow the D24 around the bend and turn left at the signs reading *Bezonvaux village détruit* and *Chapelle de Bezonvaux*. There is a memorial to André Maginot and his men on the left just after you turn towards the chapel and information about the village on the board by the stream and along the memorial path.

When war broke out the 149 inhabitants of Bezonvaux were engaged in trade, agriculture and crafts, such as stone masonry, tailoring, nail making, milling and brewing. On 27 July 1914 there were a few soldiers on leave in the village when a telegram arrived, requiring them immediately to rejoin their units. Two days later the horses were mobilized and call-up papers were received by the men who had recently completed their military service.

Soon afterwards the first soldiers were seen in the district. Among them was André Maginot, a Député [member of parliament] and former Under-Secretary of State, who had immediately joined his regiment, the 44th Territorials, as a private soldier, despite his age and parliamentary immunity. Mid-August saw him bivouacking with his company in a clearing on the top of the Meuse Heights not far from the Tranchée de Deux-Ponts, from where they could see German movements on the plain. At this period of the war the lines were not yet fixed and Maginot saw an opportunity to interfere with the enemy patrols assigned to explore the region. With his high level contacts he had no difficulty obtaining official permission to recruit an 'elite section' of men with unusual skills:

'I cannot say that everyone in the section was an irreproachable gentleman…but never mind! They were all brave, ready for anything and careless of danger. I knew that with them I could try anything…Mostly local men, knowing the country like the back of their hands, loving hunting more than anything, more or less poachers by temperament, daredevils and tearaways…Many of them were attracted to us by our relative liberty and freedom from the daily drudgery of military life.'

Maginot and his men took up residence in the former café in Bezonvaux and for three months they patrolled the deserted villages on the plain, operating between the lines, lying in wait for German patrols, informing on their movements, and fighting.

His superiors were pleased and Maginot was promoted to sergeant but German commanders were determined to put an end to his activities and on 9 November he and his group were ambushed. One of the men killed that day was thirty five year old Nicolas Gille, a native of Bezonvaux; his body was never found and his name appears on the war memorial. Maginot was badly wounded in the affray and it was nightfall before his remaining men could get him out. Although that was the end of Maginot's military career, his exploits had made him famous throughout France. After the war Maginot returned to politics and held a number of government posts, including as Minister of Pensions. Believing that

The memorial at Maucourt-sur-Ornes that commemorates the ambush of Maginot and his men on 9 November 1914. *Author's collection*

the Treaty of Versailles did not provide France with sufficient security, he advocated the building of a new line of defensive fortifications along its eastern border. This became known as the Maginot Line. He died in 1932 before the line was completed and is buried in his home town of Revigny-sur-Ornain. The memorial close to Fort Souville, inaugurated in 1935, shows the wounded Maginot, an immensely tall man, being carried away on a rifle by two of his men.

Although most of the inhabitants left Bezonvaux in August 1914, a handful of civilians remained until mid-February 1916 despite random shelling. On 25 February the village was defended by infantry and machine gunners from the 3rd Battalion, 44th Infantry, while the 2nd Battalion held positions on the plain. That morning the Germans launched a furious bombardment on Bezonvaux and the surrounding area, isolating it and preventing the arrival of reinforcements. As the defences were smashed, new ones were thrown up only to be smashed in their turn, and gradually the village was surrounded. The battalion commander was wounded, his adjutant – a sixty-six year old volunteer – was also wounded, and with the position hopeless his replacement finally ordered a withdrawal. By then the one remaining line of retreat was

The Maginot Memorial on the D112 near Fort Souville. *Author's collection*

A German image of a captured French machine gun post at Bezonvaux. *Tom Gudmestad*

covered by a German machine gun and only about thirty men managed to escape; according to the war diary, the 2nd and 3rd Battalions and the machine gun companies were almost wiped out.

Until it was recaptured on 16 December 1916, Bezonvaux formed a logistical and supply centre of the first importance for the Germans, with batteries, field kitchens, ammunition and supply dumps of all kinds, underground camps in the hillsides, medical services in the cellars of the chateau and a possibility of evacuation by light railway or road. The area was constantly shelled and as a result most movement took place at night. Ammunition columns, ration and supply parties and reserves going up to the front crossed runners, the stretcher bearers, walking wounded and others coming away, and traffic jams were frequent along the constantly repaired and debris strewn roads and tracks.

After the war

The destruction of Bezonvaux was so great that after the war the government decided that it should never be rebuilt and any salvageable debris was removed for use elsewhere. The site became part of the Red Zone and former inhabitants were not allowed to return. Nevertheless, from 1926 to 1940 there was a temporary population of foreign workers here, mostly Italians and Poles employed in clearing the battlefield and planting pine trees. That came to an end in 1940 and since then no one has lived here. Like the other destroyed villages, the site is administered by a mayor (currently appointed by the Prefect) assisted by two councillors. The only new buildings are the Maginot Memorial, the chapel, which stands on the site of the former church, and the war memorial, both of which were inaugurated in 1932. The whole site was completely overgrown for many years and it is thanks to the efforts of one of the recent mayors that the village and the Ouvrage de Bezonvaux have been cleared. At the time of writing, forestry work connected with the plague of Bark Beetle has cleared one side of the site, while winter storms have damaged some trees along the memorial path.

Clearing the camps
From Bezonvaux return to the D24, turn right and retrace your steps to the access road to the Ouvrage de Bezonvaux (13), then follow the track uphill. Continue past the entrance to the ouvrage for 150 metres and turn left downhill (14) and after another 150 metres turn right along a level path (15). Continue to the head of the first ravine and **stop**.

Cutting into this side of the Meuse Heights are three valleys, Ravin du Pré-Sud, Ravin du Muguet and Ravin de la Plume, whose steep sides offered sheltered space for camps and deep mined dugouts. This is

Using incendiary grenades to clear the camps. *Author's collection*

244

the Ravin de Pré-Sud, in which the Germans had installed permanent kitchens to supply the front lines.

The task of clearing the first two ravines had fallen to the 401st Infantry and they were determined to do a good job. Bremen Camp in the Ravin du Pré-Sud was cleared with the aid of machine gunners from the 116th Chasseurs, who swept the entrances to the dugouts and kept the occupants inside until the 401st's grenadiers arrived. The camp was under heavy flanking fire from a position by the side of the D24 and although the action was successful, in the end it came at considerable cost, which may explain why the regiment 'only took eighty prisoners. The rest were killed'. Four guns, one of them heavy, were also put out of action.

The track loops around the top of the ravine and continues to the Ravin du Muguet. Coblenz Camp, which housed troops on standby, was on the south side of this ravine. According to the war diary, there was no resistance and the camp was cleared in thirty minutes, with over 400 prisoners taken and seven guns put out of action. Cologne Camp in the Ravin de la Plume, which cannot be seen from the track, was cleared by a party from the 107th Chasseurs, who took 900 prisoners, collected a huge haul of arms and equipment of all types, and cleared fifteen deep mined dugouts as well as scores of lighter ones. When incendiary grenades failed to blow up the entrances, the artillery lent a hand. At the end of the day, the 107th's losses of 31% were typical of all those that had taken part in the operation.

Return to Vaux-devant-Damloup
Continue to the T-junction with the Chemin de la Plume **(16)**, then turn right between blocks 351 and 356. Pass the sign for the Ouvrage d'Hardaumont and after roughly one hundred metres turn left into the Ravin des Grands Houyers, heading downhill **(17)** between blocks 357 and 356. This will take you back to your car.

As a valley providing access to the Ravin de Bazil and the Vaux sector, this route was of immense importance to German troops moving to or from the front line during the Battle of Verdun and like the Ravin de la Fausse-Côte it remained under constant fire and was regarded by German troops as another of the awful death paths they had to use. Fort Vaux is on the opposite horizon as you walk down the valley. There are signs of digging on both sides of the ravine, particularly on the right a short way down from the top where there is a clear terrace and a line of collapsed dugout entrances.

Ravin des Grands Houyers
After capturing the Ouvrage d'Hardaumont on 25 February1916, a small group of men from Infantry Regiment 155 Infantry raced down

this ravine and found no one about. Without reinforcement they could do nothing, so they returned to the plateau, despite finding a 240mm naval gun in a concrete emplacement at the bottom of the hill. It was 8 March before the emplacement was occupied and the ravine was finally cleared three days later. On 15 December 1916 the gun was recaptured despite shelling and enfilade fire from German positions on the Woëvre Plain.

There were two 240mm guns at Verdun in 1916. Both had been ordered by the Peruvian government before the war but they were diverted here when the need for heavy artillery became clear and they were always known as the Peru guns. Work on the emplacement and on the spur line from the light railway through Vaux began in January 1915 and the gun was in place one month later. Officially named Marie-Louise but known to men as 'La Redoutable', it was served by two NCOs and forty two sailors under the command of *Capitaine de vaisseau* Aubert. The observation post was on the Hardaumont Plateau – possibly the one you saw earlier – and there was also aerial observation.

The first round was fired on 5 February 1915 and thereafter the gun was principally used against railways, important villages and

The 240mm gun in Ravin des Grands Houyers.

Partial remains of a heavy concrete structure in Ravin des Grands Houyers.
Author's collection

German heavy artillery, such as the 420mm howitzer which shelled Fort Douaumont in February 1915 and a 380mm 'Long Max' naval gun. German aerial observers soon spotted it and the question arose of whether to move it to a new position; but as it was too useful where it was and constructing a new emplacement meant a great deal of work, it was left in position and protected by a mobile casemate of reinforced concrete. Once the assault began, supplying it became difficult but it remained in action despite a number of casualties. However, by 25 February the gun could no longer be supplied and Aubert was ordered to expend all his remaining ammunition and blow it up. This took longer than expected because the failure of the safety fuze meant that it had to be wrapped in rags soaked in petrol and stuffed directly into the breech before it would work.

The damaged gun remained in position as a tourist attraction after the war but sometime later it was scrapped, possibly by the Germans during the Second World War. Few traces can be seen today. In February 2020 some heavy concrete remains were visible a short way from the path on the right **(18)** (where it has levelled out and before the houses), with several concrete slats and iron bars on the left, but logging debris and thick summer growth may hide them at other times. The gun's existence is recalled in the name of the street leading into the ravine from the bottom of the valley – *Allée de la Pièce de Marine* – Naval Gun Way.

GPS Waypoints Tour No 4

1. N49°12.594' E005°28.252'
2. N49°12.555' E005°28.113'
3. N49°12.477' E005°27.460'
4. N49°12.453' E005°27.297'
5. N49°12.792' E005°27.017'
6. N49°12.867' E005°26.859'
7. N49°12.945' E005°27.090'
8. N49°12.911' E005°27.633'
9. N49°12.890' E005°27.747'
10. N49°13.659' E005°28.119'
11. N49°14.112' E005°28.281'
12. N49°14.200' E005°28.224'
13. N49°13.976' E005°28.567'
14. N49°13.597' E005°28.055'
15. N49°13.609' E005°28.175'
16. N49°12.841' E005°28.260'
17. N49°12.954' E005°28.049'
18. N49°12.708' E005°28.018'

Useful Addresses

General information

Office de Tourisme, Address: Place de la Nation, 55106 Verdun.
Tel. + 33 3 29 86 14 18
Website: www.tourisme-verdun.com
Email: contact@tourisme-verdun.com

Battlefield sites

Fort Douaumont and Fort Vaux
Current opening times and tariffs are to be found on www.tourisme-verdun.com
or on http://verdun-meuse.fr/index.php?qs=fr/lieux-et-visites/les-forts-de-douaumont-et-de-vaux

Please note that opening times may change without warning. Outside visits are possible at any time, including when the forts are closed.

Mémorial de Verdun (Fleury Memorial museum)
Address: 1, Ave. Du Corps Européen, 55100 Fleury-devant-Douaumont
Tel. + 33 3 29 84 35 34
http://www.memorialdeverdun.fr/

The Ossuary
Address: 55100 Douaumont, France.
Tel. + 33 3 29 84 54 81, fax + 33 3 29 86 56 54,
Mobile + 33 (0) 6 24 73 03 90
http://www.verdun-douaumont.com
Opening times are very variable, so please consult the website before visiting.

Verdun city sites

Monument de la Victoire et au Poilu de Verdun
Rue Mazel, Verdun.
The imposing *Monument to Victory and to the Soldier of Verdun* takes the form of a cloaked and helmeted warrior who is facing east and thrusting his sword into the ground against the invader. The crypt under the monument is open from 1 April – 30 September. Entrance is free.

249

Citadelle Souterraine (Underground Citadel)
Seven kilometres of underground galleries forming a major logistical base throughout the Battle of Verdun. The visit also includes the room in which the French Unknown Soldier was chosen.
Address: Avenue du 5ème R.A.P., Verdun, France.
Tel. + 33 3 29 84 84 42
For opening times and tariffs, please consult the website:
http://www.citadelle-souterraine-verdun.fr/
Note: All visits must be reserved in advance.

Other sites in the area

Souilly
Musée de la Voie Sacrée
22 Voie Sacrée,
55220 Souilly
Tel. +33 3 29 80 52 76
www.souilly.fr/public/
Consult the website for opening times.

Tranchée de Chattancourt: interesting reconstructed trench system at the foot of the Mort-Homme
8 Rue de Baley, 55100 Chattancourt
Phone: 06 64 77 04 67
www.tranchee-verdun.com
email: contact@tranchee-verdun.com

Camp Marguerre : A German encampment and experimental concrete production station in the Bois de Spincourt, near Muzeray. N49°17.422' E005°34.088'

Site of 380mm 'Long Max' naval gun: Not far from Camp Marguerre in the Bois de Warphémont, near Duzey. : N49°21.558' E 005°36.339'

Ouvrage de la Falouse
The last permanent fieldwork to be built at Verdun, wonderfully restored.
Address: Lieu-dit Le Plat d'Houillon, 55100 Dugny-sur-Meuse, France.
N49°07.313' E 005°24.037'
Tel: 06.83.27.13.34.
http://www.ouvragedelafalouse.fr/
Email: lafalouse@orange.fr

1 April–30 September: 9–12 and 1.30–5, 1 October–11 November 9–12
Other times by appointment.

Moro Lager/Camp Moreau, Vienne le Chateau

A well restored German camp. To arrange visits contact the: Maison du
Pays d'Argonne, Rue St. Jacques, 51800 Vienne le Château, France, tel.
+ 33 3 26 60 49 40.

https://www.valleemoreau.com/en/

Email: mpa@argonne.fr

Butte de Vauquois

A wonderfully preserved site, the scene of intense mine warfare, not to be
missed. The craters may be visited at any time but to visit the museum and the
underground installations contact: **Les Amis de Vauquois et de sa Région:**
Address: 1 rue d'Orléans, 55270 Vauquois, France, http://www.butte-
vauquois.fr/

Citadel de Montmédy

A Vauban citadel on a hilltop site, first fortified in 1227. Montmédy was
the intended destination of Louis XVI and Marie-Antoinette on their flight
from Paris in 1791, which ended with their arrest at Varennes-en-Argonne.

Main de Massiges

A superbly reconstructed site on the Main de Massiges, the scene of
desperate fighting in the Battles of Champagne.

http://www.lamaindemassiges.com/ meuse-argonne1918@hotmail.com
lamaindemassiges@hotmail.fr

Private WWI Museums

Romagne sous Montfaucon: http://www.romagne14-18.com/index.
php/en/

Extraordinary and thought provoking, see the website for opening times.
Guided visits by appointment.

Montfaucon d'Argonne: meuse-argonne1918@hotmail.com
Address: 5 rue de l'Argonne, 55270 Montfaucon d'Argonne, France.
A great collection with a different focus from the Romagne museum.
Also offers accommodation and battlefield tours. See the website for
opening times.

American sites

WWI Montfaucon American Monument

Montfaucon d'Argonne.

Tel: +33 (0)3 29 85 14 18
For opening times, see the website:
http://www.abmc.gov/cemeteries-memorials/europe/montfaucon-american-monument

Meuse-Argonne American Cemetery and Memorial, with information centre
Rue du Général Pershing, 55110, Romagne-sous-Montfaucon
Tel: +33 (0)3 29 85 14 18
http://www.abmc.gov/cemeteries-memorials/europe/meuse-argonne-american-cemetery

Further Reading

As the Second Battle of Verdun has received little attention from historians, the following are suggested as general background:

In English

Verdun – The Price of Glory, Alistair Horne (London, Macmillan & Co. Ltd., 1962)

German Strategy and the Path to Verdun, Robert T. Foley (Cambridge University Press, 2005)

Verdun, Marshal Pétain (London, Elkin Mathews & Marrot, Ltd. 1930)

They shall not pass. The French Army on the Western Front 1914–1918, Ian Sumner (Barnsley, Pen & Sword Books, 2012)

My War Experiences, Crown Prince William of Germany (London, Hurst & Blackett, 1922)

American fighters in the Foreign Legion 1914–1918, Paul Ayres Rockwell (Boston and New York, Houghton Mifflin Company, 1930)

History of the American Field Service in France "Friends of France" 1914–1917, told by its Members, (Boston & New York, Houghton Mifflin Company, The Riverside Press Cambridge, 1920

Dare call it treason, Richard M. Watt (London, Chatto & Windus, 1964)

Flesh and Steel During the Great War, Michel Goya, translated Andrew Uffindell (Barnsley, Pen & Sword Military, 2018)

Fort Douaumont – Verdun, Christina Holstein (Battleground Europe series; Barnsley, Pen & Sword Books, 2002)

Fort Vaux, Christina Holstein (Battleground Europe series; Barnsley, Pen & Sword Books, 2011)

The Left Bank, Christina Holstein (Battleground Europe series; Barnsley, Pen & Sword Books, 2016)

Walking Verdun: A Guide to the Battlefield, Christina Holstein (Battleground Europe series; Barnsley, Pen & Sword Books, 2009)

Walking in the Footsteps of the Fallen: Verdun 1916, Christina Holstein (Battleground Europe series; Barnsley, Pen & Sword Books, 2019)

In French

Verdun 1914–1918, Jacques Péricard (Librairie de France, 110, Boulevard Saint-Germain, Paris VI, 1934)

Verdun 1916. Le point de vue français, Allain Bernède (Editions Cénomane, Le Mans, 2002)

Nicole Mangin: une Lorraine au cœur de la Grande Guerre, Jean-Jacques Schneider (Nancy, Editions Place Stanislas, 2011)

Vadelaincourt 1914-1918, E O Lemaire, Franck Meyer (Verdun, Connaissance de la Meuse, 2015)

In German

Verdun 1916: Urschlacht des Jahrhunderts, Olaf Jessen (Munich, Verlag C H Beck oHG, 2014)

Verdun: Die Schlacht und der Mythos, German Werth (Augsburg, Weltbild Verlag, 1990)

Select Bibliography

French sources:
Les Armées Françaises dans la Grande Guerre, Service Historique, Ministère de la Guerre, Tome IV : Verdun et la Somme, Vol. 3 (Paris, Imprimerie Nationale, 1926) ; Tome V : L'offensive d'avril 1917. Les opérations à objectifs limités (1 Novembre 1916 – 1 Novembre 1917), Vol. 1 (Paris, Imprimerie Nationale, 1926) ; Vol. 2 (Paris, Imprimerie Nationale, 1937) ; Tome V1 : L'hiver 1917 – 1918. L'offensive allemande (1 novembre 1917 – 18 juillet 1918), Vol. 1 (Paris, Imprimerie Nationale, 1931)

War Diaries [Journaux des marche et opérations]
Service Historique de la Défense references are given in brackets:

Corps
XIII corps d'armée: JMO 1 juillet – 31 décembre 1917 (26N 140/6)
XV corps d'armée: JMO 1 janvier 1917 – 28 août 1918 (26N 155/5)
XVI corps d'armée: JMO 8 juin – 6 septembre 1917 (26N 160/3)
XXXII corps d'armée: JMO 11 juillet 1917 – 27 mai 1918 (26N 208/10)

Divisions
25ᵉ division d'infanterie: JMO 20 juin 1917 – 31 juillet 1919
(26N 311/4)
31ᵉ division d'infanterie: JMO 1 janvier 1916 – 31 mai 1918
(26N 321/4)
37ᵉ division d'infanterie: JMO 27 septembre 1915 – 17avril 1916 (26N 330/4)
42ᵉ division d'infanterie: JMO 13 juillet 1917 – 31 août 1918
(26N 342/6)
72ᵉ division d'infanterie: JMO 27 août 1915 – 12 août 1916 (397/2)
123ᵉ division d'infanterie: JMO 3 mai 1917 – 9 juillet 1918 (26N 424/4)
126ᵉ division d'infanterie: JMO 12 février – 23 septembre 1917
(26N 429/3
165ᵉ division d'infanterie: JMO 5 décembre 1916 – 24 janvier 1919
(26N 457/1)

Brigades
143ᵉ brigade d'infanterie: JMO 9 février – 31 décembre 1916
(26N 533/12)

Regiments
Infantry
6ᵉ régiment d'infanterie: JMO 9 août 1916 – 14 septembre 1919 (26N 578/2)
12ᵉ régiment d'infanterie: JMO 1 janvier – 31 août 1917 (26N 585/11)
42ᵉ régiment d'infanterie: JMO 17 octobre 1917 – 31 janvier 1918 (26N 628/16)
44ᵉ régiment d'infanterie territoriale: JMO 1 août 1914 – 27 mars 1915 (26N 784/1)
54ᵉ régiment d'infanterie territoriale: JMO 28 août 1915 – 16 avril 1916 (26N 785/14)
55ᵉ régiment d'infanterie: JMO 24 février 1917 – 9 octobre 1918 (26N 644/16)
60ᵉ régiment d'infanterie: JMO 28 janvier 1915 – 25 juillet 1916 (26N 652/2)
81ᵉ régiment d'infanterie: JMO 1 janvier 1917 – 2 juin 1918 (26N 664/12)
83ᵉ régiment d'infanterie: JMO 1 janvier 1917 – 25 avril 1918 (26N 665/8)
96ᵉ régiment d'infanterie: JMO 4 août – 30 décembre 1917 (26N 672/5)
98ᵉ régiment d'infanterie: JMO 28 août 1917 – 17 mai 1918 (26N 672/27)
121ᵉ régiment d'infanterie: JMO 1 janvier – 31 décembre 1917 (26N 683/13)
122ᵉ régiment d'infanterie: JMO 1 mai 1917 – 1 janvier 1920 (26N 684/5)
154ᵉ régiment d'infanterie: JMO 1 juin 1915 – 5 février 1920 (26N 698/2)
155ᵉ régiment d'infanterie: JMO 31 mai 1916 – 20 octobre 1917 (26N 699/4)
168ᵉ régiment d'infanterie: JMO 20 septembre – 31 décembre 1917 (26N 706/11)
169ᵉ régiment d'infanterie: JMO 28 mai – 31 décembre 1917 (26N 707/9)
173ᵉ régiment d'infanterie: JMO 16 janvier 1916 – 18 décembre 1919 (26N 710/1)
211ᵉ régiment d'infanterie: JMO 1 janvier – 14 avril 1916 (26N 715/21)
259ᵉ régiment d'infanterie: JMO 18 août 1914 – 2 avril 1916 (26N 730/6)
287ᵉ régiment d'infanterie: JMO 1 janvier – 29 août 1917 (26N 739/6)
321ᵉ régiment d'infanterie: JMO 13 septembre – 31 décembre 1916 (26N 749/12)

324ᵉ régiment d'infanterie: JMO 24 octobre 1914 – 6 juillet 1916 (26N 750/4)
365ᵉ régiment d'infanterie: JMO 20 janvier – 19 juin 1916 (26N 762/11)
401ᵉ régiment d'infanterie: JMO 21 octobre – 31 décembre 1916 (26N 766/2)
412ᵉ régiment d'infanterie: JMO 19 août 1917 – 25 décembre 1918 (26N 769/3)

Tirailleurs algériens
4ᵉ régiment: JMO 1 juin 1917 –30 avril 1918 (26N 848/1)
7ᵉ régiment de marche: JMO 25 mai 1915 –16 septembre 1919 (26N 850/6)

Zouaves
3ᵉ régiment: JMO 15 février 1917 – 24 août 1919 (26N 838/14)
8ᵉ régiment: JMO 1 mars 1917 – 15 juin 1918 (26N 842/4)

Légion Etrangère
Régiment de marche de la Légion Etrangère: JMO 1 janvier – 31 décembre 1917 (26N 862/8)

Battalions
Chasseurs à pied
32ᵉ battalion de chasseurs à pied: JMO 28 février 1915 – 31 décembre 1916 (26N 826/31)
102ᵉ battalion de chasseurs à pied: JMO 2 septembre 1915 – 31 décembre 1916 (26N 835/1)
107ᵉ battalion de chasseurs à pied: JMO 8 mai 1915 – 31 décembre 1916 (26N 835/5)
116ᵉ battalion de chasseurs à pied: JMO 21 mai 1915 – 31 décembre 1916 (26N 835/10)

Regimental histories
Le 2ᵉ régiment de marche de Tirailleurs: Souvenirs de Guerre 1914-1918, Jules Carbonel, Imprimeur-Librairie-Editeur, Ancienne Maison Bastide-Jourdan, Algers, 1922
http://gallica.bnf.fr/ark:/12148/bpt6k6447026p
Historique du 2ᵉ régiment de marche de Zouaves du 2 août 1914 au 11 novembre 1918, Henri Charles-Lavauzelle, 124 Boulevard Saint-German, Paris, 1924
http://gallica.bnf.fr/ark:/12148/bpt6k63583121
Historique du 254ᵉ régiment d'infanterie, Fournier, 264 Boulevard Saint Germain, Paris 1920

http://gallica.bnf.fr/ark:/12148/bpt6k6214742z
*Historique du 362ᵉ régiment d'infanterie pendant la guerre 1914 –1918,
Imprimerie Berger-Levrault, Nancy-Paris-Strasbourg*
https://argonnaute.parisnanterre.fr/ark:/14707/a011403267962fSyAEw/
ebe07afead

General background
*Verdun. Le premier choc à la 72ᵉ division. Brabant-Haumont-le Bois
des Caures 21-24 février 1916,* Lieutenant Colonel A. Grasset
(Berget-Levrault, 1926)
Le Service de Santé de l'Armée Française. Verdun 1916, Dr Jean-Jacques
Schneider, (Editions Serpenoise, BP 70090, 57004 Metz Cedex 1, 2007)
*La Direction des Services Automobiles et la Motorisation des Armées
Françaises (1914–1919),* Rémy Porte (Charles Lavauzelle, 2004)
*French Strategic and Tactical Bombardment Forces of World War
1,* René Martel, translated by Allen Suddaby, edited by Steven
Suddaby, (The Scarecrow Press, Inc., 2007)
*Sacrifié pour Verdun: Bezonvaux, village détruit pendant la Grande
Guerre*, Jean Laparra, Jean-Claude Laparra, (Verdun, Connaissance
de la Meuse, 2006)

German sources:
Der Weltkrieg 1914-1918, Vol. 10: Die Operationen des Jahres 1916
(Berlin, E S Mittler & Sohn, 1936); Vol.11: Die Kriegführung im
Herbst 1916 und im Winter 1916/17 (Berlin, E S Mittler & Sohn,
1938); Vol. 13: Die Kriegführung im Sommer und Herbst 1917
(Berlin, E S Mittler & Sohn, 1942)

Regimental histories
Das k. B. Ersatz-Regiment Nr. 1, Alfred Enzinger, (München, Verlag
Max Schick, 1930)
*Das 4. Badische Infanterie-Regiment Prinz Wilhelm Nr. 112 im
Weltkrieg,* Oberleutnant Otto Schiel (Oldenburg i.O./Berlin, Druck
von Paul Braus, Heidelberg, 1927)
*Das 5. Badische Infanterie-Regiment Nr. 113 im Weltkriege 1914 –
18,* Udo von Rundstedt (Ratzeburg i. Lbg., Lauenburgischer
Heimatsverlag, 1933)
*Das Grenadier-Regiment Graf Kleist von Nollendorf
(1.Westpreußisches) No. 6, Deutsche Tat im Weltkriege, Band 19,*
Doring von Gottberg (Berlin, Verlag Bernard & Graefe, 1934)
Garde-Infanterie-Regiment Nr. 7, Deutsche Tat im Weltkriege, Band 5,
Otto von Kries (Berlin, Verlag Bernard & Graefe, 1934)

Die Geschichte des Reserve-Infanterie-Regiments Nr. 24 1914 bis 1918, Kameradschaft Reserve-Infanterie-Regiment 24 (Berlin, Druck und Verlag: Wilhelm F. Beese Verlagsgesellschaft m.b.H.)

Das Füsilier-Regiment Prinz Heinrich von Preußen (Brandenburgisches) Nr. 35 im Weltkriege, Verein ehemaliger Offiziere des Regiments, (Berlin, Verlag Tradition Wilhelm Kolk, 1929)

Die Geschichte des Reserve-Infanterie-Regiments Nr. 35, Kamerardschaftlichen Vereiningung R-I-R 35, (Berlin, Volkskraft Verlagsgesellschaft, 1935)

Das Infanterie-Regiment Vogel von Falckenstein (7. Westfälisches) Nr.56 im Großen Kriege 1914-18, Dr phil Martin Schultz (Berlin, Albrecht Blau Verlag, 1926)

Die Geschichte des Reserve-Infanterie-Regiments Nr.57 im Weltkriege 1914 1918, Friedrich Kölling (Wuppertal-Ronsdorf, Graphische Kunstanstal Ernst Scholl, 1934)

4. Magdeburgische Infanterie-Regiment Nr. 67, Oberstudienrat Dr Eduard Simon (Oldenburg, Verlag Stalling, 1926/27)

Kriegsgeschichte des Königlich Preußischen Reserve-Infanterie Regiments Nr. 72, Emil Hünicken (Zeulenroda (Thüringen), Bernhard Sporn Verlag,1929)

Die Geschichte des Infanterie Regiments Herzog Friedrich Wilhelm von Braunschweig (Ostfriesisches) Nr. 78 im Weltkriege, Fritz Ebeling (Oldenburg, Verlag Stalling, 1924)

Das Königlich Preußische Infanterie-Regiment Landgraf Friedrich I. von Hessen-Kassel (1. Kurhessisches) Nr. 81 im Weltkriege 1914 – 1918, Otto Schwalm, Oberstleutnant Ahlers (Berlin, Die Offiziervereinigung 'Alt 81', 1932)

Die Geschichte des Oldenburgisches Infanterie-Regiment No. 91, Major a. D. Heinrich Harms, (Oldenburg i. O./Berlin, Verlag Gerhard Stalling, 1930)

Das Infanterie-Regiment "Kaiser Wilhelm, König von Preußen" (2. Württemb.) Nr. 120 im Weltkrieg 1914–1918, Georg Simon (Belser, Stuttgart, 1922)

Das 5. Niederschlesische Infanterie-Regiment Nr. 154 im Frieden und im Kriege, Verein der Offiziere 'Alt 154' (Kommissionsverlag der Buchdruckerei Diesdorf bei Gäbersdorf, 1955)

Das Königlich Preußische 7. Westpreußische Infanterie Regiment Nr. 155, Leutnant Faden, Oberleutnant Kalkowski, Leutnant Pellner, Hauptmann Meyer-Piton (Berlin-Charlottenburg, Druck und Verlag Bernard & Graefe, 1931)

Das 8. Lothringische Infanterie-Regiment Nr. 159 im Frieden und im Weltkrieg, Ernst Zipfel (Berlin, Bernard & Graefe, 1935)

Index